G·H·O·S·T F·L·E·E·T

G·H·O·S·T
F·L·E·E·T

The Sunken Ships of Bikini Atoll

JAMES P. DELGADO

A Kolowalu Book

University of Hawai'i Press
Honolulu

Library of Congress Cataloging-in-Publication Data
Delgado, James P.
  Ghost Fleet : the sunken ships of Bikini Atoll / James P.
Delgado.
    p. cm.
    "A Kolowalu book."
    Includes bibliographical references and index.
    ISBN 0–8248–1864–4 (cloth : alk. paper)
    ISBN 0–8248–1868–7 (pbk. : alk. paper)
    1. Shipwrecks—Marshall Islands—Bikini
Atoll. 2. Operation Crossroads, 1946.
    I. Title.
G525.D38   1996
996.8'3—dc20   96–22635
                                               CIP

University of Hawai'i Press books are printed on acid-free
paper and meet the guidelines for permanence and
durability of the Council on Library Resources

Designed by David C. denBoer

For John and Beth

"In that hollow upon which now, I kept my eyes intent,
I think a spirit born of my own blood laments the guilt
which down below costs one so much."

DANTE, *Inferno*, Canto 29

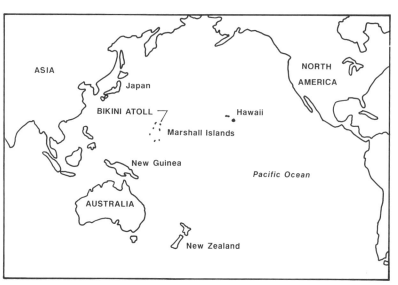

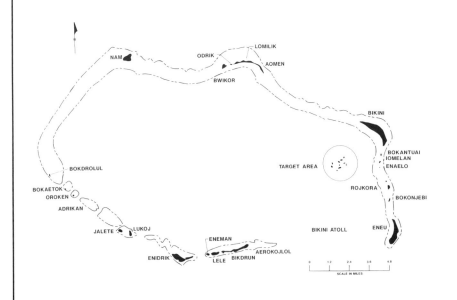

Contents

Acknowledgments

The genesis of this book was two years' field-work I spent as a member of a very special team. The Submerged Cultural Resources Unit of the National Park Service, the only federal field team of underwater archaeologists in the United States, is led by Dan Lenihan. The unit was Dan's idea, and he had always been its driving force. If it were not for Dan Lenihan's commitment to shipwreck archaeology and making shipwrecks accessible to the public, the wrecks of Bikini would never have reached the public eye. I particularly want to thank Dan for his many years of support, guidance, and encouragement.

I thank my other good friends and colleagues from the National Park Service who went to Bikini, Larry Murphy, Larry Nordby, and Jerry Livingston, for their good counsel, insights, and encouragement.

I also thank the Bikini Council, and Jack Neidenthal, Dave McCampbell, Dave Rattay, Bill Livingston, Jeanne Rawlings, Bill Curtsinger, Rowland Bowers, Doug Scovill, Ed Bearss, Kevin Foster, Jonathan Weisgall, Kent Hiner, Lee McEachern, George Lang, John Eliot, Bill Robison, Catherine Courtney, Eric Hiner, John "Alan" Brown, Lance Yamaguchi, Richard Giles, Eric Hansen, Stephan Notarianni, Wayne Olival, Edward Maddison, John Lajuan, Roger Joel, Thompson Johnson, Harry Nashon, Wilma Riklon, Kane Janer, the men of MDSU-1 and EOD-1, Detachment 62, and the captain and crew of the DOE vessel *G. W. Pierce* for their support of our team at Bikini.

For historical information and help in understanding the ships, I would like to thank Lloyd Graybar, Linda Plauner, Mike Walker, Henry Vadnais, Paul Stillwell, Mark Newton, Kevin Foster, Jonathan Weisgall, Alison McDonald, John Reilly, Burl Burlingame, Gregg Herken, Roger Meade, Charles Burdick, Russ Booth, B. J. Dorman, Tim Rizzuto, Mark Pinsel, Lawrence Wilson, Sue Moss, Carolyn Scheffer, John Smith, John Broadwater, David C. Lee, Mark Miller, Dan Bailey, and Bill Remick.

Many Crossroads veterans were extremely helpful with their time, reminiscences, photographs, and memorabilia. I would like to particularly thank Ernest Peterkin, Joe Featherston, Bob Henderson, Leon Smith, Woodrow Swancutt, Otto Schoetzow, Dick Laning, Enders Huey, Hank Arnold, Lewis Talley, A. H. Graubart, Alvin Brommer, Edward Clevenger, George Culley, Harold Demarest, Jack Lehman, and W. R. Dill, as well as the members of the USS *Arkansas* (BB-33) Association and the USS *Saratoga* (CV-3) Association.

For assistance with photographs and other graphics, I would like to thank Jerry Livingston, Larry Nordby, Bill Curtsinger, Linda Cullen, Ann Wilcox, Mark Taylor, Mark Newton, Ernest Peterkin, Steve Haller, Bruce McElfresh, Tom Freeman, and Robyn Jackson. All drawings of the wrecks at Bikini were done by Jerry Livingston and Larry Nordby as part of the Submerged Cultural Resources Unit's assessment of the wrecks, and are reproduced through the courtesy of the National Park Service, as are most of the underwater photographs.

For general advice, review, and commentary, I would particularly like to thank my personal editor, Joy Waldron, for her many years of support, and for her hard work on this book, as well as Ed Linenthal, Hugh Gusterson, Gregg Herken, Roger Meade, Betty Perkins, Susan Victor, Norman Polmar, Bill Dudley, Dan Lenihan, Larry Murphy, Candy Clifford, Ed Bearss, Jim Charleton, Harry Butowsky, Kevin Foster, Fred Schultz, and last, but certainly not least, Ann Goodhart.

I also thank the following organizations and institutions: Los Alamos National Laboratory, Los Alamos, New Mexico; Lawrence Livermore National Laboratory, Livermore, California; U.S. Department of Energy Archives, Las Vegas, Nevada; U.S. National Archives Military History Branch and Still Pictures Branch, Washington, D.C.; U.S. Naval Historical Center, Ships' History Branch Operational Archives, Curatorial Branch, and Library, Washington Navy Yard, Washington, D.C.; the Library of Congress, Washington, D.C.; the National Air and Space Museum, Smithsonian Institution, Washington, D.C.; the National Geographic Society, Washington, D.C.; the U.S. Naval Institute, Annapolis, Maryland; the USS Arizona Memorial, Honolulu, Hawaii; the J. Porter Shaw Library, San Francisco Maritime National Historical Park, San Francisco, California; Battleship Cove, Fall River, Massachusetts; Pacific Fleet Submarine Memorial Museum, Honolulu, Hawaii; the Philadelphia Maritime Museum, Philadelphia, Pennsylvania; the United States Naval Academy Museum, Annapolis, Maryland; War in the Pacific National Historic Park, Agana, Guam; Holmes and Narver, Inc., Honolulu, Hawaii.

At the University of Hawai'i Press, I want to particularly thank my editors, Pamela Kelley and Sally Serafim. For many years' work and final manuscript production, I also owe a debt of gratitude to my executive assistant, Rebecca Magallanes.

Finally, I would like to thank the three people who sacrificed the most so that I could go to Bikini: Mary, John, and Beth.

Any errors and omissions are my sole responsibility.

Prologue: Growing Up in the Nuclear Age

Like everyone else in my generation, I grew up in the shadow of the atomic bomb. I did not know a world without the emergency broadcast system, duck and cover, or the mushroom cloud. I was born relatively early in the nuclear age, in 1958, several years after the birth of the hydrogen bomb and thirteen years after Hiroshima. I remember the drills taught at school to ensure that we would survive a Russian attack. If a flash brighter than the sun itself appeared in the sky, I was to drop to the ground, roll into the gutter, or crouch under my desk, tuck my head between my knees, and cover my face, particularly my eyes. I do not recall what they told me was going to happen next, but in my naivete I assumed that an adult would come by and tell me what to do after the blast, perhaps even take me home to safety.

As the years went by, I learned more about the bomb. Its omnipresent nature intrigued me. John Hersey's *Hiroshima*, fascinating and yet repugnant, presented the image of bright red survivors staggering through the smoke and flame, their skin hanging in sheets from their arms. It brought the truth home and made me realize that, after the blast, adults or no adults, everything would not be all right. Looking at pictures of the victims of Hiroshima and Nagasaki confirmed my worst nightmares. Seeing the horrible scars and suppurating sores of those people and reading their stories made the consequences of the bomb very real. After reading how the skin slipped off burned limbs, my ten-year-old mind recoiled in horror when, at the next night's dinner, the skin slid off a drumstick of fried chicken. My parents never understood why for the next few years I could not stomach fried chicken. To this day, I can't eat a drumstick.

The bomb hung over my head every day I walked to school. Some days I lost track of the time, and when the air-raid sirens went off at noon, I froze in terror, thinking the missiles were on the way. I used to think I was alone in my fear until—years later—I talked to several of my adult friends. They all had had the same anxieties. Two of them went to Bikini with me. Dan Lenihan remembers getting dog tags issued to him in elementary school in New York so that the civil defense teams could identify his charred little body after the war. Larry Murphy stopped collecting stamps after the hydrogen bomb tests in 1958. It was pointless, he thought, if the world was about to be destroyed.

But as I got older my fears subsided. Nonchalantly, I visited the controversial nuclear power plant that Pacific Gas and Electric was building on the California coast at Diablo Canyon near Pismo Beach. Prodded by socially conscious junior-high-school teachers, I read *On The Beach, Alas Babylon,* and *A Canticle for Leibowitz* and vowed to oppose the bomb and believe in a future without it. And, in time, the bomb began to seem more like a relic that could not be used, something in the realm of far-out Hollywood movies that exploited the theme. If someone were to count the number of movies with a nuclear theme, particularly those that posit life after the bomb, I am sure it would merit a fair-size listing. These movies on one hand fed the fear, and on the other laughed at it. Last year, I watched Powers Boothe and Rebecca DeMornay in an HBO movie, *By the Dawn's Early Light.* As they flew a B-52 in the first hours of World War III to make a "grand tour" of nuclear destruction throughout Russia, DeMornay asked Boothe what would follow. "Planet of the Apes, darlin'," Boothe replied. It brought an ironic laugh to my throat.

I remember Ape City, with the Statue of Liberty half buried on the beach, the charred doll saying "Mama" in the hands of an astounded chimpanzee archaeologist, and Charlton Heston, the Omega Man himself, on his knees in agony as he gazed on the ruined symbol of his world. I watched all five of the ape movies and, later, a

number of other post-apocalyptic films. It all seemed so unreal, so far away. It took more than a new generation of films, like *The China Syndrome,* to make the nuclear threat seem real. I remember one of the first video games, "Missile Command," and how I stood with grim determination firing barrage after barrage of missiles at incoming nukes. No matter how hard I tried, the game always ended in futility. There were always more bombers, incoming missiles splitting into numerous warheads, and "smart bombs" that eluded my tracking. Again and again, they slammed into my cities, which blossomed into electronic fireballs.

As I came of age during the Vietnam War, the bomb receded in my thoughts entirely into the realm of fiction. The bloody conflict in Asia with "conventional" weapons confirmed that the threat was so great that neither side would use it. I believed that "mutually assured destruction" (MAD) was the ultimate deterrent. People were also growing saner about the bomb. After all, in the year of my birth, President Eisenhower had agreed to stop atmospheric testing of the bomb, and as Vietnam wound down, President Nixon was actually talking to the Russians and the Chinese, those bogeymen of my childhood, about reducing the nuclear arsenal. The more realistic fear, it seemed, was nuclear power plants getting out of control. Three Mile Island and Chernobyl scared me, but I still believe in nuclear power as one of few viable options after the age of oil.

Then Ronald Reagan was elected president. Considering his view of the Russians as an "evil empire," I seriously began to think that finally the United States had a leader who would actually push the button. I wasn't alone. I also knew enough to comprehend that a few sheets of corrugated tin and some dirt thrown over the top would not save me or my family if the balloon went up. I could duck and cover, all right, but when the all clear sounded there wouldn't be an adult to come along and take me by the hand. If I was caught anywhere near the impact point, there wouldn't even be a body with partially melted dog tags on it to say that this charred husk had once been me. No, millions of us would be ash, blasted high into the atmosphere to block out the sun and bring on Carl Sagan's nuclear winter.

We survived the Reagan years. The Cold War is over, the Russians are our friends, and we keep signing treaties to limit nuclear weapons. A Soviet and an American intermediate-range missile are displayed at the National Air and Space Museum along with "The Spirit of St. Louis" and the V2 rocket, as relics of the past. Visitors can walk up to the two missiles, side by side, and compare the Pershing-II and the SS-20 "Saber" ballistic weapons. Interpretive plaques explain that the mobile, intermediate-range Pershing has a 1,120-mile range and carries five 50-kiloton variable-yield warheads. The SS-20, on the other hand, can fly for 2,734 miles and possesses three independently targeted 250-kiloton warheads. These popular exhibits draw crowds through morbid curiosity and remind us of the thousands of warheads that remain pointed at targets around the globe. The Smithsonian's missiles just do not seem like relics yet.

Even as the superpowers announce plans to reduce tactical nuclear weapons and diminish the threat, we still have the bomb. And for all of us born in its shadow, that old fear and attraction will always be there. The world will probably never be shattered or globally contaminated and wasted by the bomb, whose progeny have now multiplied so that the United States alone by 1986 had manufactured at least 60,000 nuclear warheads of 71 types for 116 different weapons. Yet the world has inexorably changed because of the events of July 16, 1945, the day the first atomic bomb exploded. The capacity of nuclear weapons to devastate the planet and annihilate the human race, feared at the onset of the nuclear age, remains a grim possibility that has humanity living beneath a nuclear sword of Damocles. The sword descended twice, first at Hiroshima and then at Nagasaki, on August 6 and 9, 1945. It was then honed in more than 850 weapons tests. The era of atomic testing began in 1946, out in the far Pacific at Bikini Atoll. On July 1 and July 25, 1946, the world's fourth and fifth nuclear detonations, and the first ones to follow the bombing of Japan, forever altered Bikini Atoll. "Able" and "Baker" were part of Operation Crossroads, appropriately named naval tests of the bomb then called the "winning weapon" by politicians and generals. "Crossroads" firmly established nuclear deterrence as part of the defensive policy of the United States and, in time, the world.

After the first atomic weapons tests at Bikini in 1946, the Joint Chiefs of Staff concluded that, with atomic weapons, "it is quite possible to depopulate vast areas of the earth's surface, leaving only vestigial remnants of man's material works." Now, fifty years later, the ships of Operation Crossroads lie wrecked and Bikini Atoll stands depopulated. Its people, relocated for the tests, never returned to resettle Bikini permanently. After the 23 nuclear weapons tests that followed Crossroads, efforts to clean up the atoll led to a 1968 declaration that the islands were safe for human habitation. Yet in 1978, high levels of radioactive Cesium 137 in the soil and in the food chain once again depopulated Bikini.

Abandoned and derelict, Bikini's islands are now empty. The white coral-sand beaches are dotted with flotsam that arrives on the ocean currents to deposit traces of faraway life on these isolated shores. Crumbling concrete bunkers overgrown with vines stand open, their yawning interiors filled with cable, steel plate, and brackets where equipment once measured the kilotons and megatons of numerous nuclear blasts. Seen from the air, the dark blue of the deep ocean gives way to the emerald green of the atoll's shallows. The white sand and greenery-dotted fringe of islands is interrupted by a dark-blue circle more than a mile wide, where a 15-megaton blast obliterated two islands in March 1954. Only on Bikini itself, as opposed to the other islands in the atoll, is there any human life: a Department of Energy scientific field station there is staffed by a temporary community of workers and scientists.

Visitors to Bikini seeking to confront the tangible evidence of the first nuclear-weapons tests are at first disappointed. I was. The tall towers and quonset huts of Operation Crossroads were long ago bulldozed and erased from the surface of the land. In their place are geometrically planted palms and uniformly designed concrete houses intended for a resettlement in the early 1970s. The homes are empty shells now, their fiberboard ceilings flaking away, the acoustic tiles lying damp and rotten on bare concrete floors. In a sense these structures are a museum of nuclear-induced change, of a world faintly reminiscent of the worst apocalyptic nightmare, a world populated only by lizards and cockroaches as the fabric of human endeavor crumbles. The homes, the bunkers, the lizards—it's easy to imagine Bikini as Babylon. You land on the beach, and damned if Nevil Shute was not right about a silent land and empty houses.

Beneath the green-blue waters of the atoll's lagoon lie the visible remains of Operation Crossroads. There, 180 feet beneath the surface in a silt-filled crater from the world's fifth atomic blast, rest the hulks of ten ships, eleven landing craft and lesser vessels, all felled by the two detonations of Operation Crossroads—the "vestigial remnants" of that time and place. Left to the depths after a brief resurvey of their radioactive decks in 1947, these ships are an unmodified museum of the dawn of the atomic age.

In 1988 the Bikini Council, seeking the eventual return of its people to their homeland, inquired into the condition of these sunken relics. The ships, having been transferred to the people of Bikini by the United States, have been considered a mixed blessing by the Bikinians. Whenever they have come home for brief visits to their irradiated islands, they have been shocked by the sight of oil slicks on the once pristine lagoon surface. Contaminated by the same bombs that left the radioactive legacy in their soil which the Bikinians aptly term "poison," the ships are a source of concern and potential ecological disaster.

Like an ancient ruin in a timeless land, the blocky form of a concrete bunker at Bikini rises from the brush. The concrete bunkers looked like Mayan temples in a jungle. At times, we felt like the explorers of a world left empty at the end of the nuclear age. It reminded me of David Bradley's comment that Bikini, "which once was inhabited by a hundred Marshallese . . . now belongs to an unknown future along with Hiroshima and Nagasaki." (James P. Delgado, National Park Service)

Loaded with unexploded bombs and with bunkers leaking fuel oil, the ships had never been fully investigated before our arrival in Bikini in 1989 and 1990. That year, at the request of the Bikini Council, teams from the United States Navy surveyed the atoll, located the wrecks, and dived on them. The following year, the navy returned with a small team from the United States Department of the Interior's National Park Service. The only federal field team of underwater archaeologists, the group was asked to accompany the navy and evaluate the ships as possible diving attractions and as historic and archaeological sites. The team, led by Daniel Lenihan, the chief of the National Park Service's Submerged Cultural Resources Unit, included two other archaeologists, Larry Murphy and Larry Nordby, diving scientific illustrator Jerry Livingston, and myself. After years of dealing with the bomb as an intangible concept, for all of us the opportunity had come at last to confront it and see what it really could do. Bikini offered me the chance to appreciate the power of the atomic bomb to make abstract horror concretely real. The shipwrecks of Bikini Atoll are the physical evidence of a time and a string of events that changed our world. The same ships now bring us full circle to study and investigate them, and, in doing so, to closely examine ourselves and humanity's fascinating dance with the nuclear genie.

1

"It Is an Awful Responsibility Which Has Come to Us"

The rain had stopped a little more than an hour before. Now, in the darkness of the pre-dawn hour, the last connections were made. Electricity raced across wires, relays snapped shut, and suddenly the sky was lit by an unearthly green glow that climbed into a glowing, iridescent fireball. William L. Laurence, watching from a bunker, described the world's first nuclear detonation as a "great ball of fire about a mile in diameter, changing colors as it kept shooting upward, from deep purple to orange, expanding . . . an elemental force freed from its bonds after being chained for billions of years. For a fleeting instant, the color was . . . such as one sees only in the corona of the sun during a total eclipse. It was as though the earth had opened and the skies had split."

The steel tower that had held the bomb aloft melted and evaporated in the million-degree heat, which also scooped out a crater lined with fused pale-green glass that had once been sand. It was 5:30 in the morning on July 16, 1945, and a new world had been born in the New Mexico

desert. Physicist Robert Oppenheimer, leader of the team that had created this new weapon, the atomic bomb, gazed in awe and horror at what had been born. His mind groped for words to convey his feelings. Oppenheimer recalled the words spoken by Krishna in the *Bhagavad Gita:* "If the radiance of a thousand suns were to burst into the sky, that would be the splendor of the mighty one." Then, as he soberly reflected on the dying fireball and the rapidly rising cloud of dirt and smoke, Oppenheimer remembered other lines spoken by Krishna: "I am become death, the shatterer of worlds."

This significant, world-altering event was known only to the scientists who had assembled and now tested the bomb and a handful of military representatives who oversaw the project, as well as the secretary of war, the secretary of the navy, and the president. Only after the bombing of Hiroshima and Nagasaki did the War Department release a statement on the first successful test of the bomb a month before the attacks on Japan.

The Birth of the Atomic Age

The atomic age, born at the Trinity Site on that rainy July morning in 1945, had been conceived nearly a half-century before and was carried to fruition through the decades, slowly and inevitably advancing until the exigencies of war accelerated its arrival. The "gadget," as the atomic bomb was first called, even then was the subject of anxiety and trepidation. After three years of effort and better than two billion dollars, the thought that the bomb would not work was for some nearly as frightening as the thought that it would work. Relief, even for J. Robert Oppenheimer, was the prevalent mood of the day on July 16, 1945.

From the pioneering work of a group of scientists from around the world so small that they freely and openly corresponded with each other and shared their triumphs and failures, the secrets of the atom had been slowly unraveled, so that by 1939 the possibility of nuclear fission, powerful enough perhaps to build a weapon of hitherto undreamed of force, was foremost in many scientists' minds. The announcement of the hypothesis of fission in January 1939 so alarmed Albert Einstein and others that a letter was sent to President Franklin D. Roosevelt in October to warn him of the potential of nuclear weapons and urge U.S. action. The letter initiated an American program to build an atomic bomb. The program was kept secret so that it would not be used by the Nazi government of Germany or its Japanese allies.

By bombarding uranium with neutrons generated within a cyclotron, physicists were able to create a weapons-grade isotope, U-235. From this, scientists distilled a deadly new isotope first known only as "element 94." This element received a name in 1942—plutonium. Meanwhile, the quest to generate a self-sustaining chain reaction and thus demonstrate fission dominated the American effort. Transplanted physicist Enrico Fermi, a refugee from fascist Italy, designed a primitive reactor, which he termed a "pile," built of graphite and uranium oxide. Fermi's work was transferred from Columbia University in New York to the University of Chicago where, on a squash court, the first successful pile was built. Using 771,000 lbs. of graphite to contain the neutrons, 80,590 lbs. of uranium oxide, and 12,400 tons of uranium metal, Fermi's million-dollar pile went critical when scientists slowly slid control rods out from its core on December 2, 1942. The world's first self-sustaining chain reaction produced just a half-watt of power, though it was later allowed to reach 600 watts. The concept of nuclear fission, mathematically demonstrated in 1939, was now scientific fact. With a pile, large amounts of neutrons could now be used to bombard the isotope U-238 to make weapons-grade plutonium.

With this success in hand, the government took firm control of the secret atomic quest. The U.S. Army Corps of Engineers created a special branch, the Manhattan Engineer District, to oversee the atomic bomb project. The government's efforts were weak, however, until Major General Leslie R. Groves was sent to the project on September 17, 1942. Groves' previous assignment had been to build the massive Pentagon in the midst of a Potomac swamp. Now, although

Groves was eager for an overseas assignment, the army assigned the bluff, aggressive officer to head the Manhattan Project. Promoted to brigadier general, Groves firmly set out to push the production of the atomic bomb into reality.

Industrial facilities were created to make plutonium and U-235 at Oak Ridge, Tennessee, and Hanford, Washington. At the same time, Groves met with a brilliant physicist, J. Robert Oppenheimer from the University of California in Berkeley. Oppenheimer suggested a central isolated laboratory where all of the various scientists, physicists, chemists, and technicians would collaborate to build the bomb. Groves liked the suggestion and hired Oppenheimer to head the effort in late 1942. The team that assembled at the 7,400-foot-high Los Alamos mesa outside Santa Fe, New Mexico, included a large number of European scientists, some of them Jews who had fled Hitler's Germany as nazism engulfed the continent. Britain, a collaborator in the atomic quest, contributed British and Canadian scientists.

Groves instituted strict security measures and brought together a military organization that worked not only to preserve the secret but also to provide the considerable logistics of construction, transportation, supply, and procurement. A community of temporary homes and laboratories was hastily built at Los Alamos. Army engineers graded roads and installed security fences while the scientists and their families arrived in the spring of 1943. The goal was simply to build an atomic bomb that was a "practical military weapon." It had to cross either the Atlantic or Pacific Ocean and drop from an airplane on the enemy, be it the Germans—who were now known to be working on also developing a bomb—or the Japanese, also laboring to harness the atom.

The Los Alamos scientists labored for two years to assemble a working weapon, using both plutonium and U-235. Two basic concepts of weapons design were laid out. The first was a "gun" mechanism that fired a uranium "bullet" into a U-235 core to induce a chain reaction and detonate the bomb. This principle was used only once, when the U-235 bomb, known as "Little Boy," was built and dropped on Hiroshima. The second concept employed plutonium. Its genesis was a proposal by physicist Seth Neddermeyer, a recruit from the National Bureau of Standards who called for compression of a plutonium core through implosion to reach critical mass.

Neddermeyer's idea met with little enthusiasm, even from the naval officer selected to head the ordnance division of the project. Captain William S. "Deak" Parsons, forty-three years old and a graduate of the Naval Academy, Class of 1922, was suggested for the job by the president's science advisor, Vannevar Bush. Parsons' career before Manhattan had focused on ordnance, including service on the battleship *Idaho*, as executive officer on the destroyer *Aylwin*, and as gunnery officer on the staff of Commander Destroyers, Battle Force. Shoreside assignments of this promising officer also included duty as liaison officer between the navy's Bureau of Ordnance and the Naval Research Laboratory, working on the development of radar, and, just prior to the Manhattan Project, a stint of duty as Experimental Officer at the Naval Proving Ground at Dahlgren, Virginia. At the time of his selection for the A-Bomb project,

Parsons had just completed field testing the VT, or radio proximity fuse, for the navy's Bureau of Ordnance under Rear Admiral W. H. P. Blandy. The VT fuse would later reenter Parson's life as the trigger for the atomic bomb, and Blandy later returned as his commanding officer for Operation Crossroads.

Under "Deak" Parsons, a team at Los Alamos assembled a uranium gun bomb, which they called the "Thin Man," a name later changed to "Little Boy." As far as Parsons was concerned, his bomb was the logical emphasis of the atomic effort. Later Parsons wanted to turn his efforts toward bringing the bomb to sea, perhaps as a nuclear torpedo. One Los Alamos critic, a proponent of the implosion-core concept, felt that Parsons' attitude was "if a weapon didn't have a lanyard on it, it wasn't a weapon." The gun bomb worked on a principle that was understood and appreciated by Parsons. It was relatively simple and was guaranteed to work. The implosion-core concept was neither. There was, in particular, no proven method of simultaneously detonating explosive charges to compress a core. While development of the uranium gun bomb continued, however, work on a plutonium-core bomb also proceeded under the leadership of George Kistiakowsky. Both groups worked side by side in heated rivalry to develop a working nuclear weapon.

The success of an implosion-core weapon was made possible in the spring of 1944 when British ordnance expert James L. Tuck arrived. Tuck proposed using shaped charges to focus the blast inward in order to uniformly compress the plutonium core, providing an answer to the quandary raised by Neddermeyer. Much of Los Alamos' effort went into making the bomb work. Tests with explosives finally convinced Oppenheimer and Groves that only a full-scale nuclear test of the weapon would prove its worth. Meanwhile, the industrial plants that Groves had put on line finally reached the stage where large-scale production of plutonium through gaseous and thermal diffusion could begin at the end of 1944. Given the estimated capability of the plants, Groves hoped that by mid-1945 he would have on hand eighteen 5-kilogram blocks of weapons-grade plutonium. The first delivery of bomb-grade material was a shipment of U-235 that arrived in early 1945 to complete Parsons' "Little Boy." Enough plutonium arrived so that by the end of May, the critical-mass experiments for the implosion-core bomb could begin.

The death of Franklin D. Roosevelt on April 12, 1945, introduced his new vice president, Harry S Truman, to the bomb. Within twenty-four hours of the president's death, Truman was briefed on the now imminent weapon. Wary of his Soviet allies as the war in Europe was ending, and in need of an ace in the hole as he dealt with them and the problems of postwar Europe, Truman was also facing the need to end the bloody, hand-to-hand combat that characterized the Pacific war. He welcomed the bomb. In July 1945 at Potsdam, a suburb outside the ravaged German capital of Berlin, Truman met with British prime minister Winston Churchill and Soviet premier Joseph Stalin to discuss these issues. Only Truman and Churchill knew of the bomb's imminent arrival, and they chose not to inform Stalin. In any event, thanks to spies, the Soviets were well aware of the atomic bomb.

Japan was given an ultimatum by the allies—complete and unconditional surrender; otherwise, the Potsdam declaration offered Japan only "prompt and utter destruction." The atomic bomb would provide the means for utter destruction. It also put the Russians on notice that America's preeminent position in the world power had been assumed by providing what Secretary of War Henry Stimson termed "a badly needed equalizer." The bomb, it was also hoped, would serve as a weapon of terror, its unheralded horror shocking the Japanese into surrender. All that was needed was a successful test of the plutonium-core weapon.

The military formed a target committee in the spring of 1945 to decide where the bomb would be dropped in Japan. Targets, the group felt, should be "urban or industrial cities" that lay within a B-29 bomber's 1,800-mile range and were not obscured by clouds, so that visual bombing and photographic documentation of the attack could take place. Groves subsequently added other factors: the target had to be military, either an important headquarters, a troop concentration, or a center for the production of military equipment or supplies. The target could not have been damaged by earlier bombing raids and would have to be in an area that would confine the atomic damage, such as a city surrounded by hills. Targets should also be those whose destruction would strike at the heart of Japan's determination to continue the war.

The first target selected, after much deliberation, was the port city of Hiroshima, located at the southwest end of the island of Honshu on the shores of the Inland Sea. The bomb destined for Hiroshima was the "Little Boy" built

by Parsons and his team. As preparations were under way for the full-scale test of the plutonium "gadget" at Alamogordo, the components of "Little Boy" were crated and shipped by truck from Los Alamos to Kirtland Army Air Base, outside Albuquerque. Loaded at Kirtland on two DC-3s, the bomb parts were flown to Hamilton Field, north of San Francisco. From Hamilton Field, the crates were driven by truck across the Golden Gate Bridge into the city to Hunter's Point Naval Shipyard on San Francisco's eastern shore. There the crates were loaded on board the cruiser *Indianapolis* on July 16, the first day of the new atomic age. With the uranium-gun gadget device aboard, the *Indianapolis* sailed for Tinian in the Marianas Islands, where the bomb would be assembled and dropped on Japan.

As the pieces of "Little Boy" were being loaded aboard the cruiser in San Francisco, nearly half a continent away the day of Trinity dawned in 18.6-kiloton detonation—the world's largest man-made explosion at that time—equal to 18,600 tons of TNT and four times more powerful than the Los Alamos scientists had expected; the bomb lit the dark, predawn skies. There were no longer any questions about the plutonium bomb. In the words of one elated scientist: "It worked. The goddamn thing worked!" It was now ready for combat.

Dropping the Bomb

To drop the bomb, the army air forces intended to use the largest plane in their arsenal, the newly developed B-29. Designed by the Boeing

Aircraft Company of Seattle, the B-29 was the result of a 1940 Army Air Corps request for a long-range bomber eventually to replace the B-17 "Flying Fortress" bomber then in use. The B-29 made its maiden flight on September 21, 1942. After problems with the aircraft were ironed out, the B-29, the ultimate bomber of any nation in World War II, began to roll off the assembly line and into the field by March 1944. The United States made the decision in December 1943 not to use the new B-29s in Europe, but rather to send them to the Pacific, where the new bombers' long-range capacity made them ideal aircraft for the long overwater flights from the nearest U.S.-held airfields in the Northern Mariana Islands, nearly a thousand miles away, to hit Japan. A new command, the 20th Air Force, was created under the leadership of General H. H. "Hap" Arnold to strike at the heart of the empire. The plane that would do it: ultimately, the only aircraft capable of carrying the weight of an atomic bomb was the B-29.

With B-29s, General Curtis LeMay of the 20th Air Force had devastated Japan with a hail of incendiary bombs following the capture of the Mariana Islands. On March 9, 1945, 325 B-29s roared off from Guam, Saipan, and Tinian islands in the Marianas, which had been captured after brutal fighting in the summer of 1944. More planes followed, at times under fire from Japanese troops hiding on the islands, to deliver newly developed napalm bombs. Early in the morning of March 10, Tokyo was hit with more than 2,400 tons of incendiaries. The resulting firestorm destroyed 267,171 buildings and killed 83,000 people. Additional raids followed, raining fiery death on Nagoya, Osaka, Kobe, and Yokohama, again and again. Seas of flame lit the night skies of Japan, as the worst civilian casualties of the war mounted. In a new and vastly altered landscape of war, "strategic and precision bombing" turned into wholesale slaughter, a bloody and determined push to employ bigger, more efficient weapons of destruction simply to get the job of winning the war over with. In such an atmosphere of combat, the ultimate bomb was deployed.

While the scientists raced to develop the bomb, the Second Air Force was ordered to start training to use it. The Glenn L. Martin Company of Omaha, Nebraska, built 46 specially modified B-29s, known as "atomic bombers." Fifteen of these planes were assigned on September 1, 1944, to the newly created 509th Composite Group, commanded by Lieutenant Colonel Paul Warfield Tibbetts, Jr. The twenty-nine-year old Tibbetts was a combat veteran of the air war over Europe and had a fearless, if not brash, reputation. The sole squadron of the 509th was the 393d Heavy Bombardment Squadron commanded by Major Charles Sweeney. The 509th was a self-contained unit. Based at remote Wendover Field in Utah, the 509th drilled with riveted mock-ups of the plutonium bomb. The nearly 10-foot diameter casing for the new bomb was strikingly different from the long, almost thin "Little Boy." The plutonium gadget, short and stocky, albeit huge, was nicknamed the "Fat Man." "Fat Man" dummies cast out of concrete and painted bright orange were issued to the 509th for practice. Because of their color and shape, the dummy bombs were designated "pumpkins." The pilots called them "punkins."

In the course of training, Tibbetts developed

a getaway manuever to avoid the nearly eight-mile range of the fatal blast of an atomic bomb. After dropping the bomb, Tibbetts banked his plane, diving a thousand feet as he sharply turned 155 degrees to gain a momentum that hurtled his plane in the opposite direction from the plummeting weapon. He was then safe, eight miles away from the target when the bomb exploded. This maneuver was drilled into the 393d Bombing Squadron's pilots day after day, although none of the men save Tibbetts had as yet any idea of the type of weapon that they would drop.

Hiroshima

In February 1945, the 509th was ordered to North Field on Tinian. Arriving in May, the 509th continued drilling, including participation in regular bombing attacks on Japan and various island strongholds. As they drilled, the cruiser *Indianapolis* arrived with the parts for "Little Boy." Assembly of the bomb was completed by July 31, when "Deak" Parsons arrived to take over as weaponeer for this first combat deployment. Special 13- by 16-foot pits had been dug into the airfield, as the 9,700-pound, 10.5-foot-long, 29-inch-diameter bomb could not be loaded any other way on the runway. On August 4, the B-29 *Enola Gay*, named for Tibbetts' mother, rolled over the bomb-loading pit. The weapon was slowly winched into the reinforced bomb bay. Laden with bomb, fuel, and crew, and with Tibbetts at the controls, the overweight *Enola Gay* lumbered off from Tinian at 2:45 A.M. on August 6. With it went five other B-29s to measure the blast, photograph the results, and assess

the weather over Hiroshima and the other target cities—Kokura, Niigata, and Nagasaki—for visual bombing conditions. Inside the plane, Parsons and Second Lieutenant Morris R. Jeppson worked to arm "Little Boy." A radar fuse inside the bomb would be the primary means of detonation. Set to go off at an altitude of 1,850 feet, the radar switch would close the relays to fire the bomb. At 7:30, Tibbetts radioed back to base that the bomb was ready, then informed his crew that the new, powerful weapon they were carrying was an atomic bomb.

At 8:15 A.M. Hiroshima time, the *Enola Gay* reached its target. Hovering 30,000 feet above the doomed city, the bomber moved into position over the aiming point, the Aioi Bridge. At seventeen seconds past 8:15 A.M., Major Thomas Ferebee, the bombardier, released the bomb. As the bay doors snapped open, "Little Boy" dropped free, pulling out its arming cables. Tibbetts sharply banked his plane and began the getaway. The bomb fell for 43 seconds. Then, 1,850 feet above the city and 800 feet away from the Aioi Bridge target, the 5-pound uranium bullet fired up the chamber, rupturing a neutron-proof damper. It hit 15 pounds of target rings inside the bomb's nose. A millisecond later, the second nuclear detonation on earth took place. The 13.5-kiloton blast at 8:16:02 smashed down on Hiroshima, destroying 62,000 buildings and killing or mortally wounding 80,000 people. The burning debris of the city swept up into a boiling mass that rose into the sky. High above and now eight miles away, *Enola Gay*'s crew were hit by two shock waves. Someone shouted, "Flak!" and bombardier Ferebee yelled, "The sons of bitches are shooting at us!" Neither man could comprehend the sheer power of the solid wall of air the bomb had just thrown at them. Then, as the plane orbited above the city, tailgunner Bob Caron, speaking into a recorder, described the scene for posterity as a mushroom cloud pushed 60,000 feet into the atmosphere:

A column of smoke rising fast. It has a fiery red core. A bubbling mass, purple-gray in color, with that red core. It's all turbulent. Fires are springing up everywhere, like flames shooting out of a huge bed of coals. I am starting to count the fires. One, two, three, four, five, six . . . fifteen . . . it's impossible. There are too many to count. Here it comes, the mushroom shape that Captain Parsons spoke about. It's coming this way. It's like a mass of bubbling molasses. The mushroom is spreading out. It's maybe a mile or two wide and half a mile high. . . . It's very black, but there is a purplish tint. . . . The base of the cloud looks like a heavy overcast that is shot through with flames.

"My God, look at that son of a bitch go!" copilot Lewis exclaimed. The mushroom cloud was visible until the plane was 363 miles from Hiroshima.

"Deak" Parsons tapped out a message in code that flashed ahead of *Enola Gay*. "Clear-cut, successful in all respects. Visual effects greater than Trinity. Hiroshima. Conditions normal in airplane following delivery. Proceeding to regular base." The news reached President Truman, returning to the United States from Potsdam aboard the cruiser *Augusta*. The president turned to the sailors standing near him as he read the dispatch sent to him by Secretary of War Henry Stimson

and emotionally declared, "This is the greatest thing in history." A presidential statement, released from Washington, announced that the United States had harnessed the basic power of the universe to enforce the threat of utter destruction to Japan. It electrified the world. Truman then called on the Japanese to surrender: "If they do not now accept our terms, they may expect a rain of ruin from the air the like of which has never been seen on this earth."

Combat troops waiting for the word to invade Japan were elated. Palau, Saipan, Iwo Jima, and Okinawa had demonstrated that the invasion of Japan would surely be a blood-drenched slaughter of proportions never seen before. In the United States, the same elation, tempered with somber reflection on the immense power of the new weapon, was the hallmark of the hour. Truman doubtless spoke for many when he stated: "It is an awful responsibility which has come to us. We thank God that it has come to us instead of our enemies, and we pray that He may guide us to use it in His ways and for His purposes."

Nagasaki

Meanwhile, the "awful responsibility" entailed readying a second bomb, this time a plutonium-core "Fat Man," to drop on another Japanese city. With components on hand at Tinian, the bomb was assembled on August 7. The second atomic bombing mission, set for August 11, was rolled back to the ninth. This mission, offered to Tibbetts (he declined) went instead to his second in command, Major Charles Sweeney. Sweeney had flown the instrumentation plane for the Hiroshima strike. That aircraft, Sweeney's own *The Great Artiste*, was still fitted with scientific instruments. Sweeney borrowed the B-29 of Captain Frederick C. Bock, known as *Bockscar*. The bomb was jacked up into *Bockscar* by 10:00 P.M. on the evening of August 8. The primary target was Kokura on the island of Kyushu; the secondary target, also on Kyushu, was the port city of Nagasaki. In the interim, the 20th Air Force kept up the pressure on Japan with a 153-plane raid on August 7 and a 375-plane raid on the eighth.

Bockscar rolled down the runway at 3:47 A.M. on August 9 in the midst of tropical rain squalls and flashes of lightning. Sweeney lifted off with a fuel problem that kept him from tapping into a 600-gallon tank. Flying through the storm, the weaponeer, one of Parsons' navy assistants from Los Alamos, Commander Frederick Ashworth, charged the bomb ten minutes into the flight. Sweeney then climbed to 17,000 feet for the long flight to Japan. Once there, he waited for his escorts to show up before heading to Kokura. Arriving over the city at 10:44 A.M., he found the target obscured by haze and smoke. After three unsuccessful passes over Kokura, flak blossomed in the sky and Sweeney decided to hit the secondary target, Nagasaki. Arriving over the port city a few minutes later, Sweeney found it obscured by clouds.

With just enough fuel left for one pass, he decided, along with Ashworth, to bomb by radar. Then an opening in the cloud cover gave him a bearing on a target, a stadium several miles upriver from the initial target point by the waterfront. Bombardier Kermit Beaham dropped the bomb at 10:58 A.M. Hurtling down toward the

unsuspecting city, Fat Man detonated when the plutonium core of the last operational atomic bomb in the United States' arsenal compressed at 1,650 feet. The 22-kiloton blast swept across the hilly landscape, killing 40,000 people instantly and destroying 45 percent of the city. As was the case with Hiroshima, the casualties from radiation sickness and blast and burn injuries escalated. By the end of 1945, Nagasaki's death toll was 70,000, climbing to 140,000 within a five-year period. Hiroshima's death toll climbed to 140,000 by the end of 1945 and, in the five years afterward, to nearly 200,000. While the death toll from the combined fire raids was higher, the atomic bomb's mortality rate was 6,500 times more efficient than that of an ordinary high-explosive bomb.

On hearing the news of Nagasaki's destruction, the Soviet Union, after months of dragging its feet over the question of entering the Pacific war, declared war on Japan. A third target was considered for an atomic attack after another bomb became available; most discussions centered on Tokyo. Initial Japanese peace feelers were extended on August 10, and after much deliberation and a nearly successful coup to continue the fighting, the emperor made a recorded broadcast to his people declaring the end of the war. After four years of hard-fought battles on land, sea, and in the air, the United States had achieved "the inevitable triumph" that Franklin Roosevelt had promised the nation in its darkest hours on December 8, 1941, after the Japanese attack on Pearl Harbor. The controversy over whether it was right to drop the bombs or not was still in the future. Now, in the aftermath of the unleashing of three bombs' immense energy, the United States pondered what to do with its newfound power.

Facing the Future with the Bomb

A chilling portent already existed in the mind of Curtis LeMay when he toured the bomb-ravaged cities that his incendiary raids had burned down. "After looking at the damage done by a relatively few B-29s," said LeMay, "I thought to myself that if we'd had such a force in place on December 7, 1941, there probably wouldn't have been an attack on Pearl Harbor. From that moment forward, I believed that it would be possible to maintain peace through strength." LeMay built that force—the Strategic Air Command—to deliver the bomb with planes and missiles. With the bomb as its centerpiece, the United States built an arsenal of weapons that made it a global force. Each step of the way, America was matched by the Soviet Union, and in part by its allies, and thus the world was filled with more nuclear weapons than any future war could reasonably employ. There are now no strategic nuclear weapons of the "nominal yield" of the first three bombs, only weapons of greater power. The first step on the road of the nuclear arms race that produced these weapons was taken, in the months after the war, with Operation Crossroads and the bombs at Bikini.

2

Operation Crossroads

In the aftermath of the destruction of Nagasaki and the subsequent surrender of Japan, the awesome force of the unleashed atom and the revival of deep-seated fears of extinction brought intense scrutiny to the subject of "the Bomb." David Sarnoff, president of the Radio Corporation of America, voiced the fear of many Americans that the new weapon might someday be unleashed against them: "No nation will be invulnerable to attack. No Goliath will be safe." The *New York Herald Tribune*, in a post-Hiroshima editorial, commented that news of the bomb was "not only the most important single announcement in the course of the war; it is an announcement more fateful for human history than the whole war itself." According to the *Tribune*'s editors, "The victory or defeat of armies, the fate of nations, the rise and fall of empires are all alike, in any long perspective only ripples on the surface of history; but the unpredictable unlocking of the inconceivable energy of the atom would stir history itself to its deepest depths."

"Seldom, if ever," stated radio commentator Edward Murrow, "has a war ended leaving the victors with such a sense of uncertainty and fear,

with such a realization that the future is obscure and that survival is not assured." The atomic bomb had caught the world's attention. Foremost among those whose thinking was dominated by the new weapon were the military. The *New York Times* stated that the advent of the bomb had forever changed the conducting of war. "It should make an end of marching, rolling, and even flying armies, and turn most of our battleships into potential scrap."

Hiroshima had immediately sparked discussions in naval circles about the new weapon's effect on ships. The provocative question was finally posed on the floor of the Senate on August 25, 1945, when Senator Brian McMahon of Connecticut demanded: "In order to test the destructive powers of the atomic bomb against naval vessels, I would like . . . Japanese naval ships taken to sea and an atomic bomb dropped on them. The resulting explosion should prove to us just how effective the atomic bomb is when used against the giant naval vessels. I can think of no better use for these Jap ships."

The idea of using the bomb against ships was not new. Early in 1944, Los Alamos scientists had considered dropping the bomb on the Japanese naval base at Truk, but by that time the Imperial Japanese Navy was a decimated and largely defeated force that did not warrant the use of the bomb. But now the destruction of the forty-eight surviving surface warships of the Imperial Japanese Navy surrendered at the war's end was guaranteed, regardless of whether the atomic bomb was used. The new Japan would be demilitarized and its remaining vessels sunk or scrapped. On August 28, 1945, Fleet Admiral Ernest J. King, commander in chief of the U.S.

fleet, recommended that the remaining Japanese vessels be destroyed. Lieutenant General B. M. Giles on MacArthur's staff in Tokyo followed Senator McMahon's lead and proposed, on September 14, 1945, that atomic bombs sink the Japanese warships. His proposal was supported by Major General Curtis LeMay and General H. H. "Hap" Arnold of the army air forces. Arnold requested of the Navy on September 18 that "a number of Japanese vessels be made available to the Army Air Forces for use in tests involving atomic bombs and other weapons."

Shown here in the 1920s, *Nagato* was once the flagship of the Imperial Japanese Navy, and was at war's end the last Japanese battleship left afloat. While most other ships were scuttled at sea or scrapped, *Nagato* was selected for the atomic bomb tests because of her importance to the Japanese. (U.S. Naval Institute Photo Library)

A dead ship, partially sunk, fires out and with the bodies of some of her crew yet aboard, *Nagato* lies at anchor on Tokyo Bay at the end of the Second World War. (U.S. Naval Institute Photo Library)

The suggestion was provocative, given the developing postwar struggle between advocates of air power and naval force over which controlled the defense of the United States and constituted the nation's military strength. Advocates of air power argued that saturation bombing, particularly the fire-bombing raids in Europe and Japan, had largely won the war and would win the next without pitched sea battles or invasions. They bluntly stated that the atomic bomb had made the concept of naval power—even naval aviation—obsolete. The navy was acutely sensitive on this point. Senior navy officers remembered the Army Air Corps' staged sinking with aerial bombs of the captured German battleship *Ostfriesland* off the Virginia capes

in 1921. The navy had responded to the threat of aviation by incorporating it into its service, and now, faced again with a threat, moved to foreclose the army from embarrassing it yet again.

Navy officers felt that the tests, if conducted by them, would prove "that ships were not excessively vulnerable to atomic attack" and that "Navy carrier aircraft could be just as useful and valuable as Air Force bombers for the delivery of atomic weapons." Indeed, the navy had already toyed with the nuclear genie. Parson's Los Alamos assignment and the participation of other naval officers in the A-Bomb project, as well as Parson's own ideas of nuclear torpedoes and other ship-borne atomic weapons, were part of the navy's efforts not to let the army capture the initiative. As early as June 1945, the navy's bureaus of Ships and Ordnance recommended a "comprehensive program for testing high explosives against merchant and warship hulks, captured enemy vessels, and United States navy combatant ships about to be stricken from the active list."

The chief of naval operations approved an Underwater Explosion Program just as the atomic bomb changed the scope of the effort. On August 28, the same day Admiral King recommended destroying the Japanese ships, the chief of the Bureau of Ships, Vice Admiral E. L. Cochrane, told the Underwater Explosion Program's staff that their first priority was "to undertake broad-scale experiments with the atomic bomb to clear up its major influence on naval warfare." The chief of naval operations was then notified by the Bureau of Ships and the Bureau of Ordnance that "full-scale testing . . . both underwater and above water, against ships of various types" with atomic weapons was imperative.

A positive response from the navy to the army air forces' public airing of the proposal was therefore quick in coming. When Secretary of the Navy James Forrestal was questioned about the atomic bomb in August 1945, he strongly underscored the fact that the navy would always be a potent force, as "control of the sea by whatever weapons are necessary is the Navy's mission." The next day, the *New York Times*, reporting on naval opposition to merging the War and Navy departments, noted that the navy was amenable to joint operations regarding "scientific developments" and predicted "it would not be at all surprising" if within the next six months there would be a mutual agreement "to test the

effects of the new atomic bomb against warships. There has been some speculation . . . whether the atomic bomb might cause the bottoms of steel ships to disintegrate and thus sink the entire fleet . . . some Navy authorities say they would like to see such a test conducted against some of our old battleships for, if the atomic bomb works this way, they want to know it."

The United States had a large number of warships, including captured enemy vessels, available as target ships for an atomic weapons test. The navy's formidable wartime fleet of more than 1,200 ships was scaling down. In August 1945, Secretary Forrestal predicted that the navy would be reduced to a 400-ship force, holding its remaining ships in reserve. On October 16, 1945, with the army air forces' proposal in hand and ships to spare, Fleet Admiral King agreed to atomic bombing captured Japanese ships with "a few of our own modern naval vessels . . . included in the target array" as part of a coordinated operation conducted by the army and the navy under the control of the Joint Chiefs of Staff. The test would include an underwater detonation.

On October 24, the *New York Times* reported that the navy was about to test the bomb to assess its effect on ships, both dispersed at sea and "massed at anchorage as in Pearl Harbor on December 7, 1941." It was not until December 10, however, that an official announcement of the joint army–navy tests was made. The *Times* reported that although the details were yet to be worked out, the army air forces "have been working aggressively to get a leading role in the experiment to make sure it will not be an all-Navy affair." Though officially denied, competition between the services continually reared its head throughout the tests as each service strove for dominance. Efforts to promote an image of mutual cooperation and interservice amity at times faltered because of this rivalry. As late as July 30, 1946, after the tests were completed, an unnamed army officer attacked the "battleship mentality" of "die-hard" naval officers, firmly stating his conviction that "in the event of a future war . . . a navy as we know it now will be utterly helpless on either side."

Joint Task Force One

The Joint Chiefs of Staff ordered their staff to plan for the tests. The planners sent their recommendation to the Joint Chiefs on December 22, 1945. It outlined three nuclear detonations to assess the strategic and tactical importance of the atomic bomb's effect on naval and military forces. The tests would be placed under the control of the Joint Chiefs through a joint task force, with an independent evaluation board appointed from the ranks of the army, navy, the Manhattan Engineer District of the Army Corps of Engineers, and civilians. The plan was approved by the Joint Chiefs, who forwarded their recommendation to the secretaries of war and the navy. The two cabinet officers in turn sent their recommendation to the president, and, on January 10, 1946, Harry S Truman created Joint Task Force One.

Vice Admiral William Henry Purnell "Spike" Blandy was placed in command of the task force on January 11. Blandy, a member of the Naval Academy class of 1913, was an "imaginative but thorough planner and a resourceful, energetic combat leader" who spent most of his career in ordnance. Assigned to battleships early in his career and later serving as head of the gun section of the Bureau of Ordnance, Blandy's commands included the destroyer *Simpson* and the demobilized battleship *Utah*, then converted into a target ship and test platform for anti-aircraft weapons. Promoted to rear admiral in 1941, Blandy was chief of the Bureau of Ordnance until 1943, when his service in the central Pacific culminated in his command of all preinvasion activities at Iwo Jima and Okinawa.

At the end of the war, Blandy was promoted to Vice Admiral and Deputy Chief of Naval Operations for Special Weapons. In this newly created position he was responsible for evaluating the late war development of guided missiles and the atomic bomb, a post well suited to him. Under his guidance, the Bureau of Ordnance had previously developed the VT, or proximity fuse, for anti-aircraft weapons. He had also recommended in October 1943 that, when ships were demobilized at war's end, the navy should retain a number of U.S. and enemy warships for weapons tests. Now, tagged with the sobriquet "Buck Rogers of the Navy" by *New York Times* reporter Sidney Shallett, he took the helm of Joint Task Force One. One of Blandy's first actions, on January 12, was to name the proposed tests. "I named the project *Operation Crossroads*," he later explained, "because it was apparent that warfare, perhaps civilization itself, had been brought to a turning point in history by this revolutionary weapon."

Blandy's orders stressed that Operation Crossroads was to determine, first, "the effects of atomic explosions against naval vessels in order to appraise the strategic implications of the application of atomic bombs including the results on naval design and tactics." Next in importance were what the Joint Task Force described as "military, lesser military, and principal scientific and technical objects," determining the principal effects of the bomb on ships, ships' crews, the best means for decontaminating vessels, and gaining "sufficient data . . . to permit naval architects and engineers to design more resistant ships."

The tests would also serve as practice for the army air forces and help military planners to learn what the bomb would do to airplanes, tanks, trucks, radio and radar equipment, ammunition, food, clothing, medicine, and other equipment. The principal scientific goals included measuring radiation and its effects, diagnosing and treating radiation sickness, and studying oceanographic, seismographic, and meteorological changes. And, in a grim harbinger of the coming race for atomic power, the tests would determine "to what extent atomic bomb explosions may be detected at distances of thousands of miles." As his primary assistant Blandy selected Deak Parsons, now a rear admiral, as technical director in carrying out many of these tasks.

Tests as a Demonstration of Wealth and Power

The tests were appealing for more than technical reasons. As one account stressed, while "it is indeed routine to test each new weapon in all major applications, the novelty of the proposed

test of the atomic bomb against naval vessels would lie in the unprecedented scale and worldwide importance of the tests." Operation Crossroads was a demonstration to the world, particularly the Soviet Union, of the United States' wealth and power at a time when the nation, in the aftermath of the war, had assumed the role of global leader. The proof of power was paramount for U.S. officials, and as early as April 1946, Admiral Blandy, speaking in a live radio broadcast, stated that Operation Crossroads would "help us to be what the world expects our great, non-aggressive and peace-loving country to be—the leader of those nations which seek nothing but a just and lasting peace." Commentator Raymond Gram Swing more bluntly noted that Crossroads, "the first of the atomic era war games . . . is a notice served on the world that we have the power and intend to be heeded."

Similarly, the concept of the United States as the richest nation on earth was implicit in the tests. Presidential science advisor Vannevar Bush, writing in 1949, noted that the production of atomic weapons "requires such major expenditures and such major effort that they cannot be afforded at all except by countries which are very strong economically or industrially." By committing itself to expending three of these extremely expensive and unique weapons in the tests, the United States was demonstrating its wealth.

The size of the target fleet, expected to total nearly a hundred vessels, also underscored the image of a wealthy and powerful nation. Joint Task Force One press releases stressed that this cast-off fleet of warships represented the world's fourth or fifth largest navy, the U.S. Navy, of course, being the world's largest, a fact noted by Admiral Blandy when asked if the tests were "provocative." Blandy replied, "Some people fear that these tests may be construed by other nations as a 'martial gesture.' But the principal targets are naval ships. Great Britain, the only other country possessing a strong navy, certainly does not believe that we are planning to use the bomb against her fleet."

Even more attractive was the destruction of the surviving capital ships of the once feared Imperial Japanese Navy, which implied America's place as the principal victor in the war. The inclusion of three captured warships—notably two Japanese vessels—as target ships echoed triumphant victory parades with conquered enemies dragged in chains through the streets of ancient Rome. Moored with heavy chains in the target array, the two Japanese ships, the battleship *Nagato* and the cruiser *Sakawa*, were placed in the "fatal zone" for each test, clearly indicating that the United States would destroy them with the bomb. Indeed, one early 1946 newspaper account, accompanied by an Associated Press photograph of twenty-four battered-looking destroyers and submarines, crowed that "Trapped Remnants of Jap Fleet Face Destruction in United States Navy Atom-Bomb tests."

The two Japanese warships reflected the United States' particular enmity toward Japan, with its underlying racial overtones and bitterness over Pearl Harbor and the brutal war that ensued. It was a symbolic killing of the enemy's ships with the same weapon that had forced his capitulation. The *Nagato* especially fulfilled that role as the onetime flagship of the Imperial Japanese Navy and the scene of operational plan-

ning for the Pearl Harbor attack. The *Nagato*'s "capture" as a derelict on Tokyo Bay at the time of the Japanese surrender was intended to symbolize the complete and final surrender of the Imperial Japanese Navy. Sinking the battleship with an atomic bomb ritually "destroyed" that navy in a more potent manner than prosaic scrapping or scuttling at sea. So important was the battleship's planned fate that the navy lavished great attention on it and the *Sakawa*. At Bikini, the ships were carefully tended by support vessels alongside, as "there was some danger that the captured Japanese ships might actually sink if they were left unattended."

Massive publicity efforts by Joint Task Force One underscored Operation Crossroads' value as a spectacle and demonstration. The navy provided special facilities aboard the USS *Appalachian* (AGC-1), which became the "press headquarters ship," and the Task Force prepared more than a hundred detailed and lengthy press releases on every imaginable aspect of the test's logistics and preparations. Navy Captain Fitzhugh Lee was assigned as the Crossroads public information officer and was soon holding "open" press conferences. Furthermore, "to help those correspondents who were starting off 'cold,' Captain Lee arranged . . . various orienting schemes. Lectures were arranged; motion picture films were prepared and shown; press packets of pamphlets were prepared and distributed. No effort was spared in making this the *best* reported as well as being the *most* reported technical experiment of all time." In all, 114 U.S. radio, newspaper, magazine, and news service reporters attended the first test, Able, and 75 attended the second, or Baker, test. Ten foreign reporters

More than a hundred news correspondents from magazines, newspapers, and radio converged on Bikini for the atomic bomb tests. A few correspondents, accompanied by a naval officer, interview "King" Juda, the leader of the Bikinians, in March 1946. (U.S. Army Air Force Photo, National Air and Space Museum, Smithsonian Institution)

covered Able and eight attended Baker. Hundreds of articles and features dominated the nation's newspapers, news magazines, and newsreels. Radios transmitted live broadcasts of Able's detonation to audiences around the world.

An unprecedented invitation to foreign observers made Crossroads a world stage for the United States. Each nation with membership in the United Nations' Atomic Energy Commis-

sion was allowed to send two observers to Bikini. Ten nations accepted. Particular attention was paid by the press to the Soviet observers. There was no mistaking that the demonstration at Bikini was in large measure specifically directed at the United States' foremost rival for global domination. Although the reason for the invitation to the observers was in part to allay foreign "suspicion and disapproval of the

Shipboard "money" for the atomic age. "Short snorters" were printed for shipboard use during the war. Specially printed short snorters for Operation Crossroads quickly became souvenir items. (Ernest W. Peterkin Collection)

planned experimental use of the world's most terrible war weapon," the underlying motivation was the demonstrative power of the tests. The United States alone possessed the secret of nuclear power and a stockpile of atomic bombs.

The Best Defense

At the same time, Operation Crossroads was presented to the American public as a defensive measure. Testing the bomb on warships would "improve our navy," as, according to Admiral Blandy, "We want ships that are tough, even when threatened by atomic bombs; we want to keep the ships afloat, propellers turning, guns

firing; we want to protect the crews so that, if fighting is necessary, they can fight well today and return home unharmed tomorrow . . . the unequalled importance of the atomic bomb . . . shakes the very foundations of military strategy." The concept of defense, shaped by American anger over the surprise attack at Pearl Harbor, and a grim determination that such a surprise never happen again, produced the strong belief that the best defense was learning how to live with and use the atomic bomb.

The Cold War invocation of the necessity of nuclear capability was first stressed at Operation Crossroads. Blandy repeatedly thrust home his belief that:

The tests stand out clearly as a defensive measure. We are seeking to primarily learn what types of ships, tactical formations and strategic dispositions of our own naval forces will best survive attack by the atomic weapons of other nations, should we ever have to face them. By no stretch of the imagination can such steps of caution and economy be taken as a threat of aggression. If, because of such a false assumption, we failed to carry out these experiments, to learn the lessons which they can teach us, our designers of ships, aircraft and ground equipment, as well as our tacticians, strategists and medical officers would be groping their way along a dark road which might lead us to another and worse Pearl Harbor.

The threat of such a "worse Pearl Harbor" was not far off. In April 1946, Blandy frankly noted that "some of our leading scientists" agreed that "other nations with even a moderate degree of industrialization can manufacture atomic bombs in a few years. Our Armed Forces must be kept modern, and one of the first steps in modernizing them is to learn the full capabilities of any new weapon which may be brought against them." This underscored the domestic message of Crossroads. "The ultimate results of the tests, so far as the Navy is concerned, will be their translation into terms of United States sea power."

Planning the Tests

Most striking about the military's repeated claim of scientific interest in the Crossroads tests is the fact that it was not true. Most if not all of the scientists at Los Alamos viewed Operation Crossroads as "a show." The possible scientific benefits, according to them, were next to useless. Most viewed their participation in the tests as an opportunity to make extra money. However, Crossroads news releases touted considerable interest in the forthcoming tests on the part of scientists. In July 1946, *Life* magazine reported that "a large number of scientists are looking forward to the forthcoming explosion . . . never having had a chance to test the effects of atomic energy in their own areas of knowledge." They would now be afforded "a laboratory example of what may happen to the world and the animate and inanimate things on it in the event that war comes again."

Thus another recurrent theme of Crossroads—"scientific benefits"—was exaggerated, as the bulk of the benefits were largely for military science. The official historian for Crossroads, W. A. Shurcliff, commented:

At Hiroshima and Nagasaki a few photographs and pressure measurements were made of the explosions, but almost nothing of value to physicists was learned. Medical men, arriving on the scene late, found it difficult to tell what the early symptoms of the injured persons had been, and whether the injuries resulted primarily from flash burn, gamma radiation, or from secondary factors such as fires, and floods, and lack of food, overexertion, and lack of medical attention.

Operation Crossroads mythology insisted, and persists in doing so even today, that the tests provided the first opportunity for weapons scientists to assess, under a controlled environment, the pressure, impulse, shock-wave velocity, and optical and nuclear radiation effects of the bomb. Yet, to the scientists of Los Alamos, Crossroads was a spectacle using bombs already "tested" at Trinity, Hiroshima, and Nagasaki.

Objections to Operation Crossroads

As plans were announced, opposition to Crossroads surfaced in various quarters as letters poured into Admiral Blandy from across the country. One objection was the cost of the tests, particularly the potential loss of all the target ships. Senator Scott Lucas of Illinois criticized the tests as a "grandiose display of atomic destruction" and argued that the target fleet, if no longer useful for naval purposes, could be converted "into temporary homes for veterans." At least one writer wanted a ship of his own. Eleven-year-old Max Ladewasser "and gang" of

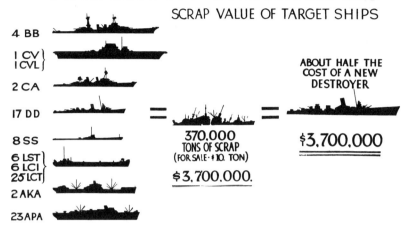

OPERATION CROSSROADS
SCRAP VALUE OF TARGET SHIPS

4 BB

I CV}
I CVL}

2 CA

17 DD

8 SS

6 LST}
6 LCI}
25 LCT}

2 AKA

23 APA

**ABOUT HALF THE
COST OF A NEW
DESTROYER**

370,000
TONS OF SCRAP
(FOR SALE · $10. TON)
$3,700,000.

$3,700,000

Anatomy of a guinea pig fleet. Sensitive to criticism that it was destroying valuable ships, Joint Task Force One issued this simple chart showing how the ships, if sold for scrap, really didn't amount to much. Of course, they had already cost the taxpayer much more. (Naval Institute Photo Library)

Chicago wanted some of the ships presented to the children of the country. Max's personal request: "I would like to have a real PT boat which we could run on Lake Michigan." Another private citizen writing to protest was angry, not over the loss of the ships, but the scrap steel they represented. He pointed out that airplane engineers tested models in wind tunnels and thus "do not need to destroy full sized planes to see just what the planes will do under certain conditions. Scientists do not need to kill elephants to determine the reactions of chemicals and drugs. They use small mice."

In March 1946, Admiral Blandy, bridling over criticism that he was an "atomic playboy," testified to the Senate's Naval Affairs Committee that, although construction costs for the ships had indeed totaled $450 million, all of the vessels were obsolete except for five of the submarines and the light carrier *Independence*. In response to continued criticism over costs, Blandy stated on April 16 that the total cost of losing the target ships would not exceed the expendi-

tures for "one large new ship." The obsolete fleet, he stressed, was only worth its scrap value, which the admiral estimated at $100 million. Form letters responding to protests over the ships' loss stressed that the fleet was obsolete and "in excess of the number required to keep our postwar navy at its proper strength." The letter also emphasized that not all the ships would be destroyed or sunk. Even "those badly damaged may be towed back to the United States and sold for scrap." Contradicting its own claim of obsolescence, Joint Task Force One also wrote that "still others may be placed back in service."

Protests also focused on the selection of certain ships as targets, specifically the battleships *New York* and *Pennsylvania*. When the *New York* sailed from its namesake city in January 1946 for Bikini, the loss of the ship was lamented by veterans' groups, and the state chamber of commerce lobbied to save it. "New York may lose forever its most useful and fitting war memorial unless something is done to prevent de-

Designed by Walt Disney, the stamp cancellation for the USS *Appalachian*'s mail was dramatic. Scientists from the Manhattan Project were afraid that the actual results would be much less spectacular. (Naval Institute Photo Library)

struction of our century's Old Ironsides as an atom bomb target. This ship should be permanently on display in New York." An unnamed officer complained that "I don't see why she couldn't have been given to the state, just as her sister ship the *Texas* was given to that state."

Joint Task Force One's response was that, "While it is regretted that ships such as the *New York* cannot be spared and exhibited as memorials, it is felt that this gallant battleship could perform no more valuable or distinguished service for our postwar Navy than it will render in the historic tests." It was also noted that "many

other ships of the target group have equally glorious battle records and are similarly distinguished historically in their respective classes. It is sincerely regretted that such ships which have served with distinction in our Navy for so many years cannot be spared."

Some nuclear scientists publicly criticized Operation Crossroads. Ships, mechanically stronger structures than buildings, would remain afloat, probably undamaged, relieving those who expected total annihilation. The greatest threat lay in creating a "feeling of false security." Yet other scientists criticized the "greatest weakness" of

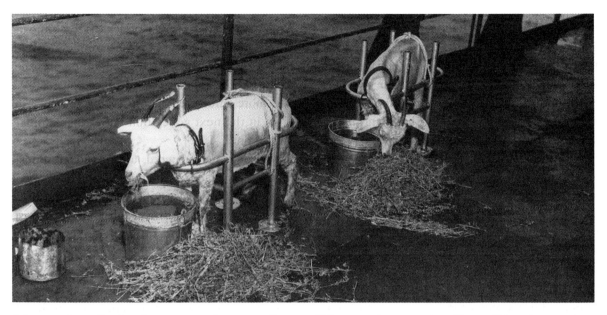

"Floating farms," a few dozen target ships were "manned" by animals to test the effects of blast, heat, and radiation on ships' crews. Some animals, like these goats, were kept penned on deck; others were locked into compartments. (National Archives)

the tests in early February 1946: "No provisions are indicated for studying the effects of the bomb's radiation on ship's crews." The scientists stressed that what would "happen in a real case, is that a large ship, about a mile away from the explosion, would escape sinking, but the crew would be killed by the deadly burst of radiations from the bomb, and only a ghost ship would remain, floating unattended on the vast waters of the ocean." Even if the crew was not "killed outright," they would "suffer such strong radiation damage as to become critically ill a few days later."

This criticism was partly met by the decision to place animals on the target ships to study the bomb's effects on them. In all, 5,000 rats, 204 goats, 200 pigs, 200 mice, and 60 guinea pigs were shipped to Bikini. The mice, "chosen from special strains showing especially great likelihood of developing cancer" were included along with the rats, those "time-honored experimental animals of radiology." The pigs were selected because of their short hair and skin, similar to that of humans. The goats were brought not only for their large volume of body fluids and closeness to the weight of an average man, but because of "their psychoneurotic tendencies."

The selection of goats underscored a basic truth that lay behind the bomb's offensive capability. Saturation bombing, fire raids, and the atomic attacks on Japan were part of a new concept in warfare, known as *Schrecklikheit*, or "terror bombing," by the Germans, who had first adopted it during World War II. In the new landscape of acceptable wartime behavior, the Allies freely adopted the concept. One welcome outcome for military planners was the absolute terror that the attacks on Hiroshima and Nagasaki had inspired. The neurotic goats were placed on the ships to provide additional information about the psychological effects of the bomb.

Protests against using animals in the tests were numerous; in all, more than half of the seven thousand letters received by Joint Task Force One involved the animals. Among these were a few letters that grimly reflected on the use of enemy vessels as targets, asking why the military did not replace the animals with "Germans and Japanese who have been condemned to death by proper courts of jurisdiction." One writer suggested that "in lieu of the 4,000 innocent animals a like or greater number of war criminals be used instead. It would seem to me to be more in keeping with the principles of justice and humanity to punish those responsible for the agonies the world was plunged into through their actions rather than to cause suffering to creatures whose only sin is existence at a lower biological level than our own." Another correspondent urged that the tests use inmates at the United States Penitentiary at Alcatraz, after a bloody May 1946 escape attempt. A few terminally ill, elderly persons and others guided by extreme patriotism offered themselves as "human guinea pigs" for the tests. One man, listing his qualifications, stressed that he had survived a ride on a champion bucking bronco. All of these offers were politely but firmly refused. Joint Task Force One's only shift in

policy was to ban the use of dogs as test animals. Man's best friend would not be atomic-bombed, but, as Admiral Blandy stressed in one press account, other animals would be sacrificed: "We are more interested in preserving the lives of men in the next generation rather than animals in this one."

As could be expected, congressional opposition also surfaced. Senators J. W. Huffman of Ohio and Scott Lucas of Illinois were the most vocal opponents. Huffman introduced a House concurrent resolution in April requesting that the president "cancel the two atomic bomb tests." The resolution died in committee. Senator Lucas criticized the tests in the face of U.S. proposals on international control of the bomb then before the United Nations: "If we are making plans to outlaw the use of the atomic bomb for military purposes, why should we be making plans to display atomic power as an instrument of destruction?" Lobbying by Joint Task Force One, the navy, and the White House convinced Congress to ignore the handful of critics. On June 14, 1946, the Senate approved a modified version of House Resolution Number 307, introduced on March 12 by Carl Vinson, chairman of the House Committee on Naval Affairs, authorizing the tests. The president signed the resolution into law the same day.

The final plan for Operation Crossroads called for three tests. The first, an airburst, was designed to duplicate the Hiroshima attack, this time over water and directed at ships. The second, a shallow underwater blast, was to simulate an attack on a fleet at anchor. The third was to be a one- to two-thousand-foot-deep detonation underneath a small group of moored vessels that would test only the underwater effects, because the blast was not expected to break the surface. The tests, in sequence, were christened "Able," "Baker," and "Charlie."

In late April, as the deadline for the tests approached, a Gallup poll, while showing that the uncertainties of the atomic age loomed large in the national consciousness, also found that 47 percent of the public were in favor of Operation Crossroads. The time had come to transform the plan into reality.

3

Bikini: The Place to Test the Atomic Bomb

The military studied sites in the Caribbean and the Pacific, and even the Outer Banks of North Carolina, before deciding where it would stage Operation Crossroads. The site it finally selected for the tests was the newly acquired atoll of Bikini in the Marshall Islands, 2,400 miles west of Hawaiʻi and 4,500 miles from San Francisco. Wrested from the Japanese during the war, the Marshalls, a former German colony, along with many other islands, formed what would become the strategically important U.S. Trust Territory of the Pacific Islands. Crossroads planners were drawn to Bikini because it met several crucial criteria. It was more than six miles wide with a lagoon of more than two hundred square miles in area, and, although under U.S. control, it was far away from established routes of oceanic travel, with only a small population of 167 people. Also, the atoll was surrounded by predictable currents that moved away from shipping lanes, inhabited shores, and fishing grounds. Bikini was selected for the tests in January 1946, and the military ordered sur-

veys and a scientific study of the atoll to assess the geology, oceanography, meteorology, and natural history of Bikini.

When Joint Task Force One was created in January 1946, it faced a race with time in order to meet a tight deadline for a first test of the bomb in May. In less than four months, the military had to find a site for the tests and assemble the ships, crews, and equipment. Most of the scientists recruited for Operation Crossroads had to be back in the United States in September in order to meet academic schedules. The demobilization of the armed forces after the war meant that enough men could not be found for the operation, particularly divers, photographers, electronic specialists, bomb disposal experts, oceanographers, veterinarians, and "various other types of technical personnel." In April 1946, the task force issued a special memorandum asking that all reserves, both officers and enlisted, volunteer to remain on active duty. Admiral Blandy promised that no one would be requested to remain on active duty after

Once isolated from the world, Bikini became well known as newsreels, radio broadcasts, and newspaper and magazine stories focused on the small atoll and its people. In this Joint Task Force One photograph, the military thoughtfully painted in the circle in which they would moor nearly a hundred ships to face the heat of an atomic bomb. (U.S. Naval Institute Photo Library)

January 1, 1947, and that "individuals will be released as soon as they have completed their task." The navy drew crews for the tests from the far corners of the globe to mount a force of 37,000 officers and men. Another 5,000 came from the army or were civilians. The total force assembled for Operation Crossroads was an impressive 41,963 men and 37 women.

Most if not all were volunteers. According to Odale Waters, captain of the destroyer *Laffey*, most of his crew were "people who wanted to be in on what promised to be a landmark event." It took Waters a month to assemble his crew, which he called "a strange assortment," at Pearl Harbor. "There were a lot of chiefs and few indians." The *Laffey*'s engine rooms were kept running by a force of eight chief machinists mates. "The normal wartime complement was one chief for each engine room. I got the eight together and said, 'Who are the two senior guys?' When they finally figured out who were the two seniors, I said, 'Well, one has the forward engine room and the other has the aft engine room. The rest of you might just as well forget those caps and buttons because you're going to be throttlemen and work for your living.' They took it well."

Officers sent for Crossroads duty in the United States were shipped across country by special trains that ran to Oakland and Terminal Island, California, to catch ships for Bikini. A lucky few caught army flights to Hamilton Field on San Francisco Bay. Each had his baggage limited to one 65-pound footlocker or suitcase. The military were told that, although personal cameras could be brought, a "final ruling will prohibit the taking of personal pictures."

Everyone was innoculated against tropical diseases in a series of shots that stretched over a few-weeks' period. One young officer, Lieutenant (j.g.) Ernest W. Peterkin, made several Crossroads trips. For some, he was fortunate enough to fly across the country in a navy C-54 transport. The twenty-five-year-old Peterkin, a radar project officer at the Naval Research Lab in Washington, D.C., was assigned to Crossroads to install icaroscopes to watch the blasts. Specially designed telescopes developed to watch for kamikazes diving out of the sun, fifty icaroscopes were Peterkin's responsibility. He left Washington on March 16, 1946, flying all night in the company of a navy commander and fighter pilot who fretted that he wasn't at the controls of the transport as it lumbered across the country. Landing at Alameda, California, on the morning of the seventeenth, Peterkin and his icaroscopes were driven to the transport ship USS *Wharton*, docked and loading equipment at Hunter's Point, San Francisco. Returning to Washington on the twentieth feeling "very tired, unshaven and dirty," Peterkin was one of many officers racing the clock to get ready for Crossroads. He worked relentlessly to overcome numerous technical difficulties with mounts, film, and his equipment until April 30, when he caught a train for the week-long trip to Oakland and joined his ship.

Besides finding enough men, the other major problem facing the task force was finding enough ships for the tests. Limited for the most part to old or damaged U.S. vessels, "for reasons of economy," the navy selected ninety-five ships for the target fleet for Operation Crossroads. The names and types of the "guinea pig fleet," as it was quickly named, were announced in a press conference in Washington on January 24, 1946. The large number of vessels was necessary, officers explained, in order to space ships of the same basic type at intervals away from ground zero and to graduate the effects of the bomb. In an apparent jab at the army, the navy announced that the necessity of a large fleet for the first test "was especially clear after it had been decided to drop the bomb from an airplane. It was clear that there would be uncertainty as to the point of detonation."

Congress limited the number of U.S. combat vessels used as targets to thirty-three ships when it authorized the tests, because "considerable public feeling developed to the effect that valuable vessels were going to be destroyed." Joint Task Force One increased the number of test vessels by including "merchant type" attack transports and landing craft. The target fleet that sailed for Bikini included two aircraft carriers, five battleships, four cruisers, twelve destroyers, eight submarines, nineteen attack transports, forty-one landing craft, two yard oilers, and an advanced-repair drydock.

The navy had stressed that the target fleet included many vessels that for the most part were "over-age or of obsolete design—which would otherwise have been decommissioned and sold for scrap." Similarly, ships heavily damaged and repaired during the war also made their way into the target fleet, among them, for example, the *Lamson* and the *Anderson* and the carrier *Saratoga*—all victims of late-war kamikaze attacks—and the cruiser *Salt Lake City*, shot up in the Battle of the Komandorski Islands. Eight submarines, all wartime products of various yards, were included because they were specifically built to resist pressure and would therefore serve as effective test instruments when submerged for the second, underwater test. The subs were taken from a group of "those scheduled for the reserve fleets or for disposal by scrapping."

The landing craft were placed in the target fleet to see how they would fare in nuclear-generated tidal waves. Two, however, were placed in the target array for the Able Test to serve as

"catchers to collect samples of any fission products which might fall out of the atomic cloud." Three reinforced concrete vessels were also included. The yard oilers YO-160 and YOG-83, and the advanced-repair drydock ARDC-13 were taken from a group of ships slated for disposal and placed in the array to satisfy the navy's Bureau of Yards and Docks' interest in "the damage of reinforced concrete structures at Hiroshima and Nagasaki. The lack of suitable land areas at Bikini made construction of similar installations impractical, even if there had been time."

In the scramble for ships, the navy reassigned vessels still at sea busy ferrying troops home from the Pacific, and dragged others from the mothball fleet. Captain David S. Bill was just completing the stripping of his command, the destroyer *Hughes* (DD-410) when the order came to make the ship ready for Crossroads. Its ammunition, fresh water, food, and all fuel except one tank for an emergency diesel gone, the *Hughes* was sitting on a mudflat off Pearl City in Pearl Harbor. Then, "the day the Admiral was coming over to haul down the flag and decommission the ship, we got a message, 'get underway ASAP. Proceed to the shipyard and prepare for the Bikini tests.' Well, to say the least, I was unhappy at that stage of the game. There were about 30 men on board and I think three officers, and that was it." Bill got the *Hughes* under way and prepared for sea, but when he sailed, he did so with half the crew he needed, and half of them were recruits straight out of boot camp.

These constraints notwithstanding, Joint Task Force One moved ahead to meet the date set for the first test—May 15, 1946. On March 22,

President Truman postponed the date of the first test for six weeks, moving it to July 1. This was done partly to allow time for the United States' U.N. representative, Bernard Baruch, to present a U.S. proposal on international control of atomic weapons, and partly to allow members of Congress to attend the tests as observers. Furthermore, the work of preparing Bikini and the ships for the tests was taking much longer than expected, despite the fact that the crews assigned to Joint Task Force One were working around the clock.

Final Preparations

Preparations for Crossroads were completed in the early summer of 1946, as the political wrangling continued and the navy struggled against its rapid demobilization and impending postwar budget cuts to find personnel and ships. A fleet of 242 ships was organized into three groups—target ships (combatants), target ships (auxiliaries), and support ships—and sailed for Bikini. Some had gone as early as March 4; others arrived between mid-May and early June. The support ships, 149 in number, included the force flagship, the transport *Mount McKinley* (AGC-7), the target vessel control ship USS *Fall River* (CA-131), and a special technical group of transports—all remodeled to serve as laboratories. Another transport, the *Appalachian,* was the press ship, and the *Burleson* served as a "great, dirtless farm" for the test animals. Two carriers, the USS *Shangri-La* (CV-38) and USS *Saidor* (CVE-117), were sent to handle naval drone and

other aircraft. Ten destroyers were assigned as a surface patrol group; 16 transports were sent to carry personnel; and a large contingent of tugs, diving support vessels, fuel barges, and other craft were attached to the service and salvage groups. Two hospital ships, the *Bountiful* (AH-9) and the *Benevolence* (AH-13), were sent to Bikini, as was a fleet of landing craft to serve as dispatch boats and "taxis" between the ships in what was described as a "Venice-like transportation system" that saw hundreds of small craft crisscrossing the lagoon daily.

Through the spring of 1946, the 53d Naval Construction Battalion prepared Bikini for the tests. The Seabees erected twelve 75-foot-tall steel towers on Bikini and Enyu islands to mount cameras and gauges. Bikini island was sprayed with DDT as bulldozers leveled the ground and crews of Seabees built dozens of huts and workshops, an officer's club, an enlisted men's club, a trap-shooting range, six basketball courts, sixteen volleyball courts, lifeguard platforms on the beach, a seaplane ramp, a water distillation and distribution system, pontoon causeways, and a weather station. In the lagoon, hundreds of moorings for ships were constructed and laid. Each mooring consisted of a 10-ton concrete block connected to three 10-ton anchors by 500 feet of chain and a short strand of riser chain leading to a can buoy on the surface.

As the target ships were assembled at Philadelphia, Bremerton, Washington, Terminal Island (Los Angeles), Hunter's Point (San Francisco), and Pearl Harbor, they were readied for the tests. This included surveys of structural and watertight integrity, installation of test equip-

Ice-cold beer at ten cents a can. Every afternoon, thousands of sailors and scientists swarmed ashore to buy a drink or relax as best as they could in the stifling heat. The officers' club "Up and Atom," shown here, was lined with souvenir life rings from the ships that had gathered for the tests. (U.S. Army Air Force Photo, National Air and Space Museum, Smithsonian Institution)

ment, and the stripping of unneeded ordnance, equipment, and "certain items of historic interest or of a critical nature," usually the bells, nameplates, commemorative plaques, and ships' silver services, which were transferred to the curator of the Navy Department in Washington, D.C. The target ships were then loaded with fuel, ammunition, gasoline, and water "as closely as possible to the battle or operating displacement. . . . Varying percentages of the wartime allowance of ammunition and the normal capacity of fuel oil and gasoline were carried in the ships' magazines and bunker tanks." Plans to fully fuel and arm the fleet were not approved for fear that post-blast detonation of ordnance would mask the bomb's effects or that the spilled fuel and gasoline from a fully loaded fleet would ignite and damage or destroy the instruments and test equipment, as well as "hamper the collecting of samples of contaminated water." At the same

time, the navy objected to heavy loading of fuel and ordnance because this would create an unjustifiable hazard for crews returning after each test to assess damage, salvage, or decontaminate the ships.

A special army unit drawn from the Signal Corps, Ordnance Department, Chemical Corps, Quartermaster Corps, and the army air forces was placed under the command of Colonel J. D. Frederick. This group installed tons of equipment, ranging from tanks, heavy and light artillery, tractors and airplanes, to guns, mortars, ammunition, radios, fire extinguishers, telephones, gas masks, watches, uniforms, canned foods, and frozen meat stored in refrigerators and later exposed for the tests aboard 22 selected vessels. Swatches of cloth were mounted on plywood sheets to face the blast. The seventy-one target airplanes, all naval types, included two seaplanes moored in the water off Bikini. Some of

The military was particularly interested in the combination of nuclear weapons and pathogenic organisms. "Special Installations" aboard target ships at Bikini included these chemical and biological warfare projectiles on the deck of LST-52. Inside these shells were "simulated" organisms to test if radiation would kill the active ingredients of biological weapons. (U.S. Naval Institute Photo Library)

the planes had sealed, empty five-gallon gas cans placed in the cockpit. "This type of instrument was roughly representative of the size and shape of a man's chest." The condition of the can after the test would be "an indication of what might have happened to a pilot with respect to crushing of the chest."

Photographers swarmed over the ships, photographing these "special installations." These also included 5,000 pressure gauges, 25,000 radiation-measuring instruments, 750 cameras, and four television transmitters. Two of the television cameras were mounted on the steel towers erected on Bikini, and microphones to pick

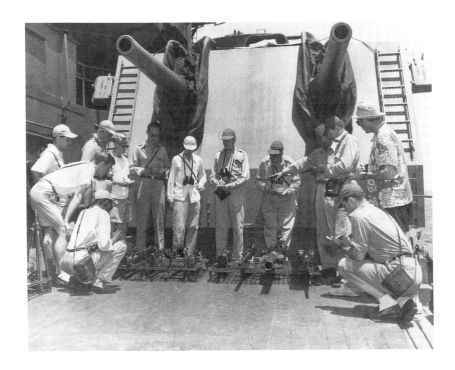

The army joins the navy. Crews loaded tons of military equipment aboard the target ships to see what the atomic bomb would do to it. Reporters shown here are looking at rifles, machine guns, and other weapons mounted on racks on the deck of the cruiser *Pensacola*. (U.S. Naval Institute Photo Library)

up the blast's sound were installed on the decks of the *Pennsylvania* and the destroyer *Rhind*.

The Ships of Operation Crossroads

The ships assembled for Operation Crossroads represented thirty-four years of naval design and development, from the oldest ship, the dreadnought battleship *Arkansas*, built in 1912, to the newest vessel, a concrete floating drydock rushed to completion in March 1946 for the tests. The ships, as the tests' planners had intended, reflected a range of types, construction methods, and hull forms, and represented in microcosm many of the elements of a typical naval force of World War II, comprised of aircraft carri-

ers, battleships, destroyers, submarines, attack transports, landing craft, and most types of carrier aircraft, including fighters and dive-bombers.

Many of the ships had had long and impressive careers, beginning with the U.S. invasion of the Mexican port of Veracruz in 1914 and World War I. Some of them, such as the carrier *Saratoga*, reflected the changes wrought by naval arms limitation treaties in the 1920s that sought to alleviate international tension and arms races. Most also had extensive World War II histories, including roles in major engagements and battles—Pearl Harbor, Midway, the Aleutians campaign, the Battle of the Coral Sea, the Battle of the Philippine Sea, the D-Day landings at Normandy, and the Battle of Leyte Gulf. The ships represented some of the most significant aspects of the war at sea: wolf-pack attacks in the submarine war of attrition against Japan, the development of the fast carrier task force, the seaborne line of supply and replenishment, shore bombardment, amphibious assaults, and the death struggle of desperate kamikaze attacks.

Arkansas

The battleships brought to Bikini were a select group of old, famous ships of the line. The dreadnought *Arkansas* was one of six near-sister ships built prior to and during the First World War that included the USS *Pennsylvania*, *Nevada*, and *New York*, also employed as Crossroads targets, and the USS *Arizona*, sunk during the Japanese attack on Pearl Harbor. The *Arkansas* was laid down in January 1910 and was launched nearly a year later, on January 14, 1911. Commissioned on September 17, 1912, the battleship's early career had included supporting the U.S. landings at Veracruz, Mexico, in 1914 at service in the 6th Battle Squadron of the British Grand Fleet in World War I. As war clouds gathered on America's horizon in early

A venerable battlewagon sent to Bikini to die. The battleship *Arkansas*, launched in 1911, fought in both world wars. *"Arkie"* ended the war shelling Iwo Jima and Okinawa before being selected as a Crossroads target ship. She was the first casualty of the second test, sinking in little more than a second. (U.S. Naval Institute Photo Library)

1941, the battleship served on neutrality patrol. During the Second World War, *"Arkie"* escorted convoys to Europe and Africa and bombarded German shore positions at Omaha Beach and Cherbourg. After a 1944 modernization, the battleship headed for the Pacific, where its 12-inch guns pounded Iwo Jima and Okinawa. Returning to the United States in October 1945, the veteran battleship made three "Magic Carpet" voyages ferrying troops home before being selected as a target ship for Operation Crossroads.

Nevada

The battleship chosen to be the target for the first test was the veteran *Nevada,* the second warship to bear that name. *Nevada* was laid down at Quincy, Massachusetts, at the yard of the Fore River Shipbuilding Co. in November 1912. The battleship was launched two years later, in July 1914. Attached to the Atlantic Fleet, she sailed for Ireland in August 1918 to join the British Grand Fleet for operations in the North Sea. Between 1918 and 1927, the *Nevada* served in both the Atlantic and Pacific before being modernized at the Norfolk Navy Yard between August 1927 and the beginning of 1930. The battleship then sailed to the Pacific, joining the Pacific Fleet, where it remained until the outbreak of war.

Moored aft of the USS *Arizona* off Ford Island on December 7, 1941, the *Nevada* got under way as Japanese dive-bombers from the carrier *Kaga* concentrated their firepower on sinking the battleship in the channel. Burning and sinking, the *Nevada* was beached. Refloated in Feb-

ruary 1942, the battleship underwent repair at Puget Sound before steaming to the Aleutians to bombard Attu. It then steamed to the East Coast and was again modernized at Norfolk before sailing across the Atlantic to provide fire support for the Normandy invasion. Alongside the battleships *Arkansas* and *Texas,* the *Nevada* pounded the Cherbourg Peninsula, and later southern France. Returning to the United States, it was readied for a return to the Pacific and participation in the conquest of Okinawa. Damaged but not knocked out of the fight by kamikaze attacks and direct hits from Japanese shore batteries, the battleship was off Japan when the war ended. After a brief stay as part of the occupation force, the *Nevada* steamed to Pearl Harbor, where it was attached to Joint Task Force One. Painted bright orange as the primary target ship for test Able, the veteran battleship arrived at Bikini at the end of May.

Prinz Eugen

One of the most famous ships sent to Bikini was the German heavy cruiser *Prinz Eugen.* This smaller-scaled version of the battleship *Bismarck* was laid down in 1936 as cruiser "J" at the Krupp Germania Werfft shipyard at Kiel. Launched on August 20, 1938, in the presence of Adolf Hitler and Grossadmiral Erich Raeder, the cruiser was christened for an Austro-Hungarian hero of the eighteenth century by Madame Nicholas Horthy, wife of the Hungarian dictator. Completed in 1940 and commissioned on August 1 of that year, the *Prinz Eugen* was built for high-seas commerce raiding. After a Baltic shakedown

Swastika flying, the German cruiser *Prinz Eugen* is launched from the Krupp shipyard at Kiel in 1938. After a short but famous career during the Second World War, *Prinz Eugen* was taken as a prize of war by the United States and sent to Bikini to face the A-Bomb. The ship impressed her American captors, many of whom hoped that the blast would leave her unscathed. (U.S. Naval Institute Photo Library)

cruise, the cruiser joined its "big brother," the battleship *Bismarck*, at Bergen, Norway, in May 1941. The two warships made their famous breakout into the North Atlantic on May 20, shadowed by pursuing British forces. Caught by the *Prince of Wales* and the *Hood* on May 24, the Germans engaged the British and sank the *Hood*, already ablaze from direct hits from the *Prinz Eugen* when a hit from the *Bismarck* detonated a magazine. The *Prinz Eugen* separated from the damaged German battleship as the pursuit continued, and thus avoided fate when the British caught up with and sank the *Bismarck* on May 27.

Arriving at Brest for sanctuary and an overhaul after engine trouble on June 1, the *Prinz Eugen* was targeted by the British and mauled by aerial bombing raids that damaged the ship and killed fifty-two men. Hitler ordered the *Prinz Eugen* and the battleships *Scharnhorst* and

Guns that once blazed away at HMS *Hood* and ended the war shelling advancing hordes of Russian troops were removed from *Prinz Eugen* at Philadelphia in February 1946 for testing. The Crossroads media releases stressed that these weapons had once exemplified Hitler's "guns instead of butter" policy. Now they remained ashore to test their efficiency while the ship faced an even more powerful force. (U.S. Naval Historical Center)

Gneisenau to break out from Brest and make for the Baltic. In a daring dash up the English Channel between February 11 and 13, 1942, the three German warships were harassed by British aircraft, ships, and coastal batteries as they made their way to safety. The *Prinz Eugen* stayed in the Baltic for the remainder of the war. Torpedoed by HMS *Trident* in a Norwegian fjord on February 23, 1942, the *Prinz Eugen* made an-

other harrowing run to Germany for repairs, again pursued by British planes. In October 1943, it became the flagship for Germany's Baltic forces and provided fire support for German troops and panzers in Lithuania and Latvia in 1944. The *Prinz Eugen* spent the last months of the war on the Baltic coast, firing more than five thousand rounds as it supported ground troops retreating from the Russian advance. Running short on ammunition, it then retreated to Denmark. The cruiser surrendered to British forces at Copenhagen on May 7, 1945. Granted to the United States at Potsdam as a prize of war, the *Prinz Eugen* was commissioned into the U.S. Navy as the USS *Prinz Eugen* (IX-300) at Wilhelmshaven, Germany, on January 5, 1946.

The U.S. Navy had no burning desire to add the German cruiser to its fleet, but had asked for the *Prinz Eugen* to keep the Russians from getting it. The original plan had been to operate the cruiser for a few months. Captain A. H. Graubart, the American commanding officer of IX-300, described his orders as a plan "to run her for a couple of months and try out everything that was better than our stuff" before discarding the *Prinz Eugen*. With a German crew working aboard along with Graubart's men, it was put through its paces off Boston Harbor before the Navy Department decided to make the cruiser a Crossroads target. After a stopover at Philadelphia, when the two 8-inch guns in turret A, a secondary battery of guns, and a range finder were removed for testing, the *Prinz Eugen* sailed for Bikini by way of Long Beach, where the last of the German crew was sent home, before crossing the Pacific with a skeleton crew of Americans. Steaming on only one shaft, the former German cruiser arrived at Bikini on June 11, 1946.

Apogon

The Crossroads submarines included two destined to become the bomb's victims, the *Apogon* and the *Pilotfish*. The *Apogon* was laid down at the Portsmouth Navy Yard in 1942 and launched in March 1943. After fitting out, it was commissioned on July 16, 1943, and proceeded to the Pacific. The boat made eight war patrols, sinking three Japanese vessels totaling 7,575 tons. It was one of ten submarines deployed for Operation Galvanic in November 1943 on its first patrol. In a coordinated action, a carrier task force, amphibious landing force, and the submarines worked together during "Galvanic" to ensure the successful invasion of Tarawa while preventing a Japanese counterstrike. At this time submarines were developed in wolf packs, and the *Apogon* was one of three boats stationed off the Japanese naval stronghold of Truk to sink ships that might attempt to strike at the U.S. fleet. Not long after, the sub scored its first kill on December 4, 1943, when it sank the *Daido Maru* north of the Marshalls.

In June 1944, the *Apogon* sailed with three other boats—*Guardfish* (SS-217), *Piranha* (SS-389), and *Thresher* (SS-200)—in a wolf pack known as the "Mickey Finns." Working off Formosa, the three boats sank 41,000 tons of shipping, but the *Apogon* did not get a kill. The boat's next sinking was on September 27, 1944, when the freighter *Hachirogata Maru* was torpedoed. The *Apogon*'s last successful attack was in June 1945 as it blockaded the coast of Japan along with other submarines and commenced finishing off the rapidly diminishing merchant marine of the nearly defeated nation. North of the Kuriles, the *Apogon* ambushed a 2,614-ton transport and sent it to the bottom on June 18. It returned to Pearl Harbor from its last patrol on September 2, 1945. Arriving at San Diego on September 11, the *Apogon* was consigned to Operation Crossroads.

Her crew lined up on the deck, the submarine Pilotfish returns home from the war to a hero's welcome on San Francisco Bay in November 1945. Instead of being laid up, Pilotfish was ordered back into the Pacific for Operation Crossroads. Moored underwater for the second bomb test, she was partially crushed and sunk. (U.S. Naval Institute Photo Library)

Pilotfish

The *Pilotfish* was laid down at the Portsmouth Navy Yard, New Hampshire, on March 15, 1944. The submarine was launched on August 30, 1943. After fitting out, it was commissioned on December 16, 1943, and proceeded to the Pacific after training, arriving at Pearl Harbor on April 26, 1944. On its first patrol, the *Pilotfish* was sent out with the *Pintado* and the *Shark* as one of "Blair's Blasters," under the tactical command of Captain L. N. Blair of the *Pintado*. The boat made five war patrols, beginning the first, to the Marianas, in May 1944, where submarines were sinking Japanese merchant vessels as they desperately tried to reinforce, supply, and ultimately withdraw stranded forces cut off as the war turned against Japan. Subsequent patrols took the *Pilotfish* to the Bonin islands, the East China Sea, Marcus Island, and off the southeast coast of Japan.

The submarine was not able to make a successful attack until the third patrol, when it hit and damaged a Japanese cargo ship off the Bonins. In 1945 the *Pilotfish* served as commander for a coordinated attack group in the East China Sea that helped to assure the successful invasion of Iwo Jima. On its last war patrol, it served on lifeguard picket duty off Japan, armed with antiaircraft guns and standing by to rescue downed airmen who had been returning from bombing Japan. After provisioning at Guam for a sixth patrol, the *Pilotfish* was off Japan when hostilities ceased on August 15. After cruising off Kii Suido on both lifeguard duty and cease-fire enforcement patrol, it motored into Tokyo Bay as part of the fleet formally occupying Japan. With eleven other submarines, the *Pilotfish* was moored alongside the tender *Proteus* (AS-19) during formal surrender ceremonies on September 2, 1945. Sent to San Francisco for layup, the boat was ordered to Bikini.

Gilliam

A large number of attack transports were sent to Bikini, including the USS *Gilliam* (APA-57). Lead ship of the thirty-two-member *Gilliam* class of attack transports, the *Gilliam* was a 426-foot long, 6,800-ton, specially designed amphibious assault ship that unloaded cargo and troops directly over the side into the landing craft. Launched on March 28, 1944, at the Wilmington, California, yard of the Consolidated Steel Corporation, the *Gilliam* was acquired by the navy on July 31 and commissioned the next day at nearby Terminal Island on the Los Angeles waterfront. It departed San Francisco on October 16, 1944, on its first voyage, with 750 army troops bound for New Guinea. The *Gilliam* then ferried troops to the Philippines in support of the reconquest of those islands before serving as a receiving ship for injured and stranded crews of warships and attack transports lost during the Battle of Leyte Gulf. The *Gilliam* ferried troops and supplies to Okinawa, and at

war's end carried occupation troops to Sasebo, Japan. The ship then made one Magic Carpet voyage home before being chosen as a Crossroads target. Arriving at Pearl Harbor on February 16, 1946, the ship was readied for the tests.

A few targets still left incomplete at war's end were rushed to completion for the tests. One of them was the concrete drydock ARDC-13, readied in March 1946. The vessel was only 60 percent complete when towed to Bikini. No armament was fitted to the floating drydock, and the main discharge pumps and cranes were never installed. Only one anchor windlass was fitted. But the dock was complete enough to serve as a target ship.

Relocating the Bikinians

As tons of equipment and hordes of military personnel came ashore, the final hours of the Bikinians in their homeland were being played out. Once German, then a Japanese-controlled territory, Bikini was now remade in an American image. The atoll was surveyed early in 1946 by the USS *Bowditch* (AGS-4) and *Sumner* (DD-692), and at that time many of the atoll's twenty-six islands were renamed, as the earlier names "were difficult to spell and would have been almost impossible to handle in dispatches." Thus Airukiiji became Arji, Bokobyaadaa became Boby, and Ourukaen became Oruk.

Aboard the *Bowditch*, scientists from the Smithsonian Institution, the Fish and Wildlife Service, the University of Michigan, the Scripps Institute of Oceanography, and Woods Hole Oceano-

The largest number of ships used at Bikini for atomic targets were attack transports like USS *Gilliam*, shown here. Heavy-duty workhorses of the sea, these transports had ferried troops, tanks, and ammunition across the Pacific and Atlantic to fight. (U.S. Naval Institute Photo Library)

graphic Institution catalogued the atoll's plant and animal life, conducted geological surveys, and collected specimens by the ton for shipment back home. The ships' crews also detonated thirty-five Japanese mines, still bobbing in the lagoon. Other hazards to navigation, 180-foot-high coral heads growing in the lagoon, were blasted to clear channels and provide a clear basin for the target fleet. In preparation for the big

blast, a hundred tons of dynamite gave Bikini its first blows.

One of the factors in selecting the atoll for the tests was its "nearly uninhabited" status. But the 167 people who did live on Bikini had to leave. These "natives" were overtaken by what *National Geographic* writer Carl Markwith described in 1946 as "modern civilization": "The outside world they knew little about, and cared less. . . . Then the U.S. Navy decided that Bikini was the place to test the atomic bomb, and almost overnight the natives found themselves in the Atomic Age." Commodore Ben Wyatt of the U.S. Navy met with the Bikinians and convinced them that the use of their homeland as the test site would help to assure world peace. Juda, sometimes referred to as the "king" of Bikini by the military, agreed, as did the *alaps* (elders), to be "relocated" for the tests.

On March 7, 1946, the people of Bikini left their homes. Their belongings, outrigger canoes, and residences were removed from the island and loaded aboard LST-1108 as the Bikinians said goodbye to their dead at the island cemetery. Once the Bikinians had boarded, the LST pulled off the beach of Bikini on the afternoon of March 7. The voyage of LST-1108 was the first of several moves for the Bikinians, as well as the beginning of what is now a fifty-year exile. Arriving at Rongerik, 128 miles to the east, on March 8, the Bikinians landed that afternoon. Only Juda would return home, briefly, during Operation Crossroads for a visit. For the others, however, "there would be no returning," at least in the foreseeable future, according to *National Geographic*'s Carl Markwith: "Civilization and the Atomic Age had come to Bikini, and they had been in the way."

The Ships Arrive

The advance crews on Bikini worked hard to have the islands and lagoon ready for the tests by the end of April, despite the postponement of Able on March 22. The first target ship to arrive was the *Nagato*, closely followed by the Japanese cruiser *Sakawa*. As the last battleship of the Imperial Japanese Navy, the *Nagato* had been hastily prepared in Japan for its final voyage. An American crew readied the ship, while hundreds of starving citizens from the streets of bombed-out Tokyo were herded aboard to remove garbage and debris. Quartermaster George Culley, pulled off the cruiser *Topeka* to man the *Nagato*, or "the Nasty Naggy," as her Yankee crew called the battleship, remembered years later that "We also had Japanese coming alongside in boats, begging for our daily garbage—which we

Battered and derelict, when at Bikini the Japanese battleship *Nagato* needed another ship alongside at nearly all times to pump out water from the leaking hull and patch in electricity to keep things running. Without this effort, *Nagato* might have sunk before the atomic bomb even touched her. (Los Alamos National Laboratory)

Guarding a ghost ship. Two marines stand guard on the deck of *Nagato*. Visitors were struck by how battered the Japanese battleship was when she arrived at Bikini. (Los Alamos National Laboratory)

gave them." Culley and his mates spent their time pumping out and repairing damaged compartments and fitting the ship out for the voyage to Bikini. The *Nagato* was, according to Culley, "almost a hulk, but able to navigate and propel herself," nothing more.

One macabre reminder of war reared its head when the *Nagato* sailed for Bikini with some of its dead crew left aboard. Previously, the American crew had opened a compartment "that was filled with dead Japanese," members of the crew killed in the last bombing raids against Japan. "The crew had to wear gas masks, but I guess that the stench was too overpowering and they had to seal up the compartment." With as many as a hundred or more corpses aboard, the *Nagato*

A fleet big enough to be the world's sixth largest naval force was assembled at Bikini for the atomic bomb tests. W. A. Shurcliff, official historian for Operation Crossroads, noted that the lagoon was "anything but quiescent. In among the target vessels and ships of the supporting fleet innumerable puny boats ploughed the water from dawn to dusk ferrying men and equipment." Every day, nearly ten thousand men went ashore. (Los Alamos National Laboratory)

sailed from its homeland with the 200-man American crew living in the officers' cabins. Too badly damaged to be used, the bridge was boarded up and the crew sailed the ship to Bikini from the armored conning tower.

The *Nagato*'s imminent arrival was noted in the April 27 issue of "Crossroads," the semi-official newsletter of the task group setting up for the tests. "Once the lofty pride of the Japanese fleet, the battleship *Nagato* will strike an ironic contrast as she enters the atoll shortly. Flying an American ensign and manned by an American crew, she will be the first of the 'guinea' ships to take her position for what may well be her last mooring. Then, humbly, she will await the fateful day when the blow, mightier than the greatest salvo ever produced by man, will descend."

After arriving, the battleship was eagerly explored by the sailors at Bikini. The "one-time pride of the Japanese Navy," reported "Crossroads," "appears to have already undergone the blast. Visitors will find that she is pretty well shattered, her decks and bulwarks rusty, and her equipment highly picked over. An LST alongside supplies all her water and electricity." The

Sakawa's arrival was delayed when the cruiser ran out of fuel and had to be towed to Bikini by the USS *Clamp* (ARS-33). Five members of the cruiser's American crew were charged with attempted sabotage when it was discovered that they had been planning to scuttle the ship prior to reaching Bikini. Two of them were sentenced to eighteen-month prison terms.

The final act of preparation was a full dress rehearsal. Originally set for June 23, the date was postponed because of heavy cloud cover that obscured the target. The weather had cleared sufficiently, however, for Admiral Blandy to reschedule the dry run, "Queen Day," for June 24. The aircraft—camera, observation, and radiological monitoring planes, and the bomb-carrying plane—flew from Kwajalein through thick clouds that thinned as Bikini was reached. The first practice run for "How Hour," the planned moment of detonation, ended when clouds obscured the target battleship *Nevada*. The second run was more successful. At 9:14, a high-explosive practice bomb dropped from the opened bomb-bay doors, plummeting slightly aft and to starboard of the battleship before detonating. "Mike Hour," the actual moment of detonation, had been reached. Observation planes flew overhead, radiation monitoring drone boats swept into the lagoon, and the task force maneuvered into position for reentry into the atoll from its point of safety fifteen miles off. The stage was set for the first use of an atomic bomb since the attack on Nagasaki less than a year before. Barring bad weather, "Able Day" would proceed on July 1.

The crew of the battleship Pennsylvania leave the ship for "Queen Day." To ensure that no one was left aboard, each man removed a tag. When the tags were gone, the ship was clear and only animals remained to face the atomic blasts. (U.S. Naval Institute Photo Library)

Officers depart from *Prinz Eugen* during the "Queen Day" rehearsal for "Able Day" on June 24, 1946. Smiling faces abound as the last officer comes down the gangway. After the tests, there were no more smiles, and evacuation was a quicker task as high levels of radioactivity drove scientists and sailors from the cruiser's decks. (U.S. Naval Institute Photo Library)

4

Able and Baker

"No one really knew what would
happen when you blew up an atomic bomb"

At 5:55 A.M. on July 1, B-29 No. 7354, better known by its informal designation "Dave's Dream" and piloted by Major Woodrow P. "Woody" Swancutt, took off from Kwajalein. It was followed by a fleet of aircraft that would document the detonation from the air, pursue the mushroom cloud and measure its radiation, and control drones that would dive into the radioactive plume to collect samples. The drones—Navy F6F Hellcats and Army B-17 Flying Fortresses—also served as "airborne target aircraft." Inside the B-29's specially reinforced bomb bay sat the bomb about to be dropped on Bikini. It was set to detonate at 515 feet, the altitude calculated to produce damage over the greatest possible area and sink only the innermost ships. A thousand-foot altitude had been considered, then rejected because of uncertainty about whether the bomb would sink any ships from that height. The 515-foot altitude was a compromise.

The bomb was named "Gilda" after the newly released Rita Hayworth movie in which the actress played a beautiful, destructive heroine in exotic South America. The movie, flown out from the States, played each night on many support ships to eager, woman-hungry crews, as Rita crooned "Put the Blame on Mame, Boys." According to Los Alamos scientist Bob Henderson, "Gilda" was "the queen of the atoll," and the movie "really kept the boys running." Leon Smith, who armed the bomb, remembers to this day that Gilda was, "Well, she was the sexiest thing around." The bomb was stenciled with the likeness of the buxom actress and her name.

The Baker bomb, assembled at the same time, was named "Helen of Bikini." The naming of the two bombs reflected the strong desire to "humanize" the weapons and consciously draw the analogy between the bomb and sex. Naming the Able bomb after the star of the sexually charged movie *Gilda* followed an erotic pattern set in the days after Hiroshima. It was evident in burlesque houses advertising "Atomic Bomb dancers," in *Life* magazine's September 1945 "unveiling" of scantily clad starlet Linda Christian at a Hollywood poolside as the "anatomic

The crew of the B-29 "Dave's Dream" poses in a jeep at Kwajalein prior to the first test. Major Woodrow P. Swancutt, the pilot, is fourth from the left in the passenger's seat. In front of him on the hood is Major Harold Wood, the bombardier. Their smiles would disappear when the bomb missed its target and they were initially blamed by the military. To this day, no one knows why the bomb missed. (U.S. Army Air Force Photo, National Air and Space Museum, Smithsonian Institution)

bomb," the 1947 pop song "Atom Bomb Baby" (which social historian Paul Boyer notes made the bomb a metaphor for arousal), and, of course, in the French bathing suit, dubbed the "bikini" after its 1946 introduction into the world of fashion. All testify to the sexual imagery of the bomb and a perennial equation of sex with death. For instance, the Elizabethans compared orgasm with dying. The idea endures in the term "femme fatale." In a world in which the potential for obliteration equals sexual power, the atomic bomb, as the deadliest weapon, also had to be the sexiest thing on earth.

The target ships were moored on the atoll's lagoon. The arrays for each test had been selected "to provide the best instrumentation possible, rather than be placed in a tactical formation. This policy was approved for both tests." The plan grouped the ships closer to the center of the array because of "the decrease of pressure with increase in distance from the zeropoint."

Eros Meets the Atom. The atomic bomb quickly became a metaphor for sex. At Bikini, the two bombs were named for women—the first for the recent Rita Hayworth movie, *Gilda*, and the second, *Helen of Bikini*. Both were particularly destructive females. In *Gilda*, Miss Hayworth crooned "Put the Blame on Mame, Boys" as she sang the song of a woman who, among other things, burned Chicago down. Helen, of course, had launched a fleet of a thousand ships and caused the Trojan War. The nose art of the B-29 "Up an' Atom," its double entendre clearly illustrated, also shows a femme fatale in front of a mushroom cloud. The "fat man" profiles to the left of the plane's name indicate that it had dropped five "pumpkins," or "fat man" dummy bombs, in practice runs. (U.S. Army Air Force Photo)

The grouping placed twenty-four ships within a thousand-yard radius of the Able zeropoint. The target fleet was moored at regular intervals from each other, along single, curved lines running out like spokes on a wheel whose hub was 5,400 yards off the beach of Bikini Island. The intent was to keep the ships from shielding each other from the blast. The center of the hub for Able was the battleship *Nevada*, selected as the target because it was "the most rugged ship available." Painted international orange (the same color as the Golden Gate Bridge) and outlined with white paint, the *Nevada* stood out in vivid contrast to the rest of the dark-blue and haze-gray fleet.

The Drop

Climbing to 32,000 feet, "Dave's Dream" reached Bikini at 8:03 A.M. and made several practice runs before making the final approach on 45 degrees true fifty miles out of Bikini. Miles away from the atoll, the crews of the ships waited aboard the support vessels. Most stood on deck and wore welders' goggles to protect their eyes against the flash. Others without glasses were cautioned when the four-minute warning was given: "All hands face aft and away from Bikini Atoll. Look down at the deck. Shut your eyes. Cover your closed eyes with the bended arm against your face. Remain in this position until after the flash."

At 8:59 A.M., "Dave's Dream" reached the target fleet. The bombardier, Major Harold H. Wood, released the bomb. It hurtled down toward the anchored fleet. When Wood shouted, "Bomb

"Turn away from the bomb. Cover your eyes." The crew of the carrier *Saidor* practice for Able. When the bomb was dropped on the target fleet, broadcasts warned observers to "duck and cover." The flash, ten times as bright as the sun, would instantly blind anyone who looked at it. (U.S. Naval Institute Photo Library)

away, bomb away!" Swancutt banked to the left at 155 degrees and dived at a 60-degree angle to increase his speed. As "Dave's Dream" sped away at 300 miles per hour, dropping 2,000 feet in the 48 seconds it took for "Gilda" to fall to the lagoon, the plane flew eight miles from the target. The bomb missed the intended zeropoint,

the *Nevada*, by 2,130 feet, detonating 518 feet above the lagoon just fifty yards off and slightly to starboard of the bow of the USS *Gilliam*. Miles away, observers on the ships saw a pinpoint of light through their goggles. "Then, suddenly, a whole hemisphere of air catches fire, ten, twenty times the size of the first burst. Through the

Facing a "brave new world," observers on the deck of a support ship watch the Able test. The thick, black Polaroid glasses blocked most light, so that those who wished could gaze directly into the heart of an atomic explosion. The dense lenses were too effective. Most observers saw only a pinprick of light. We found a pair of the glasses, discarded, in the silt on the deck of *Saratoga*'s bridge. (U.S. Army Air Force Photo)

goggles it looks fiery red. Must have been white to the naked eye. Seems to cover the whole target fleet." The bosun's mate of the USS *Pilotfish* turned to his skipper and blurted out, "Look at that, captain, oh shit!"

The firing of the bomb's detonators and high explosives compressed the 3.2-inch diameter, 6,100-gram plutonium core into a supercritical mass. Its self-sustaining chain reaction produced within a millionth of a second a tremendous release of energy equal to 19.1 thousand tons of explosive force. The burst reached temperatures reported to be close to several million degrees, nearly those at the center of the sun. Miles away, the flash was followed two minutes later by the blast's dull roar. Aboard the USS

Haven, as the flames and smoke climbed into the sky, one observer wrote: "There was an air of unreality about the whole thing. There was hardly a sound on the ship. Then the bomb went off and the continuing silence, the awful, dead, flat silence amidst all that conflagration, gave the whole thing a dream-like quality." Dick Laning, skipper of the target submarine *Pilotfish*, also watched through his goggles in awe. As a wave of heat hit him in the face, and "having been addicted to science fiction from the age of eleven and read tons of the pulps, I was swept by a feeling of nostalgic awe. . . ."

The *New York Times'* account of the blast claimed that the flash was "ten times as bright as the sun." The heat converted all matter in the area into a gaseous form that instantly expanded within the next several millionths of a second into a spherical, luminuous "ball of fire." The ball of fire continued to grow until, just a half-second after detonation, it was nearly 1,500 yards in diameter, engulfing the *Gilliam* and vaporizing the seawater below it. As the ball of fire collapsed, a cloud of vapor, reddish-brown and laden with nitrous acid and nitrogen oxide, rose above the lagoon at a speed of two hundred miles an hour. Neutrons streaming from the fireball struck the ships and water, ionizing them and creating intense but short-lived radioactivity.

At the time of the detonation, a high-pressure "blast wave" of air moving little faster than a mile per second swept 750 feet ahead of the fireball, smashing into ships as it raced out over the water. Dark roiling clouds of dust and soot from the inside of stacks shot into the sky as the ships were beaten like dirty rugs hung outside a window. "Dave's Dream," several miles away, was hit twice by the shock wave. Army observer Colonel Jack Sutherland, watching the detonation through the telescope eyepiece of a drift meter, was warned to look up by the veterans of the 509th. He didn't, and as the plane slammed into the shock wave, the colonel received a black eye as his souvenir of Able. The lagoon surface itself was pushed down several feet by the shock wave. At 1.25 seconds, the blast wave's shock front was a third of a mile distant. As it hit the lagoon surface, it bounced back, creating a reflected shock wave called the "mach effect." Dense and powerful, the mach effect moved quickly. Three seconds after detonation, it was nearly a mile from the zeropoint and towered

185 feet high, creating 165-mile-an-hour winds that swept across the atoll.

Ten seconds after detonation, the blast, now two-and-a-half miles distant and moving at forty miles per hour, had passed the ships. Now the hot, gaseous ball of fire rose, drawing air into strong "afterwinds" that sucked up water and debris, forming the stem and the top of the famous "mushroom cloud" of an atomic bomb. Thirty seconds after detonation, the cloud was a mile and a half high. As it cooled, a scant ten minutes after detonation, all the water that had been sucked up into the cloud or vaporized by the bomb condensed into a light radioactive rain that fell over Bikini. Despite the deadly rain, officials reported the level of radiation on the ships as "minimal." This they attributed to the fallout's dispersion in the atmosphere and its gradual diffusion in the rain.

The press, fifteen miles away on the support ships, described the blast as a "fascinating picture." High above the lagoon, one press representative wrote that "for a few minutes, it looked like a giant ice cream cone as it turned completely white. Looking at it then through binoculars, it seemed like floating layers upon layers of whipped cream. Again it changed colors, now to peaches and cream. It broke into two mushrooms. . . . In 30 minutes, the cloud began to disintegrate into a crazy pattern of fat Zs. In an hour, the wind had so battered it that the disintegrating cloud began to look like a giant, willowy dragon in a small boy's dream." Radio-controlled planes diving into the cloud measured radioactivity, while two navy PBM seaplanes flew toward the lagoon, their crews wearing gas masks in the stifling hot, sealed aircraft. The radiation monitors watched their geiger counters as the planes raced toward the target fleet, dodging "hot" plumes of smoke that rose from burning ships. Radio-controlled "drone" boats performed the same duty on the lagoon surface, commanded by joysticks held in the hands of fighter pilots cruising high above the atoll.

Planes followed a radioactive oil slick from the fleet as it flowed out of the lagoon, while others chased the mushroom cloud as it drifted south, away from the atoll. On the ocean, a squadron of destroyers—the "Radiological Downwind Patrol"—sprang into action. On the *Laffey*, Odale Waters later recalled with relief, "Once the mushroom cloud started blowing downwind, we ran tracks that crisscrossed back and forth under this downwind sector and took Geiger counter readings of the fallout. We were surprised by how little there was; it was practically indiscernible. But of course, no one really knew what might happen when you blew up an atom bomb. It had only been done three times before, and only twice in anger." The radiological monitors sounded the "all clear," declaring the lagoon "Geiger sweet" by the early afternoon. Slowly, in a stark line, the support vessels came steaming back into Bikini Atoll.

The Aftermath of Able

Ernest Peterkin, aboard the USS *Wharton*, reentered the lagoon at 2:30 that afternoon. "We still couldn't make out all the ships, but we could see that a couple of them were burning." Look-

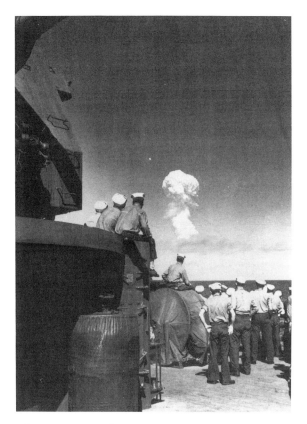

Fifteen miles out from Bikini, the crew of the cruiser *Fall River* watch the mushroom cloud from Able climb into the sky. As the cloud moved out to sea, a group of destroyers chased it, instruments on their decks ready to catch and measure fallout. On other ships, crew members recall fallout landing on them as they stood in the open. (National Archives)

ing through binoculars at ships still too radioactive to approach, Peterkin saw "bent masts, missing stacks and twisted or flattened superstructures. . . . Our ship passed close to the edge of the target array and we could [then] get a good view of the damage. It seemed strange to see ships that we had been on a few days or

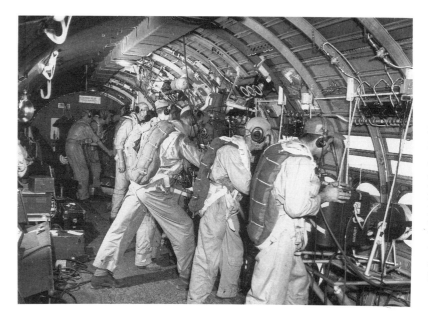

From an armada of aircraft, observers trained cameras and instruments on the bombs at Bikini. Circling above the atoll at various elevations, they filmed the blast and measured radioactivity and pressure. Some "drone" planes, without a living soul aboard, were piloted by radio into the radioactive cloud rising above Bikini, while others swooped low over the lagoon. (U.S. Army Air Force Photo, National Air and Space Museum, Smithsonian Institution)

hours before lying in the water a twisted, charred mess." As the *Wharton* passed the carrier *Independence*, flames shot out of the hangar as firefighters from other ships were rushed aboard to combat the flames.

Despite the miss, the bomb sank five ships and "immobilized" six others, while eight other ships suffered "short or long term serious loss of military efficiency" when their boilers, stacks, radio, and fire-control radar antennae were damaged. The fireball started twenty-three small fires aboard ships, some as far as 2,265 yards away, and paint on other ships 3,700 yards distant was scorched. The attack transports *Gilliam* and *Carlisle*, the closest ships to "surface zero," sank almost immediately. The *Gilliam*, caught in the incandescent fireball and battered down into the water by the shock wave, was "badly ruptured, crumpled, and twisted almost beyond recognition," and sank in seventy-nine seconds. The *Carlisle* was swept 150 feet to one side as the superstructure and masts were nearly wiped off its decks. The hull was twisted and broken. It began to burn, and five minutes and thirty-three seconds after the blast began to list to starboard. The ship sank in thirty minutes.

Two other ships close to surface zero sank quickly. The destroyer *Anderson* was hit hard by the blast and the fireball. The superstructure was torn and twisted and the stack collapsed as a

Washing away fallout, an army air force ground crew at Kwajalein sprays a radioactive aircraft with high-pressure hoses and foamite. A number of planes were contaminated, and as the water washed off some of the radioactive particles, they clung to water droplets, to clothing, and dried into the sun-baked concrete. (U.S. Army Air Force Photo)

Miles above Bikini, the mushroom cloud of the Able test climbs several thousand feet into the air as a fast-moving ring of condensation sweeps out from ground zero toward the islands that surround the lagoon. (U.S. Naval Historical Center)

fire blossomed aft of the bridge. The flames subsided for a moment, then flared up again just nine seconds after the nuclear detonation as the destroyer's ammunition exploded in two separate blasts. This was the only time a target ship's on-board munitions detonated. Burning fiercely, the *Anderson* capsized to port and sank by the stern within seven minutes. After the test, navy divers found its battered hulk lying on its port

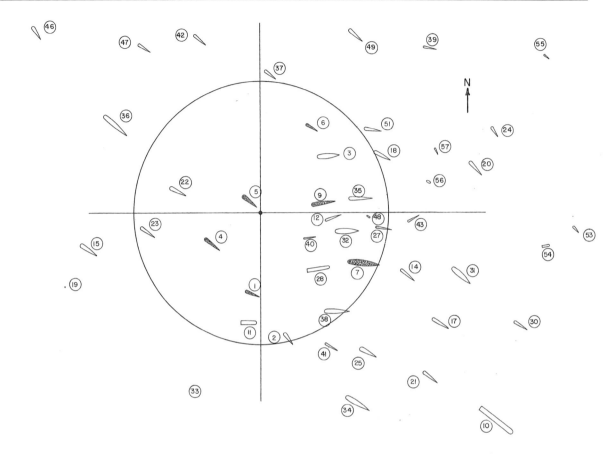

The position of the target ships at the moment "Gilda" exploded. The circle extends a mile from ground zero. The ships sunk and damaged are shown dark. No. 5 is *Gilliam*, closest to the blast. Also sunk during Able were *Carlisle* (No. 4), the destroyers *Lamson* (No. 6), and *Anderson* (No. 1), and the cruiser *Sakawa* (No. 9). The battleship *Nagato* (No. 7) was badly damaged by the bomb, as was the submarine *Skate* (No. 40) and YO-160 (No. 12). To the right of the detonation point is the intended target, USS *Nevada* (No. 32). (JTF-1 drawing redrawn by Robbyn Jackson, Historic American Engineering Record, National Park Service)

side in 176 feet of water, the bow buried in the silt. The starboard hull's shell plating was wrinkled and "several seams . . . were leaking oil and air." The deck houses were crumpled, bulwarks on several superstructure deck levels were torn away, the mainmast was stripped of its fittings, the yardarm was bent in half, and the No. 2 gun

shield was split open. Depth-charge launchers on the starboard side were torn away from the deck, and the torpedo crane was bent at a 90-degree angle.

The other ship was the destroyer *Lamson*, moored 760 yards away from the blast. Twelve minutes after the burst, the destroyer was afloat

Blasted and partially melted by an incandescent fireball, the attack transports *Gilliam* and *Carlisle* were instantly sunk by the Able bomb's burst. U.S. Marine Corps combat artist Grant Powers, assigned to Operation Crossroads, painted this impression of their destruction. (U.S. Naval Historical Center)

but heavily damaged. The lighter portions of the superstructure and the mainmast and stack were torn off the ship. The destroyer capsized to starboard, and sank with a large oil slick trailing from its ruptured hull. The *Lamson* slowly pivoted as it went down, so that when the stern hit first, the hull plates buckled and tore as the hull twisted counterclockwise. The battered destroyer's hull was wrinkled and dented along the port side, and the foremast was bent at a 90-degree angle. Navy divers visiting the wreck after the test found the depth-charge racks "twisted and torn almost beyond recognition" and unexploded depth charges littering the seabed. The ship's 21-inch torpedo tubes were undamaged and armed with a broken torpedo hanging out of one tube.

The fifth ship to sink after Able was the Japanese cruiser *Sakawa*. Moored off the port quarter of the *Nevada*, the *Sakawa* was caught by the blast, above and slightly to starboard of the cruiser's stern, 490 yards away. As the smoke cleared, observation planes flying over the target fleet saw that *Sakawa*'s superstructure and hull had suffered major damage. The superstructure aft of the bridge was smashed down, and the stack collapsed forward. The mainmast fell forward and to port, hanging over the side. The tops of the gun mounts aft were crushed, and the tops of the gun houses forward were pushed down into two-foot deep, "V-shaped" dents. The observers reported that "the stern was most badly damaged. . . . Its deck plating was crushed inward and shell plating around the counter was twisted and torn open in several places." A fierce fire, fed by the ship's fuel oil, raged on the stern for more than two hours after the blast. The *Sakawa*'s stern sank two feet into the water as the fire burned.

Through the night the cruiser slowly settled in the water and listed to port. The next day the *Sakawa* was boarded by a navy salvage team. The crew didn't stay long. The chief, as they hastily worked on the deck, exclaimed: "I don't like it; something's wrong with the goddamned ship. She's a dead ship." He ordered his men off the *Sakawa*. A line was passed to the tug *Achomawi* (ATT-148). The tug had just started towing the cruiser when the *Sakawa* rolled over onto its port side. Half-submerged, its stern resting on the bottom, it was being pulled toward Enyu Island when the order was given to cut it free. Ernest Peterkin, watching nearby, watched the foremast hit the water. "Then, as that disappeared, the bow came up vertically and she began to slide down. Big bubbles of air gushed up to the surface and in about ten minutes she disappeared from view." The only "item" recovered from the ship was a test animal, Pig No.

Twisted, battered, and on the bottom. Navy divers photographed the destroyer Lamson just a few days after Able sank five ships. Observers expecting massive destruction discounted the power of the bomb after these "disappointing" results. According to David Bradley, the divers examining the sunken ships in 1946 were "satisfied that the Bomb is not an overrated weapon." (U.S. Naval Institute Photo Library)

311, which sailors found swimming in a radioactive sea of oil. Locked in an officer's head for the test, Pig 311 had somehow escaped the foundering ship. After a series of tests, the lucky pig was shipped east to the naval hospital at Bethesda, Maryland, to live out her days. The still-thriving but sterile pig posed at Bethesda for *Life* magazine in 1947.

The other badly damaged ships were all within a thousand-yard radius of surface zero. The attack transport *Crittenden*, only 165 yards farther out from the zeropoint than the ill-fated *Carlisle*, was battered, dished, and warped but did not sink like its sister ship. *Crittenden*'s bow

Scrambling and stumbling across pitching decks, scientists and officers board the battleship *Nevada* to collect samples and equipment after Able. Aboard the ships, they found "plenty of evidence of the fury of the blast wave," according to David Bradley. Dying test animals, overturned airplanes, wrecked lifeboats, shattered instruments, toppled masts and scorched paint were everywhere. This cartoon, by Lieutenant Ernest Peterkin, captures the reboarding with humor and a realism missing from carefully posed and staged newsreels. (Ernest W. Peterkin)

had faced the bomb, while *Carlisle*, moored beam-on, took the force of the blast on an unprotected side. The two ships to suffer the worst damage and remain afloat were the light aircraft carrier *Independence* and the submarine *Skate*. The carrier's hull was "blown in and there was buckling of bulkheads." Radiation monitor David Bradley wrote that the *Independence* had been blown into a "cocked hat." The flight deck was "badly warped and buckled, and the sides enclosing the hangar were blown through." Bradley described the ship as "an impressive edifice of junk."

"Initial Boarding Teams" followed the firefighters to collect instruments and test animals from eighteen target ships. Loaded down with two flashlights, leather gloves, a knife, first-aid packet, notebooks, canteen, two "K" ration meals,

"Blown into a cocked hat" was how David Bradley described the carrier *Independence* after Able. Still too hot to board, the carrier was inspected by journalists from a safe distance. (National Archives)

and a helmet, the teams worked in haste. They did their job racing from ship to ship, scrambling aboard from landing craft that pitched precariously in the swell, then dumping their equipment back aboard to race to the next ship. During the next week, as radiation levels dropped, inspection teams followed them, poring over every ship, visiting each compartment, photographing damage, and filling out detailed forms that assessed the effects of the bomb.

For Ernest Peterkin, it was a strange scene. Boarding the target ships, Peterkin found a scene of "disorder." "Soot and burnt gear was littered all over the decks. Bulkheads pushed in, railings twisted, decks charred, ports smashed. One of the strangest odors was that of the goat and pig pens. Hay was strewn over the decks." Commenting about the bomb and the "many . . . unexplainable things," Peterkin noted: "This blast was so hot and rapid that curious things happened. A huge smoke stack hanging over one side, while below a light bulb is still intact."

Skate, the closest submarine to the blast, was moored on the surface when "Gilda" detonated. The conning tower was bent to one side, the superstructure "badly stripped and crumpled," the gun mounts torn free, and the leaking submarine could not submerge. It was towed to Enyu Island where it was beached, bow resting in fifteen feet of water, lodged in coral and "gently lifting on the incoming swells." The battleship *Arkansas,* moored off *Nevada*'s port beam, also suffered major damage. As the task force steamed back into the lagoon, clouds of smoke rose from fires on the battleship's decks, "but the shock wave did the worst damage. Stacks, masts and mast-supporting structures suffered, as well as pipe rails, bulwarks, stowage spaces. Much dishing occurred. Many doors, stanchions, and bulkheads were badly damaged." The ship was also the site of the maximum recorded radioactive contamination from Able. A pool of water on the deck was measured at eight roentgens per eight hours. The radioactivity declined sharply, however. By two days after the test, the rate of natural decay was such that only fourteen ships measured more than .1 roentgens per twenty-four hours, the set daily maximum permissible dose for the tests.

Even the concrete ships were damaged. YO-160, a yard oiler with a well-deck-designed concrete hull, was hit hard by the blast and thermal radiation. The concrete deckhouses had their bulkheads overheads blown in, and the decks and hull were spalled and cracked. Large chunks of concrete rained into the machinery spaces, smashing equipment. The vessel also caught fire. The wooden catwalk burned, along with "practically all inflammable material and equipment on the maindeck and above . . . the living and berthing spaces, steering engine room, engine room, wooden bridge." Although left afloat,

YO-160 was for all intents and purposes a total loss. Later swamped and sunk during Baker, the yard oiler was actually a casualty of Able. The other concrete target was also damaged. The wing walls of ARDC-13 were cracked, and the drydock listed from a cracked bottom.

Nuclear scientists who had feared that the great expectations for the bomb, when measured against less than cataclysmic results, would create a false sense of security had their suspicions confirmed. The *New York Times*' account of Able, filed just after the the blast, stressed that the bomb "only" sank two ships, capsized one, and damaged eighteen others. The foreign observers were particularly unimpressed, or did their best to seem so. The Russian observers shrugged their shoulders, and the Brazilian representative said he felt "so-so" about the blast. An Argentine radio announcer tooted a child's whistle as a stand in for the sound of the Able detonation. Admiral Blandy sheepishly reported that wags in the support fleet began to call Bikini "No Atoll Atoll" or "Nothing Atoll." Left unstated were the then classified assessments of "combat readiness," which found that many of the surviving vessels would, if manned, be "virtually dead in the water, their boilers, radios, radar, and equipment out of commission, and their crews dead or dying from radiation."

The submarine *Skate,* "blown to hell," was reclaimed by its crew. Enders Huey, its skipper, led his men aboard the ship with radiation monitors. Tangled debris from the superstructure was cut free, the hatches opened, and the *Skate* pumped out. David Bradley, going below to measure radiation and finding none, instead saw

The cruiser *Pensacola* shows the effects of Able. The masts and stacks droop in the aftermath of the intense heat and crushing pressures of the bomb. The deadliest effect of the bomb became obvious only a few days after the test when animals left aboard the ships began "dying like flies" from radiation sickness. (Los Alamos National Laboratory)

Her crew mustered on a radioactive hull, the submarine *Skate* cruises past Admiral Blandy's flagship, USS *Mount McKinley*. The "can-do" attitude of Captain Enders Huey and his crew struck some observers as a "hairy-chested" and futile effort. (U.S. Naval Institute Photo Library)

Briefing the secretary. Secretary of the Navy James Forrestal (second from the left) attended the Able test. Here, Admiral Blandy and other officers inspect aerial photos of Able with Forrestal. (U.S. Army Air Force Photo, National Air and Space Museum, Smithsonian Institution)

broken dishes, broken phonograph records, papers, and books amid pictures scattered over the decks. The battered submarine, its bow resting on the bottom, was righted. The engines were started. With an American flag tied to the bent periscope shears and Enders Huey balanced between them to con his ship, the *Skate* once again moved under its own power. The crew stood at attention on deck as the *Skate* made what Dick Laning of the *Pilotfish* described as a "triumphant full speed run around the task force even though his topside had been bent over about 20 degrees."

Divers working from salvage ships and tugs started surveying the sunken ships for "a full assessment of the damage done by the air blast." David Bradley, working on a "solid slimy seagoing bucket made for submarine rescue work," monitored divers as they worked below. "Those who had seen the hulk in the milky twilight of

the lagoon floor described her as being broken in three pieces and almost unrecognizable as a ship," reported Bradley. "The divers at least are satisfied that the Bomb is not an overrated weapon." The first dives were made on the *Gilliam*'s wreck on July 7, followed by dives on the *Carlisle, Anderson,* and *Lamson.* The sunken *Sakawa* was never dived.

The greatest problem facing the Joint Task Force was how to measure the effects of Able. The instruments aboard the *Gilliam* had not fully documented the blast and pressure effects or the thermal radiation, because they were more sensitive and fragile than the instruments placed aboard the *Nevada,* the intended zero-point. A large number of the test gauges and other instruments recovered from the *Gilliam* had simply gone "off the scale." Considerable time was spent analyzing Able, and every piece of evidence that could be scoured from the bottom was eagerly gathered. Divers sent to the *Gilliam* to recover instruments groped their way in "with great difficulty through the almost formless wreckage" three times before the gauges were found. Inspection of the ships, recovery of the test instruments and gauges, particularly from the *Gilliam,* and underwater photography continued until July 14, when attention turned to preparations for the Baker test.

Baker

If Able had been a disappointment, expectations were high for Baker to be a spectacle of destruction. Secretary of the Navy James Forrestal, soon to be named the nation's first secretary of defense, toured the target ships in early July. Responding to press inquiries about why the blast had not sunk the entire fleet, he remarked that "heavily built and heavily armored ships are difficult to sink unless they sustain underwater damage." Forrestal and Joint Task Force One were counting on Baker to do just that. The target array was shifted as the ships were remoored for the second test. Press accounts from the battered targets, notably the *Independence,* stressed the forces unleashed in the Able blast and the potential for Baker.

Ignored for the most part, however, was a short news item filed by the Associated Press on July 15. The test animals recovered from the target ships were now "dying like flies. . . . Animals that appear healthy and have a normal blood count one day, drop off the next day, an officer said." Twenty-five percent of the test animals on the ships were killed outright—10

percent by the blast, and 15 percent from radiation. Another 10 percent died in the laboratories aboard the USS *Burleson.* If the ships had been manned, a 25-percent casualty rate would have climbed into the thousands, not counting those crew members who would have died later or been left incapacited by radiation sickness. This scarcely noted account of radiation, more so than the blast effect, was a harbinger of a future unveiled on Baker Day.

Many of the target ships in the array were moved for Baker. Tugs shackled ships to the mooring buoys while divers connected the submarines to their submerged positions. Aboard the *Wharton,* Ernest Peterkin spent a week designing and gathering equipment to measure blast damage aboard the target ships. "As usual," Peterkin wrote in his diary, "the day before the blast we were in a frenzy of activity." The rehearsal for the test was "William Day," July 19. Five days later, the practice paid off when the fleet abandoned Bikini and the target ships for Baker. As had been done weeks before, for Able, the crews of the target ships filed off, picking up numbered tags from huge boards next to the gangplank. When all the tags were gone, the officer of the deck knew he was leaving no one behind to face the bomb. The support fleet then sailed from Bikini, through the narrow channel past Enyu Island and into the Pacific. "We are now veterans of atomic bombing," Ernest Peterkin wrote, so "there isn't as much tension as before."

Baker Day arrived on July 25. The Baker test bomb, nicknamed "Helen of Bikini," was encased in a watertight steel caisson. The caisson, prepared by Los Alamos engineer Robert Henderson, was an ingenious contraption. The conning tower of the submarine USS *Salmon*, scrapped at the naval shipyard at Long Beach, California, in April 1946, had been transformed into the caisson when one end was cut off and a hinged top made to fit over it. Rails were laid inside the emptied tower, and the bomb, with its tail fin removed, was placed on a cart and rolled inside. Tested in California's Channel Islands before being shipped to Bikini, and certified to be lowered to depths of more than a thousand feet, the caisson had been made for the third and final deepwater test, "Charlie." Early on, however, the decision was made to use the caisson for Baker.

With "Made in New Mexico" chalked on its side by U.S. Senator Carl Hatch (D-NM), an observer at the tests, the bomb was suspended ninety feet below the steel-hulled landing ship LSM-60. The LSM had been extensively refitted for its role, with special rigging facilities, a laboratory, and radio and electronic equipment. The bomb was linked to the ship by wire cable, electrical wire, and a coaxial umbilical that transmitted the ultrahigh frequency signal that detonated the bomb. At "How Hour," approximately 59.7 seconds after 8:34 A.M., tone-modulated signals from the USS *Cumberland* outside the lagoon closed circuits that armed and powered the bomb. Triggered by the signals, the bomb detonated to form a fireball that illuminated the water for a millionth of a second with intense, white-orange light.

The fireball, now a high-pressure bubble of superheated gas, erupted from the surface of the lagoon. Ernest Peterkin described it as "a huge spout and mushroom" that shot upward. Lieu-

tenant Commander Bob Underwood, a *Saratoga* officer, watched "a flash of a small boat exploding" next to the carrier. A mass of steam and water mounded up into a "spray dome" that climbed at a rate of 2,500 feet per second into a column. The center of the 975-foot thick column was a nearly hollow void of superheated steam that rose faster than the more solid 300-foot-thick water sides, climbing 11,000 feet per second and acting as a chimney for the hot gases of the fireball. The gases, mixed with excavated lagoon bottom and radioactive materials, formed a cauliflower-shaped mushroom cloud atop the column. Four seconds after the detonation, the column was 4,100 feet high. At sixty seconds, the column had climbed to its maximum height of 7,600 feet. With the column and in the cloud went two million tons of vaporized and boiling water, and at least two million cubic yards of sand and pulverized coral from the bottom. The blast excavated a 700-yard-wide, 20-foot-deep crater in the ocean floor.

The force of the eruption and the shock of the blast formed a "blast slick" of white water in a rapidly advancing circle of millions of water droplets hurtled into the air. At the same time, as the spray dome erupted into a full column, it was obscured by a vast cloud of condensation—known as the "Wilson Cloud"—that formed eighteen seconds after detonation and then quickly dispersed into a ring of wispy clouds that vanished after thirty seconds had elapsed. The blast was recorded thousands of miles distant on the mainland of the United States as an earthquake measuring 5.5 on the Richter scale. The shock wave, sweeping through the water, also induced pressures at 90 feet that equaled

Baker erupts from the lagoon. Less than a second after detonation, a million tons of water and coral shoot into the sky. The "blast slick" of white foaming water races across the surface of the lagoon, while a thick cloud of condensation begins to form, blotting out the target ships. (U.S. Naval Institute Photo Library)

those of more than a mile down. The *Pilotfish*, closest submarine to the blast, had every bulkhead ruptured as the air inside the boat was squeezed out by a peak overpressure of 5,200 pounds per square inch. Air and water rushed through the submarine before punching out the bow, as the vessel, built to withstand the repeated hammering of enemy depth charges, was partially crushed and sunk.

The shock wave on the surface was equal to a four-kiloton blast, hitting and damaging an unmanned plane passing overhead at 10,000 feet above the water. On the lagoon surface, the shock wave and the erupting force of the column created a series of waves that swept across the surface at 45 knots, smashing into the moored ships. The first wave, 94 feet high, slammed into the *Saratoga* and *Arkansas* seven seconds after detonation. Thirteen seconds later, a 47-foot wave hit the ships, followed by a 24-foot wave 47 seconds after the blast. Increasingly smaller waves followed, gradually diminishing to a 9-foot wave that crested 12,000 feet from surface zero. Bikini Island was hit by a 15-foot wave that swept over the beach, dragging and pounding the landing craft moored on its shores.

Then, just as the dull rumble of the blast reached the support ships, the two-million-ton column succumbed to the forces of gravity. As it collapsed with a tremendous roar, a doughnut-shaped cloud of water drops "like the spray at the base of Niagara Falls . . . but flowing almost as if it were a . . . fluid" poured across the lagoon and the target fleet before stopping two to three thousand yards from surface zero. Moving at speeds of 45 miles per hour, this "base surge" of

highly radioactive fog rolled into the ships, drenching them in a 10,000-roentgen spray that poured into sealed compartments. As it blew past the fleet, the dense fog slowly lifted, exposing a cluster of listing, half-sunk ships in a pool of water that was as "hot" as a pile of 2,500 to 8,300 tons of radium. At that moment, Bikini was the deadliest spot on the planet.

A fatal dose of radiation is generally assumed to be 400 roentgens per twenty-four hours. Anyone aboard the target ships that were within 700 feet of surface zero would have received a fatal dose between thirty to sixty seconds after detonation, if the shock and violent motion of the ships did not kill them first. If not, within an hour, a dose twenty times fatal—8,000 roentgens—would have been received. On the atoll's islands, anyone left would have received a fatal dose within seven minutes. Four hours after the blast, radiation levels fell off to 65 roentgens per twenty-four hours, as the contaminated water was flushed out of the lagoon and mixed with the formerly uncontaminated ocean. The overall radiation level in the lagoon's water five days after the blast was just .1 roentgens per twenty-four hours. Below, however, a four- to eight-foot-thick layer of contaminated sediments coated the bottom, the result of 500,000 tons of pulverized coral from the crater that had fallen back into the lagoon after the blast. In some spots the radioactive mud was deeper: a diver working along the port side of the sunken *Arkansas* sank up to his armpits.

The first casualty of the Baker bomb was LSM-60, which literally disintegrated in the blast. Some observers thought they saw pieces of the landing ship climb the water column, but no tangible trace of the bomb-carrying ship was ever found. Sailors boarding the target ships that survived Baker found radioactive globules of melted metal on their decks—a large number were found on the *Prinz Eugen*, nearly a mile distant. These, said the radiation monitors, were all that was left of the LSM—a vaporized cloud that had once been a ship had condensed and fallen like rain to pelt the lagoon surface.

The *Arkansas*, moored close to the LSM, was hit hard by the blast. One of the more pervasive myths of Bikini is how the veteran battleship was lifted, end on end, to stand straight up in the blast column. A dark spot in the column at the *Arkansas'* position, taken by remote camera little more than a second after detonation, is cited as proof of the force of the bomb. Actually, time-lapse photographs and archaeological examination of the battleship show that the vessel was battered and capsized by the blast waves before the column lifted into the atmosphere.

At .024 seconds after the explosion, as the spray dome burst to the surface, the blast slick had nearly reached the *Arkansas*. At .22 seconds, the shock wave hit the battleship. The stack and the foremast began to bend, and at .27 seconds the stack toppled over the side. At .38 seconds, the blast slick was racing past the ship as the foremast bent forward. Just .1 seconds later, a wave broke over the bow, inundating the battlewagon all the way aft to midships. At .68 seconds, the *Arkansas,* rolled by the shock wave that hit fully along the starboard hull, was overwashed by waves. At .81 seconds, the "last vestige" of the capsizing hulk was seen. At one sec-

ond the vessel was gone, its bulk partially blocking the upsurging steam and water in the column to form a gap; the dark spot visible as the Wilson Cloud lifted to show the nearly thousand-foot-wide stem punching into the sky.

Another ship, the destroyer *Hughes*, was close to the *Arkansas*. To this day the captain firmly believes that a dark spot in the water column was his former command, "flopped end over end and then dropped." Reboarding his irradiated command after Baker, the *Hughes'* commander, David S. Bill, found lines shattered and his ship filled with water. For Bill, the issue of radiation was a moot point. Had his ship been manned, "not a single soul on board could have survived. Their skulls would have been fractured and their legs broken" as the ship was heaved out of the water by Baker.

Two other ships hit hard by the blast took longer to die. The first was the *Saratoga*. Initially placed just 300 yards off the zeropoint, the aircraft carrier's mooring had been changed because it was likely to sink too rapidly for photographic observation. Shifted to a position 500 yards off LSM-60, the *Saratoga* was well within the 900- to 700-yard "lethal zone" for the test blast. Because of slack moorings and a wind change, it slowly drifted closer, so that at detonation it was probably within 300 yards of the bomb, as if it were the carrier's fate to be so close. As the spray dome erupted from the lagoon, the first blast wave lifted *Saratoga*'s stern 43 feet and the bow 29 feet, as the carrier was swept by water. The second wave slammed into the starboard side, sweeping away the five aircraft, armored cars, tanks, and other equipment bolted

The curtain rises. As the cloud of condensation lifts, the thousand-foot thick stem of Baker's burst rapidly rises above the ships, dwarfing the battleships *New York*, *Pennsylvania*, *Nagato*, and the cruiser *Pensacola*. To the right, the dark spot in the column marks where the battleship *Arkansas* has just capsized and sunk. Contrary to popular belief, the spot is not *Arkansas*, but a hole in the column made when the water was displaced by the mass of the sinking battleship. (U.S. Naval Historical Center)

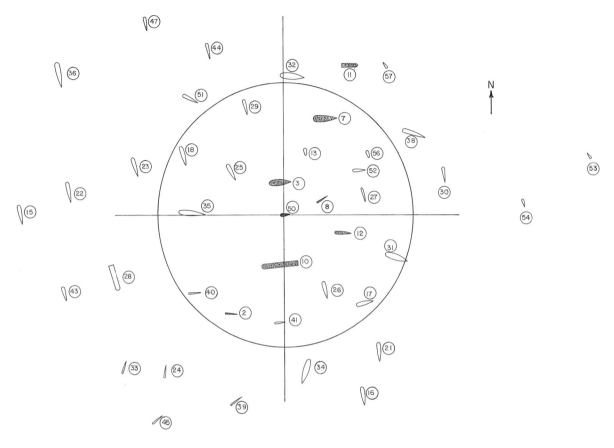

The position of the target ships for Baker, when "Helen of Bikini" erupted from the lagoon. The bomb was suspended beneath LSM-60 (No. 50) and almost immediately sank *Arkansas* (No. 3) *Pilotfish* (No. 8), and *Apogon* (No. 2). YO-160 (No. 12) sank shortly after the test, as did *Nagato* (No. 7), *Saratoga* (No. 10), and ARDC-13 (No. 11). All of the ships shown on the chart were hopelessly irradiated, including *Prinz Eugen* (No. 36), the battleships *Nevada* (No. 32), *New York* (No. 31), and *Pennsylvania* (No. 34), the carrier *Independence* (No. 28), and the destroyer *Hughes* (No. 27). (JTF-1 drawing redrawn by Robbyn Jackson, Historic American Engineering Record, National Park Service)

to the deck as the *Saratoga* was dragged and blown 800 yards, finally stopping three and a half minutes after the burst. Then the ship was obscured by the base surge. When the cloud of dense fog lifted thirty-three minutes after the detonation, the *Saratoga* had drifted back to-

ward the zeropoint, listing to starboard and leaking oil. "Deak" Parsons and other officers argued that the carrier should be beached to prevent its sinking. However, the radiation levels were too high to allow the support ships to approach any closer. As the 42,000 men of Joint Task Force

With a final gasp, belching air and oil, the bow of *Saratoga* lifts as she sinks after Baker. The loss of the carrier was a bitter blow to the Navy, who felt that if they had been able to board the ship and start the pumps, she could have been beached and saved. But *Saratoga* was a "radioactive stove" and her sinking a forgone conclusion. (National Archives)

One listened to speaker broadcasts of observers training their binoculars on the ship, the *Saratoga* took nearly eight hours to die.

Listing first to starboard and settling by the stern, at 2:10 P.M. the *Sara*'s flight deck at the stern was within 10 feet of the water. Listing three more degrees to starboard, the deck settled more, and at 3:45 was within three feet of the water. Ten minutes later, the *Sara* filled rapidly as water poured down the boiler intakes and elevator. The stern struck bottom at 4:00 P.M. Then the carrier righted and "hung momentarily with the mast, the top of the pilothouse, and approxi-

mately 150 feet of the bow out of the water." Air trapped in the ship's compartments "all along the port side bubbled violently to the surface, throwing spray into the air." *New York Times* correspondent Hanson W. Baldwin, watching with the rest of the task force at a safe distance as the carrier slowly succumbed, described the scene:

There were many who had served in her in the observing fleet and they fought with her through the long hot hours as the sun mounted. . . . Outside the reef—a safe distance from the radioactive waters in the lagoon—the observing ships cruised, while the "Sara" slowly died. There were scores who wanted to save her—and perhaps she might have been saved, had there been a crew aboard. But she died a lonely death, with no man upon the decks once teeming with life, with pumps idle and boilers dead.... From three o'clock on she sank fast, her buoyancy gone, as the fleet kept the death watch for a "fighting lady." "Sara" settled—the air soughing from her compartments like the breath from exhausted lungs. At 3:45 P.M. the starboard after corner of her flight deck was awash; then the loud speakers blared: "The water is up to her island now; the bow is high in the air." She died like a queen—proudly. The bow slowly reared high; the stern sank deep, and, as if striving for immortality, the "Sara" lifted her white numeral "3" ... high into the sun before her bow slowly slipped under. Her last minutes were slow and tortured. She fought and would not sink, but slowly the "3" was engulfed by the reaching waters ... the tip of her mast was the last bit of "Sara" seen by man....

The bow went under at 4:06, and four minutes later the mast sank from view.

The *Nagato*, moored 400 feet off *Arkansas'* port beam, was swept sideways 400 yards by the blast. As the base surge lifted, observers saw that the Japanese battleship was slowly sinking. Left alone, the ship continued to list slowly, taking on water from holes punched in the bottom of the hull. Whereas efforts were made to save other ships, and considerable anguish was felt when the *Saratoga* could not be saved, the *Nagato* was unconcernedly left to its fate. The Director of Ship Material reported to Admiral Blandy on July 29, when foundering of the battleship

Facing disaster with humor. The sinking of the target fleet made their officers and crews both angry and sad, particularly when radioactive ships were scuttled because they were too hot to handle. As Ernest Peterkin's cartoon shows, naval bureaucracy remained intact, along with a stiff upper lip, much to his and other observers' humorous delight. (Ernest W. Peterkin)

seemed imminent, that "radiological hazards prevented salvage operations on *Nagato* ... he intended to concentrate decontamination efforts ... on other damaged ships which in time would require salvage measures." That evening, the *Nagato* sank unobserved. David Bradley offered a eulogy: "I, for one, am not sorry to see the *Nagato* gone. She was a massive and brutal structure, having neither grace nor beauty. She gave no comforting illusion that war is anything but an ugly, brutal, and totally insane occupation of man."

Although Baker's blast was impressive, like Able it had failed to achieve total destruction. Able had claimed five ships, whereas Baker had a few days afterward taken nine vessels to the bottom. Reporter William L. Laurence described a new public attitude as a result of Operation Crossroads. Returning to the United States, he found that, whereas "before Bikini the world stood in awe of this new cosmic force . . . since Bikini this feeling . . . has largely evaporated and has been supplanted by a sense of relief unrelated to the grim reality of the situation." Laurence felt this was because the average citizen grasped at "the flimsiest means that would enable him to regain his peace of mind. He had expected one bomb to sink the entire Bikini fleet, kill all the animals . . . make a hole in the bottom of the ocean and create tidal waves. He had even been told that everyone participating in the test would die. Since none of these happened, he is only too eager to conclude that the atomic bomb is, after all, just another weapon."

"DOCTOR, WILL YOU BE HERE FOR CHARLIE?"

Lampooning the scientists. The detailed observations and numerous experiments at times made it difficult to see the forest for the trees. As ships toss and sink, and a family of ducks toddle into the water, an intent scientist measures waves while his assistant asks if he will be staying on for the third test, Charlie. (Ernest W. Peterkin)

5

The Radioactive Aftermath

Less than a week after Baker, most of the observers departed. The press, some of the laboratory ships, and the support carriers left on August 1, followed by most of the other ships and their crews on August 10. On the tenth, the last animal survivors of Operation Crossroads were shipped in the USS *Burleson* to Norfolk, Virginia. The creatures would be turned over to the navy's laboratories and medical center at Bethesda, Maryland, outside Washington, D.C. Left behind were the salvage and service vessels, the transports *Haven* and *Wharton*, and the target ships.

While official reports stressed that little long-life radioactive material was found on the target ships after Able, such was not the case for Baker. The water had absorbed nearly all the bomb's heat and almost half its nuclear radiation. Even the salt in the water was transformed into radioactive material. The target fleet was reboarded a few hours after Able, but after Baker only five vessels at the extreme ends of the target strings—*Cortland* (APA-75), *Fillmore* (APA-83), *Bladen* (APA-63), *Geneva* (APA-86), and *Niagara* (APA-87)—could be boarded. They lay just beyond the outer limit of the base surge's reach. Access to the rest of the fleet was denied by high radiation readings. By July 26 and 27, salvage teams were able to beach the sinking destroyer *Hughes* and the transport *Fallon*, each close to the now sunk *Arkansas* and foundering. Both vessels were so radioactive "that taking them in tow . . . required fast work. The forecastle of *Hughes*, for example, had a tolerance time of about eight minutes." The submarine *Dentuda*, also leaking, was beached on Enyu on July 28. Three days after the test, surveys of most target ships had to be made from 50- to 100-foot distances. Radiation exposures on some ships were intense: autopsies of test animals from the *Gasconade* measured fatal exposures of 2,700 roentgens per day.

Initial efforts to decontaminate the ships were hampered by the lack of plans for organized decontamination, as "the nature and extent of the contamination of the targets was completely un-

A fire-fighting navy tug sprays down USS *New York* in an attempt to wash off radioactive particles. Water didn't work, nor did soap, nor foamite (a fire-fighting foam), nor lye. (U.S. Naval Institute Photo Library)

expected." The first efforts with the beached *Hughes* employed navy fireboats to wash down the exteriors of the ship, because "water might take up some of the radioactive materials in solution." Washings reduced the radioactivity by 50 percent on the *Hughes*. The exposure rates were diminished to a still deadly 9.6 roentgens per day on the forecastle and 36 roentgens per day at the stern. Subsequent wash-downs had no measurable effect. Foamite, a water-mixed firefighting foam, was sprayed on the ship and washed off. Two washings reduced the *Hughes'*

readings to levels between 2.0 to 8.5 roentgens a day.

Radioactive material adhered to the ships' wooden decks, paint, tar, canvas, cordage, rust, and grease. Although some of it could be washed off, the only really effective means of removal was sandblasting the ships to bare metal, stripping off every piece of planking, and bathing brass and copper in nitric acid. At Bikini, decontamination work was done in stages after several experiments, including the washings. After an initial inspection, work crews came

"Decontaminating" the irradiated Prinz Eugen after Baker. The bare arms, ankles, and brooms tell it all. A large number of men received substantial doses while futilely trying to clean the ships. "The chief turned his booted, sweating, profane and laughing crew loose with brushes, water and a barrel of lye," wrote David Bradley, and yet Geiger counters showed that radiation levels remained high. (National Archives)

aboard and removed "all exposed organic materials," such as canvas and rope, as well as wood. A paint-removal mixture of 450 pounds of lye, 650 pounds of boiler compound, and 75 pounds of cornstarch was mixed with a thousand gallons of fresh water and steamed. The mixture was applied in two washings, once with an inch-and-a-half firehose general purpose or fog nozzle, and two hours later with monitor nozzles at maximum force to blast loose paint free and into the water. Spots with adhering paint, rust, and scale were then removed by the ships' crews with long-handled brushes, holystones, and any other "available means."

Scrubbing the ships by hand proved ineffective. The work on the battleship *New York* was a case in point, as radiological monitor David Bradley discovered:

The main deck forward had not been touched as yet . . . I made a careful survey of the deck, finding the intensity to vary a great deal in a matter of feet. One gets the impression that fission products have become most fixed in the tarry caulking of the planking and in rusty spots in the metal plates. When the survey was complete the Chief turned his booted, sweating, profane, and laughing crew loose with brushes, water, and a barrel of lye. Yet when the hydraulics were done and the deck rinsed clean again, another survey showed the invisible emanations to be present. . . . The portly Chief stood watching the dial on my Geiger counter, completely bewildered. The deck was clean, anybody could see that, clean enough for the Admiral himself to eat his breakfast off of. So what was all this goddam radioactivity?

The scrubbing efforts were also hampered by the short times the crews were allowed to remain aboard because exposure to radiation on most ships was limited. An early goal of the decontamination effort was to bring the level down to allow at least two hours aboard the ships to conduct surveys, recover test instruments, and continue decontamination. It was hoped that during these two-hour work periods the crews could "apply detailed scrubbing, abrasive, and paint removal action as necessary to reduce the radioactivity sufficiently to permit continuous habitation of the ships." But only complete removal of the contaminated surface reduced the radiation. The navy discovered, too, that "paint-

ing over the surface produced no reduction in activity."

"Lightly" contaminated ships—*Conyngham, Wainwright, Carteret,* and *Salt Lake City*—were the first vessels subjected to "detailed" decontamination on July 30. Other ships followed; by August 5 several ships were being pumped out, and "secondary decontamination" of others followed. Meanwhile a few target vessels that could not be saved were deliberately sunk. LCT-1114, capsized and drifting in the lagoon, was sunk with demolition charges on July 30. The concrete floating drydock ARDC-13, half-submerged and capsized, sank on its own on August 6. Five other landing craft were sunk inside the lagoon with demolition charges, while another landing craft and the landing ship LST-125 were sunk outside the atoll entrance by gunfire on August 10 and 14.

On August 15, two landing craft being towed from Bikini were sunk by gunfire near Rongelap. Meanwhile, inspection dives began on August 24 on the sunken target ships, with salvage efforts focused on the three submarines sent to the bottom during Baker: *Apogon, Pilotfish,* and *Skipjack.* Though the first two boats could not be raised, the *Skipjack* was successfully brought to the surface on September 2 after more than a week's hard work. It was the only Crossroads casualty successfully salvaged. Nearly 80 percent of the test instruments "lost" with the sunken ships were recovered and assessments made of the damage to the vessels, but radiation in the water kept the divers' times to a minimum. A full year after Crossroads, the diving equipment used after Baker was found to be radioactive.

Divers descend into the depths, 1946. The navy sent two-man teams into the lagoon to recover instruments and record damage to sunken ships. In the "milky twilight" of the lagoon, they walked through broken hulls, on radioactive decks, and in one case, sank chest-deep into radioactive mud next to the overturned *Arkansas*. (U.S. Naval Institute Photo Library)

The major problem, however, was the lack of radiation monitors and equipment. Crossroads radiological safety, a concern of test planners who had sought to ensure that "no successful suits could be brought on account of the radiological hazards," had set up a team under Colonel Stafford Warren, a veteran of the Manhattan Project who had also been a member of the first American assessment teams to enter Hiroshima and Nagasaki. As Crossroads planning proceeded, Warren assembled a team of sixty radiation monitors—half of them from the Manhattan Project, the other half military doctors. The scope and magnitude of the tests, however, dictated the need for more monitors, and Warren scoured universities and the armed forces for additional personnel. After training, these men, some learning their jobs en route to Bikini, were shipped out.

A variety of instruments, including film badges and electric-charge dosimeters for determining individual exposures, were shipped with them. Delays in obtaining enough monitors meant that they arrived nearly last at Bikini in mid-June, just two weeks before the first test. At Bikini the monitors faced several problems. The first was that the film badges only recorded exposures of 0.04 to 2.0 roentgens: higher exposures gave the same reading as no exposure. Heat and moisture, present in great quantities at Bikini, also clouded results. The order went out to place the long, pencil-like dosimeters inside tied condoms to keep them dry. When the dosimeters were collected and read, the discarded condoms were thrown into the ocean along with other garbage. This led to a monumental misunderstanding. En route to a briefing, *Pilotfish* skipper Dick Laning passed the hospital ship in a landing craft. "I noticed the coxswain and the crew of the boat engaged in animated conversation and pointing over the side. We were passing through a stream of floating condoms. I got close enough to hear that they were worried about the half dozen or so female nurses aboard the hospital ship. 'Them fucking officers and scientists will ruin them gals!' I found it necessary to report to the Task Force Commander at his meeting so we could avoid a scandal in the media."

After Baker, contamination on a scale larger than anticipated, inadequate equipment, inexperienced personnel, and difficult working conditions overwhelmed the monitoring effort. As teams worked to determine which ships were

"Geiger sweet," or "Geiger sour," the Crossroads' set limit for exposure, 0.1 roentgens per day, the same as for the Manhattan Project, was met within minutes, a half-hour, or a few hours. Work was curtailed aboard the target ships, but to make matters worse, increasing radioactive contamination of the support ships now anchored in the lagoon introduced the need for monitors on the nontarget vessels. The radioactive water of the lagoon was accumulating radioactive materials in the evaporators and saltwater lines of the support vessels moored and working in the lagoon, while contaminated marine growth irradiated their hulls to create readings in some cases reaching as high as 0.204 roentgens a day, twice the set limit. Bunks next to the contaminated hulls were abandoned, and nervous men limited the time they spent sitting on toilets that flushed with radioactive salt water.

As the limits were passed on the maximum permissible doses for monitors and ships' crews on the target ships, in part because of a "hairy-chested" attitude toward the radiation, Colonel Warren urged Admiral Blandy to abandon Operation Crossroads and withdraw from the contaminated lagoon and ships. The final straw was the discovery of potentially fatal alpha-emitting particles inside the *Prinz Eugen* "which were not detectable with the monitoring instruments in use at Bikini. Further investigation showed probably widespread presence of alpha emitters . . . even in spaces not obviously contaminated. Since no alpha detectors for general field use were available and the alpha emitters are one of the most poisonous chemicals known, their presence was considered a serious and indeterminate menace." Stressing inadequate crews

Baker contaminated Bikini Lagoon. The salt in the water was made into a short-lived radioactive isotope, while the algae that fouled ships' hulls were also irradiated. The ships that stayed behind after Baker to recover equipment, conduct more tests, and prepare the surviving target ships for withdrawal were also contaminated. Steel hulls and saltwater systems for fire-fighting and sanitation were radioactive. "The timid soul" in this cartoon nervously passes his Geiger counter over the toilet in recognition of the fact that too long a sitting could be hazardous to your health. (Ernest W. Peterkin)

and facilities, Warren drove his argument home. Blandy ordered withdrawal from Bikini on August 10, noting that "although all waters and land areas of Bikini are well within radiological tolerance, the tendency of radioactivity to concentrate and accumulate in ships, in evaporators and in marine growth on the hulls, makes it mandatory to remove the ships of the task force from this atoll with its small and decreasing, but nevertheless cumulative hazard."

On August 10, as Blandy departed Bikini, he gave orders to cease decontamination and move the surviving target ships to Kwajalein. The decontamination effort began to shift to Kwajalein on August 16. The fleet slowly left Bikini as the work priority at the lagoon changed to "recovery of instruments and the clearance of those ships designated for use in test Charlie." The third and final test, which was to include five submarines and five capital ships moored seaward of Oruk Island, at the southwestern end of the atoll, was tentatively scheduled for March 1947. Mooring blocks were manufactured on the island so that the ships could be "streamed" from it by long cables. Landings were built on the western islands, and construction of instrument towers began, part of the work necessary to place ten vessels over a bomb that was to be slung a thousand feet below the surface.

The work for Charlie was well under way when the president decided on September 7 to cancel the last test of Operation Crossroads. The reason cited for the cancellation was that sufficient information had been gathered during Able and Baker. Less public reasons included the opposition of Los Alamos scientists to a third test, the difficulty of holding the task force together in a rapidly demobilizing military, the necessity for many of the nonmilitary scientists to return to their universities and colleges for the fall session, and the ominous fact that all of the anticipated target vessels for Charlie remained radioactive.

The "severe" contamination problem was kept as quiet as possible. According to a secret August 10 memorandum from Colonel A. W. Betts, the observer from the Manhattan Engineer District of the U.S. Army Corps of Engineers, to his boss, Brigadier General Kenneth D. Nichols, "the classification of this memo can only be explained by the fact that the Navy considers this contamination business the toughest part of test Baker. They had no idea it would be such a problem and they are breaking their necks out here to find some solution." Gross decontamination efforts continued, which enabled the navy to complete the removal of test instruments and records, make technical inspections, and salvage the beached *Hughes, Fallon, Dentuda,* and the raised hulk of *Skipjack.* However, the navy's assessment of the decontamination efforts at Bikini concluded that the work, "although successful to a certain extent in the limited application they [the target ships] received, revealed conclusively that removal of radioactive contamination of the type encountered in the target vessels in test Baker cannot be accomplished satisfactorily."

Although the decision to move to Kwajalein had been made on August 10, it was not until the twenty-fifth that the navy's Director of Ship Material felt that all "significant information"

had been recorded and declared that all technical inspections at Bikini were complete. That day he and his staff left for Kwajalein "to establish facilities there for continued examination and radiological re-checks of the target ships." Some of the target vessels had already departed on August 19, and now the other ships followed. By August 29, only nineteen target ships—the destroyer *Mustin,* the fuel barge YOG-83, and sixteen landing craft—were left at Bikini, along with eighteen diving support and salvage vessels. All of the target vessels were gone by September 9, and on September 26, 1946, the navy evacuated Bikini. However, the chief of naval operations ordered that the abandoned atoll be kept under constant surveillance "to restrict entry of foreign, merchant, or private shipping," in large part because of fears that foreign scientists could analyze bomb residues to discover the "atomic secret."

Apart from the nineteen sunken vessels left on the lagoon bottom at Bikini, the remainder of the surviving targets were at Kwajalein, anchored in the lagoon between Kwajalein and Enubuj Islands. Decontamination efforts at Kwajalein ceased at the end of September 1946. After that, the work focused on removing ammunition left aboard the ships for disposal. Until the end of November, crews worked aboard with radiological monitors, clearing compartments in advance with Geiger counters in hand. They were followed by the work crews, clad in coveralls, rubber boots, and gloves, and wearing rescue breathing gear.

An order was issued not to drydock, weld, or cut into the hulls of the surviving target ships to

Colonel R. L. Snider of the U.S. Army Air Force runs a Geiger counter over the "hot" engine of a B-29. A number of the planes, returning from Bikini after the first test, were radioactive. (U.S. Army Air Force Photo)

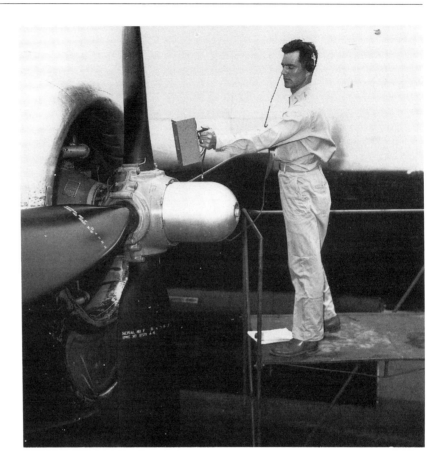

avoid exposing workers to contaminated fumes or dust. This meant that vessels damaged in Able and Baker could not be repaired or mothballed, actions that in time would have allowed the radiation to decay and subside naturally. Ernest Peterkin, aboard the battered battleship *Pennsylvania*, wrote in his diary, "It is a very peculiar sensation to be working among this activity knowing that there is a possibility of getting an overdose that could have lethal effects." "We walk around these deserted ships in a strange atmosphere," he wrote. "Loose gear and doors bang and creak with each roll. Empty decks, compartments and passageways have a haunted look. . . . Walking about on these ships gives the feeling that I imagine one would receive if they found the main street of a big city completely deserted at high noon with all the shops open. The absence of men on these ships is indescribable."

A confidential memorandum from the commander-in-chief of the Pacific Fleet and dated September 4 authorized the sinking of contaminated vessels at Kwajalein. Under no circum-

Fearing that deteriorating ammunition left aboard the contaminated target ships might go off, worried navy officials sent crews back aboard to remove the bombs and shells. Laboring in darkened compartments, in stifling heat with constantly fogging face masks and heavy coveralls, these men were only able to remove some of the ammunition before their work was halted. (U.S. Naval Institute Photo Library)

stances were any vessels to be burned. The same day, in Washington, Admiral Blandy reported at a press conference that forty-five of the target ships had been decommissioned after the tests. Only "9 of 92 ships escaped at Bikini,"

noted Blandy. The eighty-three ships that did not escape "were either sunk, damaged or contaminated by radioactivity," leaving only the submarines *Tuna, Searaven, Dentuda,* and *Parche,* and the transports *Cortland, Niagara, Bladen, Fill-*

more, and *Geneva* more or less untouched. Blandy, alluding to the confidential directive just issued, stated that he had sought and received permission to sink "a number of small landing craft damaged in the experiments, pointing out to his superiors the dangers of possible lingering radioactivity and also . . . the cost of repairs and movement from the Marshall Islands."

The target ships at Kwajalein remained there for two years in a caretaker status, rusting idly at their moorings, off-limits to all but a few personnel, and described by David Bradley as "crippled, gaunt, silent, the twisted wreckage, still untouched on deck, creaking with the slow rolling of the ships. They box the compass with the variable winds, and disappear for a while in the rainsqualls." This proved fatal for one ship. On December 22, 1946, the *Prinz Eugen* capsized and sank from progressive leaking. On the morning of December 21, the ship was boarded when it was found listing and sinking by the stern. The boarding party discovered that the ship was filling rapidly from a failed sea valve. An attempt was made to beach the cruiser on Enubuj, but underpowered tugs and strong winds pushed the *Prinz Eugen* broadside to the beach, portside to shore, where it grounded on a coral ledge at 5:00 P.M. During the evening the flooding continued, and the list had increased by late night to 35 degrees to starboard. Just forty-three minutes after midnight on the twenty-second, *Prinz Eugen* capsized and sank, finally following its "big brother," *Bismarck*, to the bottom six years after the two had separated in the Atlantic prior to the British onslaught that had sunk the German battleship.

The Fate of the Fleet

Another Crossroads target left at Kwajalein also succumbed before the decision to scuttle the ships was acted upon. On October 30, 1947, the landing craft LCI-327 stranded on Bascombe (now Mek) Island. It could not be pulled free and was "destroyed" in place with charges. The wreck remains visible on the lagoon side of the island. Eight other vessels first taken to Kwajalein were sent to Pearl Harbor, then to the West Coast "for further study of damage and for development of radiological decontamination and safety techniques by the Navy. . . . it is the policy of the Navy to carry out an aggressive active program of radiological and atomic defense research to apply the lessons of Crossroads." This left twenty-eight vessels at Kwajalein. A status report on the target fleet at the end of August placed a handful of vessels en route to Pearl—*Skate, Conyngham, Searaven, Tuna, Parche, Dentuda,* and *Fillmore,* the last five under their own power. They were followed by the contaminated *Independence, Crittenden,* and *Gasconade,* which were towed to San Francisco to join the submarines, by then at Hunter's Point and Mare Island. The battleships *Nevada* and *New York,* and the destroyer *Hughes* were towed to Pearl, and *Hughes* was sent to Puget Sound with the *Pensacola* and the *Salt Lake City.*

The experiences of the battleship *New York* were typical for these ships. Moored at the center of the southeast loch of Pearl Harbor with the destroyer *Hughes,* the battleship was subjected to eight weeks of detailed investigation after arriving in Hawaii in early March 1947. On May 11,

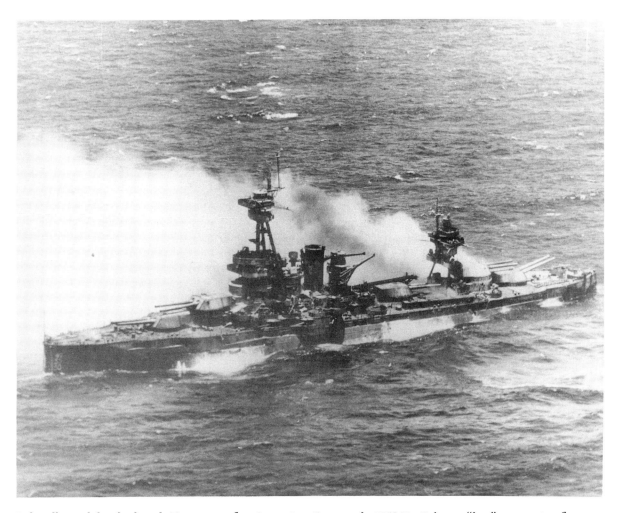

Belatedly sunk by the bomb. Two years after Operation Crossroads, USS New York, too "hot" to remain afloat, was sunk by naval gunfire off Oahu. Only a handful of ships that went to Bikini in 1946 avoided being sent to the bottom. (U.S. Naval Institute Photo Library)

the *New York Times* reported, "Since the *New York* was towed here . . . she has been gone over from stem to stern by civilian workers and scientists," who forwarded the results of their monitoring to San Francisco, where the *Independence, Gasconade, Crittenden,* and some of the submarines were also being monitored and exposed to various decontamination methods. The "rusting destroyer" *Hughes,* also analyzed, was towed to Puget Sound for disposal, but the *New York* was left behind, "stern low and covered with rust," to await its fate as a "victim for fleet target practice."

The *Independence*, heavily dosed with radioactivity, could not be reboarded after Baker until August 18, nearly a month after the test. Even then, the reboarding team stayed aboard for less than five hours. Limited reboardings prepared the ship for a tow to Kwajalein. Departing Bikini under tow by the fleet tug *Munsee* (ARF-107) on August 25, the *Independence* was moored off Kwajalein on August 27 and decommissioned the next day. After a seven-month hiatus at Kwajalein, it was then towed across the Pacific. Departing the Marshall Islands on May 15, 1947, the *Independence* arrived at the Golden Gate on June 16 and was moored at Hunter's Point, where the Navy Radiation Laboratory had been established. The laboratory was the result of an August 27, 1946, directive from the chief of naval operations to establish a radiological safety program, which included the determination of tolerances, physiological effects, and treatments for radiation exposure by the Bureau of Medicine and Surgery. The Bureau of Ships was to study the target ships and develop shipboard detection instruments for ships and individual crew members, and to develop equipment and methods for decontamination at sea as well as "industrial" decontamination at naval bases.

The temporary laboratory, established with the cooperation of the University of California's Crocker Radiation Laboratory at the San Francisco Naval Shipyard at Hunter's Point to decontaminate nontarget ships, was made permanent on November 18, 1946. On April 21, 1948, the facility became the Naval Radiological Defense Laboratory, which it was known as until 1969, when it closed. The *Independence* served as

the focal point for the laboratory's activities through December 1950, as work crews experimented with various compounds to wash off contaminated surfaces and natural rates of decay were measured. The readings had already declined to 0.06 roentgens per day by the time the *Independence* arrived at San Francisco in June 1947. The light carrier's disposition through weapons tests was suggested in January 1950. A year later, the *Independence* was towed out through the Golden Gate and sunk near the Farallone Islands in 500 fathoms with bombs and torpedoes on January 27, 1951, the last of the Crossroads targets to be scuttled. In 1990 its upright hull was rediscovered in 3,000 feet of water by a U.S. Geological Survey team surveying the Gulf of the Farallones National Marine Sanctuary. The *Independence* lay in a field of steel drums filled with the discarded clothing, equipment, and sand used to decontaminate the ship and later dumped into the ocean.

Scuttling, first suggested by Admiral Blandy and approved in September 1946, was the preferred option by June 1947. At that time, the chief of naval operations established a policy for handling and control of "radiologically contaminated material from Operation Crossroads." Noting the "real and ever-present hazard," the CNO dictated that materials be removed only for carefully considered testing, that they be specially controlled and handled, and that they not be "retained indefinitely . . . but shall be disposed of, when the tests are completed, by sinking at sea or by replacement aboard the target vessel." Eventually this policy was adhered to for all of the ships.

On August 30, 1947, the chief of naval operations reiterated the earlier decision that all ships "found radiologically unsafe" would be sunk at sea in deep water. Between 1948 and 1951, but mostly in 1948, the Crossroads target ships were taken to sea and sunk in waters thousands of feet deep, scuttled or pounded in attacks as part of training exercises and tests of new but conventional weapons. On June 9, 1948, the *New York Times* announced that twenty-three of the ships at Kwajalein had already been sunk by gunfire, nine in early May "to forestall their sinking in shoal water and blocking the anchorage." Over the next five weeks, another fourteen were sunk "to sharpen the Pacific Fleet's teeth in experiments involving the Navy's nonatomic weapons in event of an immediate emergency." Fifty target ships were sent to the bottom, thirty-six of them off Kwajalein, the others off the California and Washington coasts or in the Pacific south of Hawaii.

The *New York* and the *Nevada,* towed from Pearl Harbor, were sunk by surface bombardment and aerial torpedoes. After eight hours of severe pounding from ships and planes, the *New York* sank on July 8, 1948. At the end of the month, on July 31, the *Nevada* was towed from Pearl Harbor and moored sixty-five miles south of Oahu. It took four and a half days of bombardment to sink the battleship. Charges placed inside the hull ripped it open, and the ship was then pounded by the cruisers *Astoria* (CL-90), *Pasadena* (CL-65), *Springfield* (CL-66), and several destroyers. A 16-inch salvo from the USS *Iowa* slammed into the *Nevada,* while "rocket-firing planes blazed away." Torpedo bombers scored several hits on the ship, which "belched smoke and defiance," until a final hit amidships capsized it. The battleship sank bow first "in water five miles deep." The *Salt Lake City,* towed 130 miles off San Diego, also succumbed to "a hail of five, six, and eight-inch shells, and numerous 100, 500, and 1,000-pound bombs" fired from fifteen surface ships and dropped from scores of aircraft before being sunk with two torpedoes. In a less spectacular display, the submarines *Skate, Skipjack, Searaven,* and *Tuna* were sunk after aerial bombardment in the fall of 1948 at the navy target range off San Clemente, California.

On October 16, 1948, the destroyer *Henderson* met up with a target ship off the Farallones. Standing on the bridge was Joseph Zuccaro, a veteran of the *Hughes.* "When I saw that single stack sticking up there. I said, Oh, no!" Zuccaro later explained. Zuccaro watched as the *Hughes* was pounded by planes. The *Henderson*'s quartermaster told Zuccaro, who had turned away, "because I couldn't bear to look," that "the bastard is still there. They will never sink that son of a bitch. They're going to have to do better than sending in aircraft." The destroyers charged and fired torpedoes into the *Hughes.* "You could see her go over. I have seen a couple of ships sink, and usually, they go up—show their bow or their stern and then go down. The old lady just rolled over and said, 'the hell with you, I'm going down flat.' And that's the way she went, without any fanfare. I think it got to the old man on the *Henderson,* Commander Cunningham. He gave me a handkerchief and I don't know where the hell he got his."

Only nine ships escaped scuttling or sinking. Two of the target submarines, *Dentuda* and *Parche*, were retained in the inactive fleet and used as training vessels. The *Dentuda* was sold for scrap in January 1969. After a long career as a Naval Reserve training boat, the *Parche*, then AGSS-384 and the last of the Crossroads submarines, was stricken from the Navy Register in November 1969. Sold for scrap in 1970, the boat, one of two submarines moored on the surface for Baker, is survived by portions of its bridge and the conning tower, which are, respectively, monuments and displays at the SUBASE and the USS *Bowfin* Submarine Museum and Park at Pearl Harbor. Four attack transports, the *Cortland, Fillmore, Geneva,* and *Niagara,* which with the *Bladen* were the only five vessels not hit by the radioactive base surge during Baker, were transferred to the United States Maritime Commission, which ultimately sold them for scrap. Though two are known to have been scrapped, the fate of thirteen landing craft is unknown. If they were scrapped, this would raise the number of scrapped "surviving" Crossroads targets to twenty-two vessels. Although in numbers that would represent a fourth of the fleet, these survivors included only two combatants and actually represented a small fraction of the total tonnage assembled and lost by Joint Task Force One.

Even the support vessels did not fully escape the effects of the bombs at Bikini. The ships moving back into the lagoon slowly accumulated radiation on their hulls, both in the paint and the growth that fouled their bottoms, and inside the ships' evaporators, where the scale

acted as "a sponge for radioactive particles," along with every saltwater line—particularly the fire mains and the sewer lines. Special orders were issued for those vessels that had spent ten or more days in Bikini lagoon; they were not to go into drydock or undertake any structural repairs or maintenance until special decontamination measures were devised. Many of the support ships, particularly the destroyers, were wartime-built vessels that had seen plenty of action but had, "even in damage repair . . . skipped a lot of things that needed fixing." Prior to any of this work being done, each ship was given a safety inspection and sent to be decontaminated.

This rule applied to every ship that had been to Bikini. All were radiologically suspect and had to be cleared whether they were going back into service, being laid up, or scrapped. Most of the ships were decontaminated at the San Francisco Naval Shipyard at Hunter's Point, where the first support vessel to be made "safe," the USS *Laffey* (DD-724) was sent. Moored in a floating drydock to avoid "permanently" contaminating a shoreside facility, the *Laffey* was lifted out of the water and inspected on September 5, 1946. Only shipyard workers were allowed into the drydock when the inspection determined that the hull was radioactive along with the internal piping systems, although the levels of radiation were not as high as feared. The algae and barnacles on the hull, particularly on the waterline, and growth inside the saltwater systems were the source of the radiation, although paint on the hull was also contaminated.

Sandblasting to bare metal and flushing the *Laffey*'s pipes with nitric acid diminished the radioactivity. Work to decontaminate other ships followed at a fast pace, despite a controversy that flared up over instituting a lesser standard of safety for ships returned to sea duty as opposed to those being "mothballed." By October 1946, 55 support vessels had arrived at San Francisco, and by early 1947, 80 of 159 vessels were granted radiological clearance. By February 1947, 128 vessels had final clearance; four ships had "operational clearance," with final clearance not recommended; and three had operational clearance with more work needed for final clearance. Operational clearance meant an overall shipboard reading of no higher than .5 r/day and no more than .1 r/day on saltwater systems. Final clearance meant an unshielded .005 r/day overall and .001 r/day in the saltwater systems. In time, all were cleared, but the effort was considerable and expensive, and no doubt contributed to the decision to scuttle all the target ships, given the additional effort and cost needed to clean those by then two years unmaintained, and in some cases bomb-damaged, vessels.

Within a few decades, almost every one of the "cleared" support ships were ultimately scrapped or scuttled, most after long careers. But some had shorter careers, like the hospital ship *Benevolence* (AH-14). Mothballed after Crossroads and recalled to duty in 1950 for the Korean War, the hospital ship was renovated and undergoing sea trials on August 25, 1950, when it was rammed and sunk outside the Golden Gate in a disaster that claimed eighteen lives. It had not outlasted the scuttled target ships by more than two years. By 1990, only five Crossroads veterans remained afloat, four of them still in naval

service. The *Laffey* is now a museum display vessel at Patriot's Point, near Charleston. The *Conserver* (ARS-39), *Preserver* (ARS-8), and *Reclaimer*, all part of the diving and salvage group, are naval vessels attached to the Pacific Fleet or, in the case of the *Preserver*, to the Naval Reserve Training Facility at Little Creek, Virginia, whereas the submarine tender *Fulton* (AS-11) is attached to the Atlantic Fleet.

The Message of Bikini

To the military the message of Bikini was clear. A fleet that had physically survived the effects of two atomic blasts was nonetheless forever lost to radioactive contamination. Blast effect, though impressive, paled in comparison to the effects of radiation. "From a military viewpoint, the atomic bomb's ability to kill human beings or to impair, through injury, their ability to make war is of paramount importance. Thus, the overall result of a bomb's explosion upon the crew . . . is of greater interest." The deadly effects of radioactivity, as seen at Hiroshima, Nagasaki, and Bikini, on the human and animal victims of the three explosions and from the continued contamination of the ships and Bikini itself, meant that, in the words of the Joint Chiefs of Staff's Crossroads Evaluation Committee:

If used in numbers, atomic bombs not only can nullify any nation's military effort, but can demolish its social and economic structure and prevent their reestablishment for long periods of time. With such weapons, especially if employed

Some of the target ships were taken to Pearl Harbor, Bremerton (Washington), and San Francisco for decontamination. Sandblasting and scraping reduced radioactive levels, but the ships remained contaminated, like this transport and submarine in San Francisco. The navy, reported David Bradley, felt like "Br'er Rabbit when he got mixed up with the Tar Baby." Now they had to contend with "decks you can't stay on for more than a few minutes; air you can't breathe without gas masks. . . ." (U.S. Naval Institute Photo Library)

in conjunction with other weapons of mass destruction, as, for example, pathogenic bacteria, it is quite possible to depopulate vast areas of the earth's surface, leaving only vestigial remnants of man's material works.

The vestigial remnants of Operation Crossroads—the target ships and Bikini itself—were the first demonstrations of the power of the atomic bomb significantly to alter the world and man's works upon it, even when the atoll was scarcely touched by the heat and shock of a bomb's detonation. As historian Paul Boyer noted, this awakening slowly resulted from "the Navy's determined, frustrating, and ultimately futile efforts to decontaminate . . . by scrubbing, scraping, and sandblasting . . . the pariah fleet of ghostly radioactive ships."

Ironically, Operation Crossroads' results were in the end largely "inconclusive" for each branch of the services locked in rivalry at the beginning of the tests. The air force, citing the fact that only nine of the target ships escaped "sinking, damage or unacceptable radioactive contamination," found proof of "what it had argued all along; ships were intolerably vulnerable in the atomic age." The navy responded that the seeming knockout to its ships, so gleefully reported by the air force, was the result of unmanned and undefended ships anchored in a tight formation. It further argued that "modern" ships, "properly dispersed, executing evasive maneuvers and utilizing their own defenses, would be far less vulnerable . . . than, for instance, fixed air bases." It was also noted that "Dave's Dream" had missed the *Nevada* by "two miles."

The navy found the ideal proponent for its post-Crossroads survival in correspondent Hanson Baldwin, a navy veteran. In the aftermath of Able, said Baldwin, as terrible as the damage seemed, "the results at Bikini . . . must be qualified." The tight grouping of the ships to measure blast effect and their crewless state were stressed. Some sinkings "could have been avoided had there been fire-fighting crews and damage control parties aboard." The argument resurfaced after Baker, despite the high levels of radiation. Hence, even when the "radioactive stove" *Saratoga* sank, the loss of the ship was attributed less to the bomb by Baldwin, who opined, "perhaps she might have been saved, had there been a crew aboard. But she died a lonely death, pumps idle and boilers dead." In order to survive, "ships must seek safety in dispersion," with redesigned superstructures to better protect radar and radio antennae—the greatest operational casualties of Able—and concrete skins that would be added to armor hulls against radiation because of "the relative success of concrete structures (buildings in Japan, a floating drydock and a small auxiliary craft at Bikini) in withstanding blast, heat and radiation." Baldwin also proposed a "reversion to the turtle-back Monitor-type ship, with thick underwater plates and little exposed superstructures. . . . Shallow draft vessels were less exposed to shock damage. . . . Naval designers, therefore, may sacrifice draft for security."

But the issue of radiation kept rearing its ugly head. A more pessimistic view, expressed at the same time by an unnamed officer, noted the harsh reality that "crews doomed to slow death from exposure to lethal radioactivity are nevertheless able the first few days after exposure to continue normal duties. The seamen of tomorrow must be prepared to accept radioactivity as part of the hazards of their living and be ready to work and fight and save their ship even though they know they are doomed to slow death."

The Navy and the Bomb

The navy devoted considerable effort to the problem of decontamination and in the end was defeated by it. The need to modify ships to meet the threats of radiation, underwater shock, and blast effect surfaced as early as September 1946, when Vice Admiral E. L. Cochrane, chief of the Bureau of Ships, announced that as a result of Crossroads superstructures would be redesigned. "The results may be emphatically streamlined topside structures designed to reduce the effect of the enormous wide-area pressures produced by atomic bomb blast," while passive defensive measures such as steel decks, rounded surfaces, and washdown systems, were planned to wash away fallout and contaminated water.

In 1951, the experiences of years of decontamination research at Hunter's Point led to the issuance of procedures for "defense" through decontamination. If at sea, vessels were to be washed down with seawater; then, using steam, they were to be washed with detergents, lye, and boiler compound, or even sodium triphospate, to strip the paint off the ship with steamjets, hosing, and scraping. The object was to reduce the radiation intensity so that "it will not be a serious hazard to the ship's crew for the short period required for the completion of an urgent mission, or for return to port."

Operation Crossroads reinforced the navy's plans to bring the atomic bomb to sea. It gave the navy time to develop a nuclear capability and led to a decrease in public and political pressure for it to merge as a secondary partner with the air force or the army, or even to cease to exist altogether. By adopting the new technology, the navy assumed the strongest defensive role in the nation, particularly considering the new U.S. policies of nuclear deterrence and retaliation, which would be the hallmark of the American military.

Air-dropped bombs were made available for aircraft carriers after 1952 when the 15-foot-long, half-ton "Thor" bomb was introduced. Guns on ships were gradually replaced with nuclear-tipped missiles, such the Terrier. Developed after World War II and first tested in 1951, the Terrier was brought to sea in 1956. Nuclear depth bombs, torpedoes, and various types of bombs joined the naval tactical nuclear arsenal. Advocates of the big-gun battleships also adopted the bomb. In 1956 the navy introduced the Mark 23 Atomic Projectile. These 5-foot-long, 1,900-pound 16-inch shells were created for the *Iowa*-class battleships (the famous *Missouri* being one) as "atomic support" for marines landing on the beach. These weapons remained at sea until President George Bush ordered them ashore in 1992 as part of a reduction in nuclear arms.

A prescient comment made by Hanson Baldwin after Able augured the development of the ultimate nuclear-age weapon. Submarines, he wrote, "atomic-driven and equipped with atomic warhead missiles that could, perhaps, be fired while the craft was submerged, appear to have tremendous potentialities." Another development that underscored the superior role of tactical deployment of nuclear weapons at sea was outlined within months of Crossroads when Admiral Cochrane announced that the cruiser *Kentucky* and the battleship *Hawaii* would be guided-missile warships, particularly since "the advent of the rocket with atomic blast warheads is just around the laboratory corner." Nowadays, nuclear-capable missiles such as the Tomahawk are carried on surface warships while ballistic missiles in nuclear submarines silently patrol the depths.

Back to Bikini

The nagging issue of the long-term contamination of Bikini, and questions left unanswered by the withdrawal from the atoll in light of the decontamination problems posed by Baker, were not addressed by the months of survey and effort at Kwajalein and San Francisco on the target ships brought there. Indeed, at the end of Crossroads, the Crossroads Evaluation Board had pointed out: "It is too soon to attempt an analysis of all the implications of the Bikini tests. But it is not too soon to point to the necessity for immediate and intensive research into several unique problems posed by the atomic bomb." In early 1947, plans for a scientific resurvey of Bikini during the coming summer were drafted by the Joint Crossroads Committee, which had succeeded the now defunct Joint Task Force One, disbanded on November 1, 1946.

"Deak" Parsons, now the navy's Director of Atomic Defense and chairman of the Joint Crossroads Committee, forwarded a proposal to the Joint Chiefs of Staff on April 9, 1947. In Parsons' staff's opinion, a program of biological study was necessary "in order to determine the long term effects of Test Baker on fish and other marine organisms including corals and calcareous algae . . . and to obtain data on which to base a decision relative to possible resettlement of the native population." At the same time, diving on some of the sunken target ships was proposed to "make additional diving observations" and retrieve missing test data from Crossroads instruments abandoned there in 1946.

The plan was approved, and a group of scientists and technicians from the navy, the army, the Smithsonian Institution, the U.S. Fish and Wildlife Service, and Stanford University, among others, were placed under the command of Captain Christian Engleman, USN. The technical director was Commander E. S. Gillfillan, who had participated in Crossroads as executive officer of the *Nagato*. Overall command of the resurvey group was given to Captain H. Henry Hederman, USN. Although classified, the resurvey was publicly announced because of a strong desire by the Joint Chiefs to stress "the story of cooperation that exists between civilian and military agencies in the Bikini resurvey work. Proper handling of the Bikini Resurvey story can do much to acquaint the American public with the long range value of Operation Crossroads."

Specific tasks for the resurvey group were "to determine the amount and nature of radioactivity in the lagoon water, and of the reef and land structures of the atoll . . . to determine the concentration and kind of radioactive materials in the animals and plants of the atoll, and effects of this radioactivity," as well as additional inquiry into the botany, zoology, microbiology, oceanography, and geology of Bikini, and further investigation of the effects of the bomb on the sunken target ships. A group under the command of Lieutenant Commander F. B. Ewing, USN, was to make detailed observations of the *Saratoga*, *Nagato*, *Gilliam*, and *Apogon*. "Other vessels, including *Arkansas* and *Pilotfish*, will be inspected if time permits." The inspection plans called for extensive underwater photography and structural inspections. In addition, "it is believed that a portion of LSM-60 has been located. If time permits, an attempt will be made by divers to locate this portion and inspect it thoroughly for type of rupture, heat effects, and radioactivity. If practicable, an attempt will be made to raise this section for an inspection on the surface."

The 700-member Bikini Resurvey task group steamed from San Diego and Pearl Harbor to Bikini on the transport *Chilton* (APA-38), the submarine rescue vessel *Coucal* (ASR-8), a Crossroads veteran, LSM-382, and LCI(L)-615, on July 1, 1947. The *Chilton* arrived at Bikini on July 15, steaming through the channel to anchor in the lagoon 355 days after Baker. Careful precautions had been made for the reentry. A detailed plan, drawn up in advance, called for a single landing craft to transport an advance landing party, with radiological monitors, to Bikini. After radiation levels were checked, the landing party, dressed in long-sleeved shirts, long pants, and heavy work shoes, wearing film badges and carrying pocket dosimeters, trudged ashore at 11:45 A.M., past cast-up debris that included fenders and life rafts probably "blasted loose from ships of the target fleet last year," to reach the locked, empty buildings left behind by Joint Task Force One.

As equipment and supplies arrived, crews rehabilitated the island for the use of the resurvey team. A grader, two bulldozers, a crane, a power shovel, two wagons, and a refrigerator, abandoned after Crossroads, were "restored to operating condition," while lumber, nails, and hardware were salvaged to convert several buildings into laboratories, a galley, barracks, and an officer's club for the six-week stay on an island and atoll, which bore "few visible effects of that

blast. Except for the activities of the . . . Task Group, Bikini is the same placid palm-ringed lagoon on which King Judah and his subjects sailed in outrigger canoes."

Divers from the *Coucal* made more than six hundred dives on the *Apogon*, *Pilotfish*, and *Saratoga*. A "cursory inspection" was made of the *Nagato*. The first dives were made on the *Saratoga* on July 17, two days after the resurvey team arrived. According to a press release, "divers today walked up and down the flight deck of the gallant old aircraft carrier *Saratoga*. They reported that the 33,000 ton ship, sunk last July 25 . . . is resting on a nearly even keel. The top of her mast can be seen a few feet beneath the surface of the lagoon. They reported that the *Sara*'s flight deck is covered with coral dust. . . . Waterproof Geiger counters were lowered in the water ahead of the divers."

Radiation levels were carefully monitored. Divers wore pencil dosimeters and three film badges—one on chest, abdomen, and leg—and when lifted from the water, each diver was washed down with a hose before being hoisted aboard. The recorded radiation levels ranged from "two times background (gamma) to .1 R/24 hr. (gamma), to .6 R/24 hr. (beta and gamma)." Additional protection was provided, according to a press release, by the "inch-thick lead soles worn by deep sea divers." However, the readings were not considered high, and by July 24, a ban on swimming in the lagoon was lifted, so that on the twenty-fifth, another press release noted that "sun-tanned sailors and scientists observed the anniversary of the world's first underwater atomic bomb explosion today by going swimming in the clear blue-green 84-degree waters of Bikini Lagoon. They swam from beaches that one year ago were lashed by high and angry waves thrown outward from the explosion point."

The hours of detailed observations on the *Saratoga* and the two submarines added to the record of bomb damage. The *Saratoga* had "much more serious damage," including twisting in the hull girder, misalignment of the starboard shafts, "deeply indented" shell plating and strakes, and a crack in the torpedo blister. The *Pilotfish* and *Apogon* were entered and inspected without the limitations imposed by radiation in 1946. By 1947 shipboard radiation was "of a low magnitude."

Other work accomplished by the resurvey team included detailed geological assessments of reef structures by drilling. Cores and samples of the bottom of the lagoon were taken that plotted the distribution of the half-million tons of sediment dropped back into the lagoon after Baker. The radioactive mud was five feet deep, on average, though at one spot the mud was eight feet deep. Yet radiation levels were not high. The only spots where radioactivity was higher than the one-tenth of a roentgen per twenty-four hours tolerance limit for the group was on debris and where patches of tar had stuck to coral. Scientists attached to the radiobiology and fisheries groups were busy collecting samples of algae, sea urchins, and other marine invertebrates, insects, birds, and mammals were collected and studied for "possible radiological or blast effects upon structure, physiological processes, fertility or normal processes of development."

The Resurvey Group completed its task by the end of August. A final inspection of Bikini was made before the ships sailed on the twenty-ninth. The three-volume final report of the resurvey was published by the Armed Forces Special Weapons Project in December 1947. The results were reassuring for those who had feared that Bikini was hopelessly contaminated, just like the target ships. The radiological survey group made "a comprehensive survey of radioactivity on the reefs and islands," finding no major concentrations or "hot spots" on dry land. Likewise, the biological studies "revealed no changes in population, numbers, or composition, and no physiological damage that could definitely be ascribed to the explosion."

As to whether the Bikinians could return, however, the results were less than unequivocal. Radioactive materials were found in the fish and other animals, though not in the plants. In the opinion of the resurvey group scientists, the 1–10 percent retention of ingested radioactive materials through the food chain, and the limited amount of long-life particles there, meant that "after a few more years these islands will constitute relatively slight radioactive hazard to anyone." What had not been assessed, however, was the fact that fallout in the soil and the silt of the lagoon bottom was being passed on to plants, algae, and fish, which could then be eaten by people. This created "a set of problems whose answers lay beyond the scope and period of the 1947 Resurvey." The decision was made, with the Bikinians still absent, to continue to use their abandoned home for twenty-three more powerful and hence "hotter" tests, which considerably increased contamination of the atoll. The next U.S. nuclear weapons tests, Operation

Sandstone, took place in 1948 at Eniwetok Atoll, also in the Marshall Islands, followed by Operation Ranger, the first tests to use the newly developed Nevada Test Site in the continental United States. Tests at Eniwetok followed in 1951, with Operation Greenhouse, and in 1952 with Operation Ivy.

The bomb returned to Bikini with Operation Castle in 1954. The bombs now being tested were hydrogen bombs, however. Holmes and Narver, Inc., of Honolulu prepared several of Bikini's islands between November 1952 and February 1954. Six bombs were detonated at Bikini in 1954, starting with the deadliest. If Baker was the first nuclear disaster to befall Bikini, the Bravo shot of March 1, 1954, was the second and worst. The Bravo bomb, estimated to yield six megatons, was a monumental miscalculation. The 15-megaton burst, the largest ever exploded by the United States on the surface of the planet, formed a three-mile-wide fireball and blasted a 240-foot-deep crater a mile in diameter in Bikini's reef. Fallout spread across the Pacific for a thousand miles, dusting nearby islands and ships, including the Japanese fishing vessel *Fukuryu Maru,* the "Lucky Dragon." Inhabited by the test crews prior to Castle, Bikini was evacuated. The remaining five shots, all but one on barges moored in the lagoon, were conducted from shipboard. The last, a 110-kiloton blast code-named "Koon," vaporized the tip of Eninman Island, leaving a 800-foot-diameter crater 75 feet deep. Other tests during Operation Redwing followed in 1956, when seven more hydrogen bombs were dropped or set off on barges at Bikini. More tests followed in 1958 with Operation Hardtack, when ten bombs were shot off from barges moored in the atoll. When the last reverberations of the Hardtack-Juniper detonation died away on July 22, 1958, the era of nuclear weapons testing at Bikini came to an end. Only the traces of the past, some visible as bunkers, cable, and sunken ships, and other more deadly legacies left invisible in the soil, remained to mark that era.

Top heavy and weighted down by turrets, battleships and cruisers capsize when they sink. The stern of *Prinz Eugen*, propellers in the air, rises out of the water at Kwajalein. (Daniel Lenihan, National Park Service)

Swimming alongside *Prinz Eugen*, divers need to float with their feet to the surface, upside down, to see the ship properly. Here, a diver kneels on the overhead of a midships companionway, with the deck above him. (Larry Murphy, National Park Service)

Dan Lenihan and Larry Murphy squeezed past the narrow gunports to enter the only part of the battleship *Arkansas* that wasn't crushed by the Baker bomb. The 5-inch gun shown here in the aircastle now hangs upside down from the deck of the overturned battlewagon. (Larry Murphy, National Park Service)

Aircraft carriers have been called "floating cities" because of their large crews and the fact that the huge ships have nearly every amenity you would find in a small municipality. If so, then *Saratoga* was a city of the dead, every compartment now dark and silent. This was the scene when we entered the flag plot, where admirals once commanded air groups and squadrons. (Larry Murphy, National Park Service)

The admiral's day cabin on *Saratoga*. "Bull" Halsey and practically every other flag officer in the navy who served aboard carriers between 1928 and 1945 slept here. (Larry Murphy, National Park Service)

The only light that entered the bridge came from the slits on the battle covers on the ports. This was the nerve center of the carrier when she was a fighting ship. (Larry Murphy, National Park Service)

The rampaging forces of Baker devastated *Saratoga's* flight deck, sweeping planes, tanks, and equipment into the sea. The 90-foot high armored stack came crashing down onto the deck, leaving the twisted mass of girders and torn steel. (Larry Murphy, National Park Service)

The sea's corrosive action is slowly claiming *Saratoga*. Railings and light metal plating are disappearing, while sea fans and coral soften the warship's once sharp lines. (Larry Murphy, National Park Service)

Rusted bright red, instruments and a chart table covered with marine growth make a sharp contrast to one another on *Saratoga's* bridge. Thick silt covered everything, and we had to hover nearly motionless in the water, using our hands and legs in short, crab-like movements, to avoid kicking it up and losing our visibility. (Larry Murphy, National Park Service)

In the shallows off Bikini Island, the corridors of a swamped and battered landing craft are half-clogged with sand. I worked my way partially through, toward the engine room, twisting and turning at all angles to avoid being caught in the tight passage. (Larry Murphy, National Park Service)

As the battleship *Nagato* sank, unattended in the night, the hull capsized and went down by the stern. The tip of the stern, at the fantail, struck first and slowly tore free as the ship continued to pivot. The fantail now lies buried in the bottom, amid loose equipment that fell from the deck. (Larry Murphy, National Park Service)

Once high above the deck, the bridge of *Nagato* now lies to the side of the ship, bent and twisted, but still attached. The slow settling of the Japanese battleship on the bottom was a stark contrast to the rapid, blunt hammering of *Arkansas* into the lagoon's floor. (Larry Murphy, National Park Service)

6

Diving at Ground Zero

I was born in the same year the tests at Bikini ended. I first learned I would join a team going to the islands on my thirtieth birthday. We would be among the first people to dive there since Operation Crossroads. In fact, Bikini saw few visitors after 1958. Although divers, souvenir hunters, and filmmakers visited the wrecks at the bottom of the lagoon, swimming over the *Saratoga*'s flight deck and peering into darkened compartments, the islands were officially off-limits to all but those first invited by the Atomic Energy Commission, the Department of Energy, Holmes and Narver, and later by the Bikinians themselves.

Thirty years after the last bomb had burst over the atoll, the U.S. Navy sent a team of divers back to help the Bikinians locate the sunken fleet of Operation Crossroads. Relocating the ships was a challenge met by the navy's Mobile Diving and Salvage Unit One, headquartered at Pearl Harbor and then commanded by Commander David McCampbell, whose father was the top-ranking U.S. naval flying ace of World War II. Finding the Crossroads ships and aircraft that his father had known and flown was a consuming interest of McCampbell's, who had pre-

viously worked closely with Dan Lenihan of the National Park Service to survey the sunken remains of the USS *Arizona* and *Utah* at Pearl Harbor, inaugurating a joint program known as "Project Seamark." Seamark exercises combined navy and park service teams to assess sunken ships and other submerged relics throughout the Pacific. The concept created by the two men and by Captain J. K. "Otto" Orzech of the navy grew into a worldwide program that in time brought us to Bikini.

Dr. Catherine "Kitty" Agegian, from Holmes and Narver, the Department of Energy's contractors and representatives at Bikini, contacted Dave McCampbell in 1988 to see if the navy would resurvey the Crossroads target ships. After a long career in Pacific nuclear testing, Holmes and Narver was working with the Bikinians to clean up after the tests. McCampbell agreed to the survey and pointed out that his friend Lenihan would make a fine addition to the effort. Lenihan met with McCampbell and Holmes and Narver representatives Kent Hiner and Kitty Agegian in Honolulu in June 1988 and agreed to go to Bikini in 1989.

Meanwhile, McCampbell and his team went

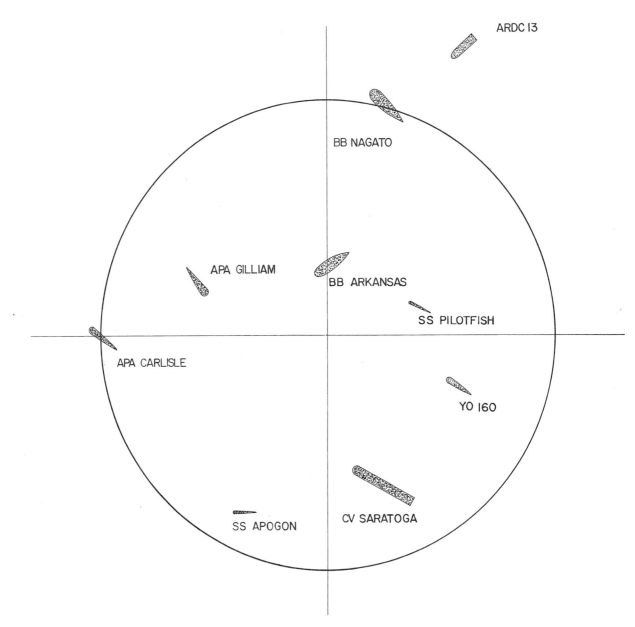

ARDC 13

BB NAGATO

APA GILLIAM

BB ARKANSAS

SS PILOTFISH

APA CARLISLE

YO 160

SS APOGON

CV SARATOGA

A graveyard of sunken ships. Plotted within the one-mile diameter target circle for the Baker test, the sunken ships of Operation Crossroads rest on the bottom of Bikini Lagoon. The locations were mapped by the U.S. Navy, working with our National Park Service team in 1989–1990. Not shown here are the destroyers *Anderson* and *Lamson*, or the Japanese Cruiser *Sakawa*, which we did not dive on. Drawing by Robbyn Jackson, Historic American Engineering Record, National Park Service).

to Bikini in August 1988. The navy relocated all the major vessels lost during or immediately after the Able and Baker tests with the exception of three: the destroyers *Anderson* and *Lamson* and the cruiser *Sakawa*. Buoys were placed on each wreck and limited dives made on each ship, accompanied by a crew from ABC television. In July–August 1989 and again in April–May 1990, the National Park Service went to Bikini, accompanied by the navy in 1989 and on both occasions by ABC. *National Geographic* magazine also sent writer John Eliot and photographer Bill Curtsinger in 1990. In the midst of all the activity, Holmes and Narver conducted a radiation survey of the sunken ships and investigated the possibility of a catastrophic release of oil from the bunkers of the wrecks. Navy divers probed and prodded unexploded bombs on the various ships, placed new mooring buoys on the wrecks, and sent robot cameras known as ROVs (Remotely Operated Vehicles) beneath capsized hulks 180 feet down. It was a frenzy of activity, and it was the most attention to be paid to the ghost fleet of Bikini Atoll since 1947.

Off to Bikini

My journey to Bikini began months before we left the States. For many weeks beforehand, I dug into the thick files of Operation Crossroads and read the published accounts of the epic tests. It all seemed as distant as Bikini itself, 9,000 miles from Washington, D.C., and a third of the world away. Flipping through the pages of *Operation Crossroads: The Official Pictorial Record,* I was struck by the images from that place and

time—black-and-white portraits of officers posing for the cameras in Washington, five politicians in suits wearing parachutes at a Washington National Airport "photo opportunity," ships clustered at Bikini, sailors hoisting a squealing pig by his hind legs aboard the USS *Burleson,* fireballs and mushroom clouds, journalists clambering over the bow door of an LCT to view the shattered hulk of the *Independence.* There were two strange and upsetting views, one of a goat strapped to an operating table while masked technicians gathered around, titled "That Men May Live," and another showing Baker's erupting column and cloud superimposed over the New York skyline. It all seemed far away, long ago, and surreal.

Like many of the men sent to Bikini in 1946, my trip began at National Airport in Washington. In 1946 Ernest Peterkin had flown all night for fifteen hours to reach San Francisco; on August 4, 1989, I boarded an L-1011 and made the trip in half that time. San Francisco, my hometown, has changed a great deal since the end of the war. Hunter's Point, where the *Indianapolis* loaded "Little Boy" for its debut over Hiroshima, where the *Saratoga* was prepared for Crossroads, and where the *Independence* came back from Bikini to spend five years being washed down with acid, is no longer an active naval base. The *Sara* and many of the Crossroads fleet steamed under the Bay Bridge and past Alcatraz before passing through the Golden Gate. The bridges still span the bay, and Alcatraz, whose inmates were once proposed as atomic guinea pigs, is empty, a tourist mecca.

As our jet lifted off from San Francisco International Airport, it turned in a slow arc to the northeast, swinging past the peninsula and the

A shoreside dump at Kwajalein has been the military's disposal ground for over fifty years. Tons of rusting trucks, tracked vehicles, and equipment have been cast into the water at one end of the island. "Deep sixing" or sinking unwanted or discarded material in the ocean included ships of Operation Crossroads that survived the blast but not radioactive contamination. After the tests, many were scuttled off Kwajalein's shores. (James P. Delgado, National Park Service)

high-rises of the city. As we climbed into the sky, the sun sparkled on the dark water beneath us and reflected on the dull orange towers of the Golden Gate Bridge. I was struck by the color—the same paint had been liberally applied to the *Nevada* as it was readied to be the aiming point for Able. Several thousand feet above the bridge, I could see why the experts had selected international orange. The bridge would have made a perfect target, silhouetted against the dark water and the narrows of the strait.

The plane touched down at Honolulu, where I met Dan Lenihan, Larry Murphy, Larry Nordby, and Jerry Livingston, my fellow members of

Time stands still at the bottom of the sea. A black plastic engraving gives the wartime emergency signal instructions on *Saratoga's* bridge. As we swam onto the bridge it was if we were journeying back into time, into a blacked-out, battle ready station. (Larry Murphy, National Park Service)

the National Park Service team going to Bikini. Taken in hand by Holmes and Narver officials, we caught an early-morning flight across the Pacific on a Continental Airlines jet. My first trip across the Pacific, it was a journey that became all the more strange and wonderful, yet chilling, as we crossed the last few thousand miles to reach the Marshalls. Johnston Island, now a storehouse of American chemical and biological warfare weapons, was an intermediate stopover. We were kept on the plane, surrounded by jeeps manned by machine-gun-toting guards, as the jet refueled. At Majuro, capital of the Marshalls, we walked out of the jet to spend a few moments drinking a beer in the humid blast-furnace climate while deciding which basket to buy at the airport giftshop.

In the late afternoon we landed at Kwajalein. Wrested from the Japanese in a fierce battle that had blasted the atoll and left only one palm tree standing, the pock-marked "Kwaj" now intercepts missiles fired from Vandenberg Air Force Base in California. Paved and covered with 1950s and 1960s utilitarian structures, the island is ruled by the military but populated by civilians who work for various defense-industry companies. Traces of the past protrude incongruously—shattered concrete pillboxes, tons of broken and rusting trucks, tractors, forklifts, and tires lying in the surf, and the stern of the *Prinz Eugen*, bronze propellers gleaming in the sun, as it rises from the cruiser's grave off Carlson Island. A team stands by to handle unexploded bombs and ammunition left behind from the Battle of Kwajalein. Just before our arrival, a section of road gave way to expose a small bunker filled with boxes of Japanese mortar rounds. The bones of Kwaj's Japanese defenders turn up from time to time. They are reburied with military ceremony at a small Japanese cemetery at one end of the airstrip.

We waited for days at Kwajalein for a flight to Bikini. When we finally got into the air, our propeller-driven plane made the crossing in little more than an hour's time. As we approached Bikini, the pilot banked to give us a view of the dark-blue Bravo crater before we swung around and landed on a hard-packed coral field on Enyu. By that afternoon we were esconced on Bikini Island, full of lunch and ready for our first dive on the *Saratoga*.

Dropping back into the depths of the lagoon to visit the sunken fleet of Crossroads was all that was required to bring the past to life. On the bottom of the sea, time stands still; and indeed, it was only through my descents onto the *Saratoga, Arkansas, Nagato, Pilotfish,* and *Gilliam* that the years slipped away. As I became intimate with the wrecks, I learned their histories as veterans of the war and atomic guinea pigs. Operation Crossroads was no longer an isolated, distant event—it was real. We dropped through the depths, and it was as if we passed through layers of time. Inside one ship, my bubbles rose to the surface, more than a hundred feet above me, mingled with oil from ruptured bunkers and trapped on overheads before my passage. My hands touched instruments left on decks when the bomb blasts sent the ships to the bottom, and I swam through dark passageways of ships lost more than a decade before my birth. Almost all of them were famous, and each was a challenge and a thrill to dive. Each in its own way offered an instructive lesson about Operation Crossroads. Three of them, the ships caught at surface zero, were evocative witnesses to the power of a nuclear detonation.

The *Gilliam* and the *Carlisle*

We made only one dive on each of the two attack transports. The significance of the *Gilliam* and the *Carlisle* was lost on many of the other divers, and only our group was interested in visiting these ugly ducklings. I wanted to dive the

Gilliam because I had spent a fair amount of time in San Francisco aboard the Liberty Ship *Jeremiah O'Brien* and also on the Victory Ship *Lane Victory* in Los Angeles. The last unaltered World War II armed merchantmen, these plucky, unattractive, and hardworked ships are also unappreciated. Like the *Gilliam* and the *Carlisle,* they were built fast and tough to carry the tools needed to fight the war to the war. Common and mass-produced, most have long since vanished from the seas. Maybe it was the romantic notion that these ships were the floating equivalent of the G.I. dogface, epitome of a Bill Mauldin cartoon and symbol of the stolid American boy next door who fought not for glory but to make the world free. It was also a certain perverse pride in diving a ship that possessed none of the sleek, sinister lines of the sunken submarines or the bristling guns of the battleships. But, most important, the two transports, along with the *Arkansas,* were the most mauled of the sunken target fleet. The Crossroads planners never intended to sink the transports. The ships just happened to be in the way when "Dave's Dream" missed the *Nevada* and "Gilda" detonated almost directly overhead. Here was a chance to see the worst that an atomic bomb could throw at a ship.

The wreck of the *Gilliam* is the most impressive dive at Bikini. This heavily built, sturdy steel ship was constructed for hard use. Yet it is the most damaged of all the ships of Operation Crossroads, its twisted steel mute testimony to the forces unleashed when "Gilda" detonated 518 feet above it. The mangled hulk now lies upright, with the highest elevation of the wreck —the remains of the superstructure—in 150

feet of water. The bow was hit the worst: *Gilliam*'s forward end was shoved under the water by the bomb. The stern extended upward as the ship was rocketed to the lagoon floor at a 70-degree angle. When navy divers visited the *Gilliam* in 1946 to recover test instruments, they could hardly recognize the ship. The front end of the ship and the sides bent down and to port by as much as six to ten feet, "mashed down," they said, "as though the blast [had] acted like the hammer and the water an anvil."

The same feeling of awe as when confronted by overwhelming power overtakes you when you follow the buoy line down to the *Gilliam.* At first, when we rolled off the side of the dive boat, the water was clear. The buoy's steel cable descended into a milky-blue deep, and I pulled myself down, hand over hand, as I dropped. At sixty feet a dim shape appeared below, looking almost like a child's broken toy discarded on the white sand of the lagoon floor. My first impression when I reached the highest point of wreckage was that I didn't know where I was on the ship. It looked like a junkyard, with torn steel and twisted skeins of electrical cable and pipe. We swam toward the bow, past what had once been the superstructure.

Passing over the hulk, I was amazed that the blast had pushed the ship into itself. Most of the wreckage lay inside the *Gilliam*—the sides of the hull were bent into the ship—and only a few fittings, a fallen mast, and small debris lay on the lagoon bottom. The *Gilliam* was hit so hard that each deck level pancaked down, bending stanchions and bulkheads along with four-inch-thick steel deck beams. For me the most impressive damage was around the hatches.

Ground zero at Bikini, the transport *Gilliam*. The Able bomb "Gilda" burst off the attack transport's bow, literally eradicating everything shown here except for the hull. Today, a twisted hulk, broken in many places, masts to one side and melted, misshapen forms everywhere, rests on the bottom of Bikini Lagoon in 165 to 180 feet of water. (U.S. Naval Institute Photo Library)

Yawning holes, once rectangular and now twisted into irregular shapes, dropped into the hull. The hatch coamings, however, had torn free of the steel deck. One of them, remarkably still rectangular, hangs over the side, an edge caught on the stub of the forward bulkhead of the deckhouse. The bow is bent and twisted, crumpled, and almost torn free of the hull. The force of the blast tore through the bow and forced the chain out of its locker, through the hawsepipes, and vomited it out onto the lagoon floor. The heaps of chain, with the hawsepipes torn off the hull and lying atop them, are attached to the wreck by single strands that rise up from the bottom and lead back into the wreckage.

At the bow, we swung around and headed back, now knowing what end of the ship we were at. Our time was short. In all, I spent half an hour on the *Gilliam*, paying for a visit that was longer than planned by hanging on a decompression line at thirty, twenty, and ten feet for nearly as long a time—twenty-seven minutes—to drive from my blood the nitrogen bubbles brought on by the depths. At depths of more than a hundred feet, the danger of diving comes from the nitrogen, which builds up the longer you stay down. If you come up too fast, your blood acts like a bottle of Coke that has been shaken on a hot day and then uncapped. I balanced my excitement about diving the *Gilliam* and the other ships with constant glances at my watch, air pressure, and the dive tables of decompression times that ruled our lives beneath the waves.

Swimming faster now, Dan Lenihan, Larry Murphy, and I quickly passed over the buckled decks. Near the bow, I spotted a bulkhead that had once marked the ship's forecastle. Bent into an S curve, the bulkhead had a single doorway, also twisted into a Salvador Dalí image that I couldn't resist swimming through. One of my favorite spots in San Francisco is Lloyd Lake in Golden Gate Park. On its shores stands the marble portico of a Nob Hill mansion, left standing before the rubble as the last intact vestige of a once proud palace after the great earthquake and fire in 1906. Moved to the park as a memorial, the "Portals of the Past" are a haunting legacy of the devastation of 1906. As I swam through the forecastle doorway on the *Gilliam*, I thought of Lloyd Lake.

Open to the sea, with much of the steel plating gone, the *Gilliam*'s holds contain the ill-fated transport's last cargo. As common and utilitarian as the ship, the cargo was a jumble of twisted iron rails and gas cylinders. The only other piece of test equipment we found was a mangled rectangular block of wreckage. It was a bulldozer that had been blown from the *Gilliam*'s decks and dropped into the water to sink next to the transport. Its cab gone and the thick steel blade bent nearly double, the bulldozer was for me the second most impressive scene on the wreck, next to the hatches and the twisted portal between a nuclear maelstrom and the calm of the sea.

The *Carlisle*

The *Carlisle* was the only other casualty of Able located and dived when we were at Bikini, although divers discovered the destroyer *Lamson*'s wreck the year after we left, in 1991. Battered by the Able burst, the *Carlisle* rests upright but lists slightly to port in 170 feet of water. It is close but just out of sight in the murk from the *Gilliam*. The blast hit the ship on its port side, toppling the mainmast, stacks, and foretopmast. The midships deckhouse was partially smashed and shifted to starboard.

On our visit, time was running out when the time came to dive the *Carlisle*, so no divers visited the sunken transport. A small robot camera was flown from the surface to reconnoiter the ship. As one approaches the ship from the starboard side, the lagoon bottom is littered with debris, including steel beams, a boat davit, ammunition boxes, and hull plating blasted free when the bomb burst on the other side of the ship, throwing debris in this direction. Unlike the *Gilliam*, the *Carlisle* is basically intact, but the port side is badly dented and broken from midships all the way to the stern. It was a surprise to find it in one piece. In 1946, divers working to raise the sunken *Skipjack* reported that the nearby wreck of the *Carlisle* had broken in three pieces. Ironically, one of the salvors was Machinist's Mate 1st Class Sid Geller, one of the *Carlisle*'s crew now assigned to the submarine rescue ship *Widgeon*. Geller is credited by his shipmates as being the last one of them to see the *Carlisle*.

The *Carlisle* was fueled and armed for the test with bombs, rocket heads, and incendiary clusters "throughout the ship." It is no surprise that the transport burned fiercely until it sank. The passage of time has hidden the ferocity of the *Carlisle*'s death. The hull is lightly encrusted with rust and coral, masking any evidence of the fires that raged on the ship. A mainmast cargo boom slopes down from the main deck to the lagoon bottom on the port side, but there is no trace of the mainmast. A broken ladder lying on the deck approximates the mast's position, which is now marked only by torn deck plating. The midships house, deformed but recognizable, seems more collapsed than 1946 under-

Mangled and almost unrecognizable, this bulldozer was swept off the deck of the *Gilliam* by the atomic blast. Only the treads and weirdly bent blade of the dozer hint at what it once was. (Larry Murphy, National Park Service)

water photographs and diver sketches indicated then. This is probably because the fire-weakened and corroded steel is slowly giving way to the sea. Bulkheads have separated, and the after-port quarter, once surmounted by a 20 mm gun mount, is now smashed down, leaving the tub nearly at the weather deck level, its gun missing. Davits on the port side, bent into the superstructure wreckage, are in part buried by steel plates and other mangled debris. The davits, like the other wreckage, were for me subtle yet impressive reminders of the force of the bomb that had bent them back into the wreckage like slender stalks of grass in the wind.

The deck has separated from the hull along the port side, and the deck plating has cracked and separated at the seams. The after hold is open, the hatch covers missing, and the coaming bent and for the most part separated from the weather deck. The decks are partly smashed down, ending in a jumble of plating and unidentifiable wreckage in the hold. The after deckhouse is smashed flat, one bulkhead bent aft and twisted so that it is nearly parallel to the deck. Bitts line the deck, and wire cable is wrapped around one—perhaps the remains of the wire rope that once cabled an airplane to the deck. Two strands of heavy anchor chain—the aft moorings that held the ship in its target position—now run aft from bitts and straight down into the lagoon bottom. The anchor chain, like those I later saw on the submarines, was a reminder that the ships had not died a noble death after a battle with men or the sea; shackled to the bottom, they had been gracelessly executed.

The wreck of the *Carlisle* was impressive in comparison with the mangled *Gilliam*. The visual impact of the extreme damage done to the latter by the bomb was accentuated by comparing it to the *Carlisle*. The awesome destructive force of the bomb, particularly its compressive forces, buckled reinforced concrete roofs at Hiroshima and Nagasaki. But the most important lesson of the two transports, as Larry Murphy told me after seeing them, is that these ships were not damaged by unique and unknown forces that, in the popular view, should have "vaporized" them. Murphy has noted that the "ships were damaged and sunk by forces governed by physical processes that are repetitive, often quantifiable, and ultimately . . . predictable." Diving ground zero took away some of the mystery of the atomic bomb, focusing my attention, as well as that of my fellow divers, on its raw power. That lesson was brought home by diving the *Arkansas,* the closest ship to Baker's burst.

The USS *Arkansas*

The ship that best represents the destructive forces of the bomb is the *Arkansas,* whose broken and crushed hulk lies on the lagoon bottom in 180 feet of water, capsized and forced into the coral and sand. Moored within 500 feet of the zeropoint, the *Arkansas* was the closest target vessel except for LSM-60, which suspended the bomb. Joint Task Force One's historian, W. A. Shurcliff, wrote in 1947 that, "in sinking, she carried with her the dubious honor of being the first battleship to be sunk by an atomic bomb, and the first battleship to be sunk by a bomb that never touched her."

Lost within a matter of seconds, the *Arkansas* was described by navy divers in 1946 as "lying buried in the silt, bottom side up. . . . Most of the superstructure, including stacks, boat cranes and mast is not visible and is presumed to have been driven into the coral silt on the lagoon bottom. . . . Little is left of the shafting and the rudder has not been found. Only the port

A floating fortress breached by 23 kilotons. When the Baker bomb blasted up, almost directly beneath USS *Arkansas,* the hull was crushed for two-thirds of its width and for its entire length. The ship flipped onto its port (left) side and went down. The falling column of water and silt from the blast thundered down atop the sinking ship, hammering it into the lagoon floor. Today, the towering masts and turrets are pushed down into thick coral and sand, forever buried. Only a few feet separate the decks from the sandy bottom. (U.S. Naval Institute Photo Library)

forward shaft without the screw has been found, and it is seriously out of line. No struts have been sighted and two large holes aft indicate the after two shafts have been completely torn out, stern tubes and all, leaving the surrounding area badly distorted and broken."

The seriously damaged hulk lies, bow to the east, with the bottom of the hull at 110 to 120 feet, the main deck at 170 feet, and the lagoon bottom at 180 feet. We made two dives on the

Arkansas and sent the camera down once. I let go of the buoy line and dropped like a skydiver onto the wreck from 60 feet. As the bottom rushed up to meet me, I was shocked to see an inverted and broken wreck. A battleship's bottom should be flat and massive. The *Arkansas* looked like sharply eroded ledges of limestone that quickly drop into the depths. The starboard side was jammed into the lagoon bottom, with splayed frames coming out of the wreckage.

The overturned hull of the battleship *New York* prepares to slip beneath the waves after being scuttled in 1948. The flat expanse of the hull stands in sharp contrast to the bottom of the battleship *Arkansas*, sunk by Baker; the bottom is crushed into the lagoon floor. "Arkie" is smashed and twisted into ridges and flat expanses of metal along *the entire area* of hull shown here. (U.S. Naval Institute Photo Library)

The battleship was unrecognizable. I wasn't sure which one we had reached at first until I dropped down past the intact port side.

The *Arkansas* had been pounded down and apart by Baker. Like the mangled *Gilliam*, poor *Arkie* no longer resembles a ship. The stern was torn off, and I was astounded to find that the propeller shafts were either missing or twisted away from the hull. Two of the shafts were gone, their 142-foot lengths yanked out of the hulk to leave gaping wounds in the bottom of the hull. The impact of the bomb was all the

The broken bones of USS *Arkansas*. The stern is torn away, along with two of the four propeller shafts. The hull has collapsed and dented into large valleys of twisted wreckage that rise and fall like eroded gulleys in a once flat plain of steel. (Larry Murphy, National Park Service)

more shocking when I compared it to scenes of the German battleship *Bismarck*, which rests miles down in the Atlantic. Attacked and sunk by a British task force in May 1941, the *Bismarck* had 2,876 shells fired at it, nearly 400 of them hitting the German battleship. Torpedoed and aflame, the *Bismarck* capsized and sunk 15,317 feet to the ocean floor. Yet when rediscovered in June 1989, it was intact and could be easily and clearly identified. The *Arkansas*, 180 feet down, took us two dives to identify.

The only identifiable feature of the ship is its row of port casemates. Called the "aircastle" by *Arkie*'s crew, these half-turrets built into the armored side of the hull were antiquated reminders of the dreadnought era of battleships when the *Arkansas* sailed to Bikini. Mounting three single 5-inch/51-caliber anti-aircraft guns, the aircastle retains its weapons. The 11 1/2-ton, 22-foot long guns hang upside down, their barrels swung to port, to protrude from the six-inch-thick armor plating of the aircastle. Finding the

Upside down and dangling from its casemate, a 5-inch gun protrudes from the darkened aircastle of USS *Arkansas*, the only intact compartment left on the battleship. Dan Lenihan and Larry Murphy squeezed in past the gun in 1990 to examine it. (Larry Murphy, National Park Service)

guns was the most exciting part of the dive, and we all gathered close to the aperture to shine our lights inside. In the darkness, the vague outlines of stanchions were illuminated by our spotlights as we moved them around to see what we could make out inside the ship.

Dan Lenihan and Larry Murphy made a second dive on the *Arkansas* in 1990 and pushed their way past the guns. I missed the dive because of a cold, but had helped plan for the entry by practicing it a few months earlier. I had visited the *Texas*, the oldest American battleship

afloat, in a shipyard in Galveston. A near sister of the *Arkansas*, the *Texas'* aircastle became the stage for practicing slipping past the guns. It was easier to figure out if you got stuck while squeezing into the aircastle 40 feet above the water than trying the same stunt nearly 180 feet down. Not going into the *Arkansas* was one of the biggest disappointments of my second trip to Bikini, but Dan and Larry's video of the dive almost made up for it.

Inside the aircastle, the deck is a forest of stubby fasteners where the teak planks have

Still lethal, live 5-inch/51 caliber shells hang from a ready ammunition rack near one of the guns inside *Arkansas*. (Larry Murphy, National Park Service)

been eaten away. Below, the overhead subtly sags and bows from the bomb's distortion, and the stanchions that supported it are slightly bent. Yet, in one of those amazing contradictions, the glass covers inside the overhead lights were unbroken. Dan Lenihan was surprised. He swam straight for one, reached down and wiped the silt away, and shined his flashlight directly into it. Watching Dan's tape, I was reminded that, in the aftermath of a tornado, people sometimes find unbent paper straws driven through tree trunks.

When we dived the *Arkansas*, we had to yet to see the time-lapse photos taken during Baker that showed the battleship capsized and driven down by the bomb. Every meal we ate in the Bikini Field Station was next to a large framed photo of Baker shot from a tower on the island, practically from where we were now sitting. The big black speck that started at the righthand side of the thick column of the blast was supposedly the *Arkansas* climbing the mushroom. That myth died hard, and only after our dive. While *Arkie*'s bow is twisted—and a few of the guys thought that might mean the ship had pirouetted in a radioactive dance of death inside the upthrust column of water and steam—the ship lies nearly flat against the bottom.

The world turned upside down. This ammunition hoist in the aircastle of the battleship *Arkansas* once lifted shells to the deck for the 5-inch anti-aircraft guns. Now inverted, its cover hangs open. The teak deck is gone, eaten by marine worms, leaving only the metal bolts that fastened it to the armored steel underdeck. (Larry Murphy, National Park Service)

More than a hundred feet of superstructure and masts towered above the deck. Now that same deck, upside-down, rests only six to eight feet off the seabed. Swimming up from the bottom, past the terrible damage to nearly two-thirds of the hull, I could see that the bomb had punched up into the *Arkansas*, rolling it over to port and capsizing it. Then the falling millions of tons of silt and water had driven the battleship down 180 feet, hammering *Arkie* into the ocean floor and either crushing or burying the superstructure and masts. We didn't try to slip under the ship, but the tiny robot camera did. Up near the bow, we were delighted to find the barrels of the No. 1 turret's twelve-inch guns sticking up out of the silt. The anchor chain stretches out of the chain locker and loops down to the coral sand before rising up again to pass through the hawsepipes. The chain runs out from the bow, disappearing into the gloom. It was another reminder that the *Arkansas*, like the other ships, had been a tethered giant at the moment of its destruction.

We were all surprised to be able to see beneath the *Arkansas*, because we thought the decks were buried. Navy reports from 1946 described a thick layer of radioactive silt that had buried the lower portions of the wreck, and we all had shuddered at the thought of the navy diver who had sunk into the "hot" mud up to his armpits. The mud was gone, flushed away by tidal action and currents, and we were the first to visit the guns of the *Arkansas*. Although we couldn't see it, we all felt the strange and indescribably thrilling sense of diving into the center of the large, shallow crater blasted out of

the bottom by Baker and partially filled by the *Arkansas*'s hulk. Swimming over the smashed battleship, I felt the same awe and fear that the *Gilliam* had inspired. The condition of the ship made it very clear that I was at ground zero, in the very maw of armageddon. I now understand what happened to the *Arkansas*, but I will never fully comprehend the forces unleashed against it. Left behind at ground zero, the remains of what once were ships brought the scratchy newsreels and photos of Able and Baker to life in a unique and unforgettable fashion.

7

Exploring the Wreck of the *Saratoga*

The most famous and perhaps most mourned of the ships lost at Bikini was the aircraft carrier *Saratoga*. *Sara,* as the carrier was known to its crew, was the focus of our work during the two years we dived the atoll's nuclear fleet. With my colleagues, I spent hours swimming over the decks, into compartments, and down the cavernous hangar into the blackness. In 1989, we made dozens of dives from 100 to 180 feet on the *Saratoga,* spending five and a half hours exploring the sunken carrier. The depths exacted a price—we had to spend almost four more hours hanging on a line that jerked up and down with the swell. As we waited, we breathed pure oxygen to purge the nitrogen from our blood.

The *Saratoga*'s birth had resulted, ironically, from a naval arms limitations treaty. It was originally planned as the second cruiser of the six-vessel *Lexington* class. Laid down on September 25, 1920, at the Camden, New Jersey, yards of the New York Shipbuilding Corporation, it was part of a post–World War I arms race with Great Britain and Japan in which construction efforts focused on large, heavily armored and armed battleships and battle cruisers. This arms race, as well as a growing interest in naval aviation, conspired to redesign the *Saratoga* before its launch.

The postwar naval arms race also inspired several international conferences, conventions, and treaties seeking to limit the expansion of the number of battleships and cruisers, the world's most powerful weapons. The Washington Naval Conference of 1921–1922 led to an international agreement to limit the numbers, sizes, and armaments of any capital ship. Under the terms of the treaty signed after the conference, battleships and battle cruisers then under construction would be scrapped except for two vessels from each nation's fleet that could be converted into aircraft carriers. The U.S. Navy's choices for conversion were the *Lexington* and the *Saratoga;* Japan chose to convert the battleship *Kaga* and the battle cruiser *Akagi* to fleet carriers. The incomplete hulls of the two American cruisers joined the converted collier *Jupiter,* renamed *Langley* (CV-1), as the second and third carriers of the U.S. Navy. The *Saratoga,* sitting under a huge shipyard shed on the banks of the Delaware River at New York Shipbuilding, had already received its armored barbettes to mount the turrets, and the decks were being laid. Almost all of that work was torn out and replaced, as the cruiser was rebuilt as a carrier.

The *Saratoga* was the first of the two carriers launched, sliding from the ways into the Delaware River on April 7, 1925. As the first of the two-ship *Lexington* class carriers, the *Saratoga*'s was the heaviest warship launch on record and among the top dozen heaviest launches for any merchant or naval vessel up to that time. Proud navy press releases crowed that "the new *Saratoga*, aircraft carrier, when completed and commissioned . . . will be the largest and fastest craft of its kind in the world." Fitting out the ship took two years before it was commissioned on November 16, 1927, at the Philadelphia Navy Yard. Departing on a shakedown cruise on January 6, 1928, the carrier landed its first plane on board five days later.

The two carriers heralded the beginning of naval aviation. Pushed into bringing the plane to sea by the army's bombing and sinking of the captured German battleship *Ostfriesland*, the navy built the two carriers, one of which would ironically die as a result of another contest between the army air forces and the navy. A generation of navy fliers was trained on the *Saratoga* and the *Lexington*, and the ships were well loved. The irascible Admiral W. F. "Bull" Halsey wrote in his reminiscences that, of all the ships he had served aboard, only two were special—the carriers *Saratoga* and *Enterprise*: "*Sara* is a queen and that is why she will always have a place in my heart. First, I loved her as a home; I commanded her for two years and flew my rear admiral's flag on her for two more, which means I lived on board her longer than I ever lived anywhere else. Second, I loved her as a ship; she helped me make my debut in the carrier Navy, and she initiated me into the marvels of fleet aviation."

The *Saratoga*'s prewar career was spent on the Pacific in training exercises that defined a strong role for aircraft carriers in naval warfare. This included staged "attacks" on the Panama Canal and Pearl Harbor, usually operating in tandem with the *Lexington* or, in later years, with the carriers that followed the two pioneers. The Pearl Harbor "attack" of 1937, which the carriers pulled off with considerable success, received much hindsight attention as proof that a surprise aerial assault on the U.S. Pacific Fleet was possible, if not probable, prior to the bloody events of December 7, 1941. On that day, as the Pacific Fleet was pounded by Japanese torpedoes and bombs, the *Saratoga* was in California, entering San Diego harbor after an overhaul at the Puget Sound Naval Shipyard at Bremerton, Washington. Within twenty-four hours, it was readied for war and on its way to the Pacific. Thus the carrier started a long campaign that lasted through the entire war.

The *Saratoga*'s career included sailing in the aborted effort to relieve the beleaguered marine garrison on Wake Island. A more satisfactory role was opening the American assault on Guadalcanal. It also pounded Japanese bases in the Gilbert and Marshall Islands, provided support for the landings at Tarawa, and flew combat air patrols over Eniwetok and Wotje. The *Sara-*

The setting for *Sara's* greatest tragedy. In February 1945, during a kamikaze attack, *Saratoga's* marine gun crew manned this 5-inch gun, as well as the others in the starboard-bow sponsons, just below the flight deck. Plane after plane dived into the carrier and exploded. As burning gasoline poured off the deck onto them, the men at these guns kept firing to keep other kamikazes at bay. They were burned alive. (Larry Murphy, National Park Service)

toga's aircraft struck the heavily defended Japanese port of Rabaul and airfields at Buka, neutralizing Japanese counterstrikes at Bougainville in what the navy termed "perhaps her most brilliant strike of the war." Operating with a British and French naval force, the *Saratoga* then struck Japanese-occupied Sumatra and Java to hit port and oil production facilities. After several months training in nighttime operations, the *Saratoga's* pilots flew diversionary strikes at Iwo Jima, combat air patrol over Chichi Jima, and nighttime raids on the Japanese home islands.

Despite its reputation as a "lucky" ship, the *Saratoga* was hit three times by the enemy. Torpedoed twice by Japanese submarines, the *Saratoga* limped back to Bremerton for repairs and

refits in January and August 1942. However, its darkest hour came off Iwo Jima on February 21, 1945, when five kamikazes hit the carrier, killing 123 men and wounding another 192. Burning gasoline from planes parked on the flight deck rained down onto the forward starboard sponson, drenching the marines manning the guns. Forty-five years later, it was a grim and disquieting experience to swim over those same guns.

Repaired once again at Bremerton, the *Saratoga* was steaming for Japan to strike the home islands in August when the war ended. Sent to the West Coast for decommissioning, it was instead ordered to "magic carpet" service in November 1945. As part of Operation Magic Carpet, the *Saratoga* ferried home 29,204 veterans, more than any other vessel. Another impressive record also heralded the end of the carrier's active service career: 98,954 aircraft landings in seventeen years, the record for the greatest number of planes landed on a carrier.

The *Saratoga* was selected as a Crossroads target because it was obsolete, having been replaced by a fleet of wartime-built Essex-class carriers. The *Lexington* had been lost during the Battle of the Coral Sea in May 1942. The sentimental value of being a famous surviving sister-

USS *Saratoga* leaves for Bikini. A photographer caught this last look at *Sara* as the carrier passed beneath the San Francisco–Oakland Bay Bridge. The flight deck is now shorn of its aircraft and test equipment. The stack has fallen, and the thick steel deck is dented into a 200-foot long, 70-foot wide, 20-foot deep valley that runs from the superstructure aft to the stern. (San Francisco Maritime National Historical Park)

ship notwithstanding, the choice of the *Saratoga* was also justified because it had more than a thousand watertight compartments and underwater protection that was "very similar in arrangement to that of modern battleships and large carriers," which made it tough to sink. Prepared for the tests at Hunter's Point, San Francisco, the *Saratoga* sailed through the Golden Gate on April 30 after an emotional farewell that included a tribute broadcast from the flight deck by Jack Benny.

The *Saratoga* steamed to Bikini with the destroyer *Anderson*. The choice of the destroyer as an escort was highly ironic. The *Anderson* had screened *Sara*'s sister *Lexington* at the Battle of the Coral Sea in May 1942 when the carrier was sunk. It had then helped to screen the USS *Yorktown* (CV-5) at Midway, and despite the destroyer's shooting down four attacking torpedo bombers, Japanese planes got through and hit the carrier, which sank the next day. Sent again into the front lines, the *Anderson* was with the USS *Wasp* (CV-7) when that carrier succumbed to torpedo attack on September 15, 1942, and with the USS *Hornet* (CV-8) in October 1942 when that carrier was sunk during the battles of the Eastern Solomons and the Santa Cruz. The *Anderson* had sailed with and defended several carriers, even at the cost of the ship's own crew at Leyte, when the *Anderson* survived a kamikaze attack that killed eighteen and wounded twenty-one members of the crew. During a hard-hitting career, the *Anderson*'s crew had also watched four carriers die. Now it sailed to die with a fifth. The two ships arrived at Bikini on May 31. In less than ninety days, the *Saratoga* was dead.

Revisiting the *Saratoga*

Speeding across the sparkling blue-green waters of Bikini Lagoon, the first clue that a sunken wreck is nearby is the telltale smell of diesel fuel wafting across the water. Forty-four years after Operation Crossroads, the *Saratoga*'s bunkers continue to leak oil. Our boat slows at the first sniff of oily air, and all aboard peer intently into the water. The first bit of the *Saratoga* seen is the tip of the mast, rising within twenty feet of the surface as a pale-green shadow. It was usually here, abaft the island, that the dive boats tied up. There, tethered to the *Saratoga*, we donned our scuba gear and held last-minute discussions to confirm the plans for the dive. Then, two by two, we rolled out of the boat, arching backward into the clear, warm water as hundreds of tiny fish darted out of the way. At the mooring line, we always stopped to collect all our team members before slowly letting the air out of buoyancy-compensating dive vests as we headed down the line, plummeting into the depths as the impressive bulk of the carrier loomed up.

At fifty feet, we passed the open deck of the air-defense bridge, its toppled mounts and chairs lying on the rubble-strewn steel plates. Behind them, the turret-like Mark 37 gun director, shorn of its topping radar antennae, rises toward the surface, its observer hatches sealed shut by coralline encrustation and corrosion. From the air-defense bridge, the island stretches below, deck after deck, to reach the yawning black pit of the open elevator shaft on the flight deck. A hundred feet beneath the surface, the flight deck, its wooden plank sheathing now gone, is marked only by bits of consumed wood

The wrecks at Bikini are deep—most lie 180 feet down. The flight deck of *Saratoga* is at 100 feet. At that depth, we could only spend 25 minutes from the time we left the surface before decompressing. We usually spent an hour down there because it took a long time to map and photograph the wreck. We paid for our time in the water by hanging on decompression lines for what seemed like an eternity. Jerry Livingston and Larry Nordby compare notes, while Dan Lenihan, video camera clipped to his vest, hangs behind them. (Larry Murphy, National Park Service)

adhering to the bolts that once fastened them down to the steel deck beneath. The pole mast, bent and partly twisted, no longer gaily flying ensigns and signal flags, points to port, its radar

The Mark 37 gun director atop *Saratoga's* island. From their high vantage point, the crew used radar and their sharp vision to direct the fire of the ship's anti-aircraft gun batteries. This is the first portion of the carrier encountered by divers after following the mast down from the surface. (National Archives)

Fifty feet below the surface of Bikini Lagoon, a diver swims past the mast and the air defense level on the superstructure of the carrier *Saratoga*. Once the highest level in the ship, this is the first area divers encounter when they drop into the blue waters of the lagoon. (Larry Murphy, National Park Service)

Inside the aft 5-inch gun house on *Saratoga*, a group of cartridges waits in a ready ammunition magazine for a battle that will never come. Everywhere we went on the carrier, we found live ammunition. (Larry Murphy, National Park Service)

antenna and rigging also stripped. Forward is an open expanse of flight deck, interrupted by the forward five-inch gun house, the remains of the palisades that once caught errant planes, and the toppled crane. Near the bow the deck has partially collapsed, huge cracks and yawning gaps leading into officers' country forward, below deck.

The flight deck, as well as the ship's stack, shows the worst bomb damage. It looked to me as though Godzilla had stomped the deck. When the *Saratoga* rolled in the trough of the atomic bomb's tidal wave, the force of the falling column and the tons of water and sand that fell out of the sky collapsed the flight deck into a single, large dent that is 70 feet wide, 200 feet long, and 20 feet deep, ending near the after end of the stack. Although navy reports in 1946 stated that "the indentation is gradual with no abrupt breaks or bends," and despite the fact that "the wood decking has been splintered and broken," and there was "no indication that the steel deck has ruptured," the steel deck *is* now ruptured. It might have been cracked in 1946 and the splintered wooden deck hid the evidence. Now a large break in the deck runs athwartship about 100 feet from the stern, while cracks alongside the edges of the dent, which was called "the valley" by navy divers in 1946, are separating as the weakened steel slowly collapses.

At the aft end of the stack, the deck has collapsed into the hangar. Here, a roughly square depression lined with broken steel, is the location of *Saratoga*'s No. 2 elevator, which was closed off in the carrier's 1945, pre-Crossroads refit. The elevator platform was left in place when the bay was sealed off. The platform lies in the hangar, covered with debris, as the edges of the flight deck bend around in a veritable frozen shower of rusty, encrusted debris. The *Saratoga*'s main flight elevator, forward of the stack, lies at the bottom of its shaft, diagonally bent nearly 90 degrees. Weakened, cracked, and bent by Baker, the platform succumbed to decades of immersion in the salt water and finally collapsed, one edge lying against the port bulk-

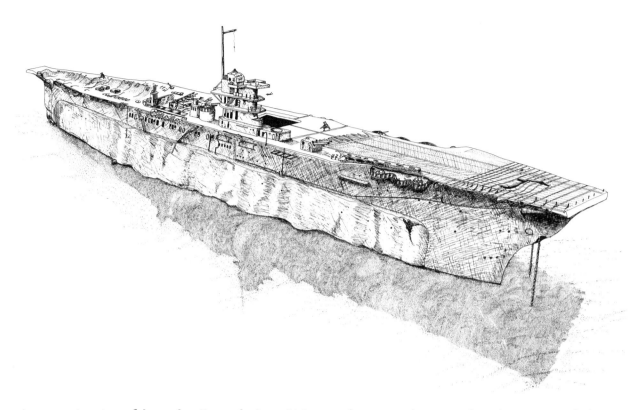

A perspective view of the sunken *Saratoga* by Jerry Livingston documents the tremendous damage wrought by the atomic bomb. The starboard hull is partially crushed and "washboarded," the flight deck has collapsed into a 200 by 70 foot, 20-foot deep "valley," and the stack is knocked flat. The drawing is based on thousands of hours of work by Livingston and archaeologist Larry Nordby. (National Park Service, Submerged Cultural Resources Unit)

head of the shaft, and then bending down so that the other edge lies flush at the bottom of the shaft. On our first dive, we all looked eagerly at the dark hole in the deck, wanting to drop down it and into the hangar, but we had decided to see as much of the ship as possible going no deeper than a hundred feet.

The *Saratoga*'s stack was a massive steel-plated structure that towered eighty feet above the flight deck. It is now a twisted mass of wreckage that dominates the deck in a different way.

When the stack was hit by the blast wave, it split and fell to port across the flight deck, slightly angling toward the bow, indicating a lateral twisting, probably from the angle of the wave that hit it. Diver reports from 1946 noted that the after-quarter of the stack, still erect, was "twisted about 20 degrees counterclockwise." The stack tore free at its base, exposing the boiler intakes. As I swam over them, I peered down more than sixty feet into the engineering spaces, but saw little. The intakes are clogged

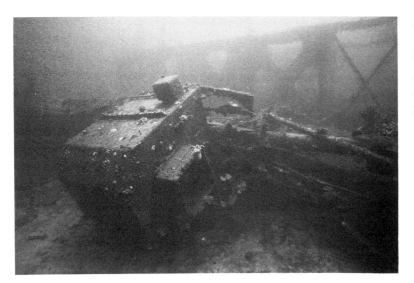

The wreckage of *Saratoga*'s collapsed stack lies across the deck. This armored gun director once stood at the forward end of the stack. (Larry Murphy, National Park Service)

with debris. Any thought I had of entering the engineering spaces was abandoned.

The stack punched into the flight deck when it fell. The deck bent and then cracked. The cracks are now slowly widening, as the weight of the stack bends the rusting deck beneath it. A noticeable bowing of the flight deck around the stack and elevator indicates that the deck will eventually collapse into the hangar. The deck beams, large steel girders riveted and welded to the steel deck, have begun to break free and fall into the ship, evidence of the inevitable decay of the *Saratoga*. One of the most striking aspects of the ship was this deterioration. All of us had dived steel ships that were sunk in salt water years before the *Saratoga* had taken the final plunge, but nowhere else did we see as much rust and decay of metal. Pieces of the ship broke free when we brushed against them, and every time we went inside the hangar on later dives our bubbles loosened a rain of rust flakes. My guess is that the steel was shattered by the burst, opening millions of microscopic cracks that hastened rust and decay.

The hull of the carrier, particularly below the waterline, also shows the fatal blow from the Baker bomb. When the *Saratoga* was first dived by the navy in August 1946, divers reported that the ship lay at a ten-to-fifteen degree list to port, just as it does now. The bow tilts up five degrees, as it did when the *Saratoga* slipped beneath the surface. The navy divers reported major damage, particularly to the hull, which had ruptured, especially near the outermost starboard propeller shaft. The shaft had bent, tearing out the strut that supported it along with plates. The starboard side of the hull was dented and "washboarded" by the blast wave.

Our dives in 1989 and 1990 showed just how much "washboarding" there was. Below the flight deck, particularly along the starboard torpedo blister, the hull is dented in between the frames, in some cases as much as six feet along the blister. The denting increases toward the

Where feet once pounded, fish now swim. This ladder, running from the flight deck down *Saratoga's* starboard side, is now a haven for whip coral and small tropical fish. The shadowy form of the carrier's superstructure rises in the background. (Larry Murphy, National Park Service)

stern, where the plating is actually cracked and torn. The damage is impressive, but it hit me only after spending time swimming along the side of the ship. The *Saratoga* itself overwhelmed me once I was alongside the carrier. One hundred and forty feet down, the flight deck towered forty feet above me, and for as far as I could see, forward and behind, the massive hull stretched into the gloom. The magnitude of the damage slowly unfolded as I swam past dents, pushed-in hatches, and broken portholes.

On one dive, I squeezed past a collapsed hatch and into an open passageway as Lenihan shined a light in to guide me. Debris covered the deck, half-detached pipes hung from the overhead, and fuzzy white whip coral waved in the wake of my passage, raising red and angry welts on my skin. It was my first foray into the *Saratoga*, and the darkness and deterioration brought home the finality of the carrier's death.

Though the bomb left its mark on the *Saratoga*, other changes are attributable to time and the sea. The flight deck, once covered with teak planks, is now an expanse of steel, the small fragments of wood adhering to the fasteners, metal tiedowns for the planes, steel battens, and hydraulic catapults. Aft, bitts and wire-rope arresting gear run athwartship, dipping into the depression of Baker's dent into the deck. The arresting gear and the jumbled remains of the palisades forward of the island are evidence of the tens of thousands of aircraft that once flew off this deck. The airplane crane is collapsed and lies on the deck. On the other side, the airplane jettisoning ramp, athwart the island, slopes off to port. On February 21, 1945, the bodies of the men killed in the kamikaze attack that knocked *Sara* out of the war were slid, eight at a time, into the sea next to the ramp, while burned-out hulks of planes were shoved with less ceremony off the deck. In little more than a year *Sara* would join them in the depths.

As we swam along the ship's decks and sides, we searched the lagoon bottom below for airplanes washed free of the deck, but found only scattered debris. Pieces of plating, pipe, and sheared sponsons carrying guns and range-finders lay to starboard, some of them in the gloom of the ship's shadow, close to the half-buried screws. Part of a trailer, with still-inflated rubber tires, rested on the port side. Near the bow, where the ship's anchor cable drapes down from the bow into the silt, some strands dangling free, one of the twenty-ton clumps used to moor the ship lay on the lagoon floor, dragged with the carrier as it was swept from its target position by the blast. At *Sara*'s stern, a partially crushed mooring buoy rested on the bottom, while a huge navy stockless anchor, also used to

hold *Sara* in position, lay on the deck, sucked up and dropped there by the upthrust of the blast. Everywhere I went, evidence of the bomb was at hand.

I was interested in searching for test equipment and instruments and spent as much time as I could hunting the decks. Very few pieces remain of the test equipment stowed on the *Saratoga*'s flight deck by the Army Ground Group. The empty steel mounting slots for the wheels and tracks of missing tanks, trucks, an armored car, and two field guns were the only traces of what was once a crowded testing ground. An army 90 mm anti-aircraft gun lay next to the edge of the deck, close to the still cabled but crushed and corroded remains of a pallet with a generator's engine and radiator rising from it. These pitiful remains were the fragments of the packing case and "safety trough" for a radio set and its air-cooled diesel generator. They were, amazingly enough, a link with the living past of the *Saratoga*. A member of the crew, interviewed at the annual reunion in 1989, recalled that he and some friends had listened to the broadcast of a Joe Louis fight on that radio while sweltering in Bikini's tropical heat. Discoveries like this held the most satisfaction, because they allowed me to share a sense of them back in the States with men who remembered *Sara* when the carrier belonged to their world of sun and air.

We all had no trouble spotting and identifying two roughly pyramidal, nine-foot-high, steel-pipe blast gauge towers. Known during Crossroads as "Christmas trees," they mounted aluminum foil gauges used to measure shock waves. The gauges were "ruptured foil peak pressure" instruments made of quarter-inch-thick brass

Measuring the incomprehensible. This simple instrument is known as a "ruptured foil gauge for recording peak pressure in air." Doctor C. W. Lampson (on the gauge) and Captain A. E. Uehlinger "inspect" a gauge for a Crossroads press photo. The tower the gauge rests on was called a "Christmas tree." We saw several on the decks of the sunken ships at Bikini. (U.S. Naval Institute Photo Library)

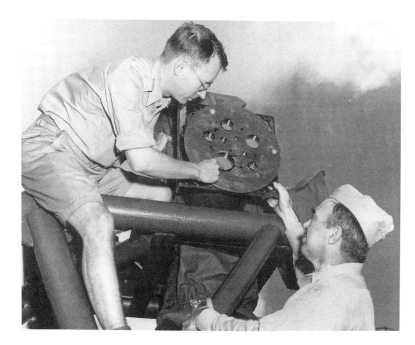

plates with round holes of various diameters bored through them. Tinfoil was sandwiched between the plates, which were mounted atop the towers on a steel box that was kept "air tight . . . to prevent instantaneous equalization of pressure." The greater the pressure, the smaller the diameter of the ruptured foil. Looking at the many holes in the chambers atop each tower, I was struck by how simple, seemingly unsophisticated, and yet ingenious these instruments were. At the beginning of the nuclear age, aluminum foil, tin cans, and aluminum disks that scratched the marks of a ship's tossing in an atomic tidal wave were evidence of people's first attempts to understand and measure the incomprehensible forces unleashed by the bomb.

Another type of gauge for measuring peak overpressure left numerous pieces scattered across the *Saratoga*'s deck. These are one-inch-thick lead plates, some with square holes cut in them, like mats for a picture about to be framed. The remains of indentation peak pressure gauges, they lay crumpled, bent, and scattered aft of the funnel, atop the mount for the No. 3 five-inch gun house, and on the house itself, where a steel mounting bracket for the plates was still welded at the forward edge of the house. Measuring overpressures, either from 20 to 1,000 psi, or 100 to 6,000 psi, depending on their thickness, these gauges recorded "in terms of indentation produced by a small steel ball forced against the sheet of lead. The greater the pressure, the deeper the indentation." It reminded me of the fairy tale of the princess and the pea.

Other test instruments left on the sunken ship after Baker lay broken and nearly unidentifiable on the platforms that surround the car-

Pausing to investigate a smashed test instrument on the deck outside of flag-plot on *Saratoga*'s island, or superstructure, the author kneels to take measurements and draw it on his clipboard. (Larry Murphy, National Park Service)

rier's island. I found two parabolic, chromed aluminum disks in a jumble of rusted metal. They were the remains of a "pendulum type inclinometer" developed by the material laboratory of the New York Naval Shipyard to record the angles of the target ships as they pitched and rolled after the blasts. Mounted on steel plates with a weighted arm designed to remain vertical

Every compartment we entered in *Saratoga* was sealed shut, with every hatch dogged down. Condition "Z," for battle, had been set to keep the ship from sinking. Yet cracks and twisting from the Baker blast opened *Sara's* thousand compartments to the sea, and she sank in seven hours. (Larry Murphy, National Park Service)

at all times, the discs were scratched by the arm to leave a record.

In 1989 we penetrated the *Saratoga*. Our first forays into the ship's many compartments began on the island. Lying in shallower water, the island was an excellent site for the second dive of the day when we didn't want to make a second deep descent. We swam through open doorways into the flag plot, where the *Saratoga*'s admirals manned their station during combat. All the hatches and doors that led into the flag plot were down, blown off their hinges and lying on the deck. Radar and communications equip-

ment filled the compartments, while electric-light fixtures dangled, half detached, by their conduits. A chart table, bolted to a bulkhead, mounted a drafting machine missing its drawing arm. Moving aft, the bulkheads themselves were gone, probably to corrosion, opening up the tiny day cabin. The bunk and a gleaming white porcelain head and sink were all that was left in the cabin, which is now open to the sea because the exterior bulkheads have also partially collapsed. As we entered the cabin and passed the head, Larry Murphy grinned. Later, when we were back on the boat, he told us why.

Saratoga's bridge during the war, somewhere in the South Pacific, 1942. The seaman at the helm steers the carrier by means of the small handle. Nearly fifty years later, I rested my hand where his once was. The indicators in front of the helm have now fallen free; one lies nearby. (National Archives)

We all wore standard National Park Service dark-green overalls as our dive suits. The suits, used by park maintenance workers, were light, protected our skin from coral and rusty metal, and were cooler than a wet suit in the tropical water. We joked that they made us look like "underwater janitors," particularly when the ABC-TV and *National Geographic* crews asked if we would lose the suits because they made us look too dark in their photos. We couldn't, of course, because we hadn't brought bright neon-colored wetsuits. We were there to do a job, not look pretty for pictures. As he swam past that toilet, though, Murphy looked at it, saw it was a little dirty, and had the insane thought of cleaning it for a photo opportunity as an "underwater janitor." We all cracked up when he told us. But Lenihan wouldn't let Murphy carry a toilet plunger down with him on the next dive to clear that head.

From the cabin, I dropped down another level past a half-fallen door and twisted onto my side to enter the bridge. Inside, many of the instruments that had once navigated and conned the ship at this nerve center of the carrier remained in place—binnacle, engine-room telegraphs and revolution indicators, chart tables, and a lighting panel on the aft bulkhead, its switches denoted by black plastic engravings that read "mast head," and "man overboard." Aft of the bridge in the chartroom, toppled equipment blocked access into the compartment. By sticking our lights inside, we could make out the chart table and a ladder that leads below.

Time stood still, and as I hovered over the helm, my hand rested on the simple switch and its handle that had steered *Sara*. It took little imagination to picture a late-night watch on the bridge, as the ship hunted the Japanese in the South Pacific. Closing my eyes, I could almost hear the low murmur of voices coming from the chartroom as the dim red lights and the glow of the compass in its binnacle before me marked a course as we cut through phosphorescent seas.

Outside the bridge, on the vast expanse of the port side, the plates once held the painted legend of the *Saratoga*'s battle flag, recounting the number of enemy planes splashed, targets hit, and campaigns completed. I spent several minutes with my gloves trying to wipe away the grime of forty-five years, in the hope of glimpsing a small Japanese flag or the painted outline of a sitting duck (the symbol for aircraft destroyed on the ground). But the proud record is now erased by corrosion, and my attempts to remove the accumulated growth met with the hardened resistance of coralline algae.

Lenihan and Murphy swam into the bow, past the anchor bitts still wrapped with the mooring chain that runs from the hawses toward the lagoon bottom. The emergency radio room, packed with equipment, is a museum of vacuum-tube

The thick steel of the flight deck is bent and crushed after being hammered by atomic tidal waves, and yet inside the hangar deck, light bulbs are unbroken. Dan Lenihan shines his dive light on an intact light fixture inside *Saratoga*'s hangar deck. (Larry Murphy, National Park Service)

relics now dusted with silt and slowly rusting in the eternal darkness of the ship's interior. Beyond it, in other compartments, hatches are dogged shut, physical reminders of the ship's fully battle-ready condition—"Z"—for the test. The hatches were a reminder of why the *Saratoga* had been sent to Bikini: with a thousand watertight compartments, the carrier was nearly impossible to sink. But Baker's blast opened the bottom, twisted the hull, and popped open many of the hatches, allowing the water to fill the ship slowly. The same destructive power left a string of light bulbs hanging unbroken from the hangar deck's overhead—in yet another paradox of the bomb.

Into the Hangar Deck

The elevator shaft drops twenty feet down to the seventy-foot-wide cavern of the hangar deck, which sweeps aft for a few hundred feet. Just inside the hangar, on the starboard side, a rack of 500-pound aerial bombs lie in the silt, next to a steel drum and a 350-pound depth bomb that rolled from port to rest against the nose fuses of the five aerial bombs. The other depth bombs, four of them, lie in a row on the port side of the hangar. We all gingerly swam past the bombs. In 1989 one of the navy's Explosive Ordnance Disposal Mobile Unit One, Detachment 63's divers, HT1 Pape, wrapped a fuse in underwater putty in a daring maneuver to "gag" it. We all relaxed. The next year we felt even more relief when I found photographs in the National Archives showing the same bombs in 1946 with INERT painted on their sides.

The hangar deck is littered with fuel drums, loose torpedo racks, and sections of pipe. On the overhead above, sprinklers hang loose, their pipes broken free, while light fixtures with their bulbs intact remain attached. The survival of the light bulbs in the midst of a smashed and sunken ship was an unexpected discovery of delicate features left untouched by the bomb. But the overhead also showed signs of the ship's death. It is smeared with fuel oil—the carrier's life blood—that oozed from the bunkers as the *Saratoga* settled in the water. Fuel oil coats every overhead. Our air bubbles, as we exhaled, pushed the oil into swirling slicks and tar balls.

The biggest thrill was swimming up to four airplanes that remain stowed, wings folded, on the hangar's starboard side. The first three planes are navy dive-bombers—SBF-4E "Helldiver" single-engine aircraft, placed aboard the *Saratoga* in 1946, combat-ready with ten rounds of ammunition in the twin 20 mm cannon mounted to the wings. Every instrument except the aviator's clocks remained mounted in the instrument panels—even the bomb sights were there. I wondered about the clocks until an officer who had been present at Crossroads told me that they might have been taken out to prevent the clocks—much sought-after souvenirs at the time—from being pilfered by the crew. In January 1992, after a slide lecture I gave at the 1991 crew reunion, a "Sara," Jack Lehman, sent me two polaroids of one of the clocks with the rejoinder to remember "what was told to you by some officer." "Well, guess what?" wrote Mr. Lehman. The clock was "still running and keeps good time." Once again I had the feeling of the years telescoping to the few seconds my eyes had swept over the instrument panels of those planes on the hangar deck.

The planes' identities are known because the

Saratoga's flight deck, once the scene of noisy activity. On our dives, the open well of the elevator gave us easy access to the hangar, 130 feet below the surface of the lagoon. We pushed back into the interior to find planes, torpedoes, rockets, and unexploded bombs mixed up with fire-fighting equipment, carts, and hand-trucks. (National Archives)

Wings folded up and bent back, this Curtiss "Helldiver" rests in the hangar deck of USS *Saratoga*. The canopy open, live bombs in the bomb bay and slung under the wings, and tires yet inflated, the plane is one of five left aboard the carrier. It is incredibly fragile; the pressure of a finger punches through the aluminum skin. (© Bill Curtsinger)

From the production line to aerial combat over the Pacific. The "Helldiver" was an effective dive bomber and several were tested at Bikini. We examined them inside USS *Saratoga* from the same vantage point of the workers on the wings. Floating without gravity, we hung upside down and sideways above the canopy as we studied the instrument panel. (U.S. Naval Institute Photo Library)

navy's Bureau of Aeronautics carefully recorded each aircraft's serial number: plane 31894 is first, stowed at frame 90; followed by plane 31850, stowed at frame 100; and plane 31840, stowed at frame 110. After Baker, each was noted in the meticulously kept bureau notebooks as "missing—sank with *Saratoga*." Each was built to carry a thousand pounds of bombs in the bomb bay and another two bombs on the wings. *Sara's* planes each have full bomb bays. The planes on

Unexploded and jumbled next to one another, live "Tiny Tim" rockets lie next to the edge of *Saratoga*'s flight deck in this rare 1946 underwater view of the sunken carrier. We avoided the still volatile rockets on our dives. (National Archives)

the carrier were also Canadian Fairchild-built versions of the SB2C; identical, they were designated "SBF." Only one hundred of the SBF-4E Helldivers were built between 1944 and 1945. The rapid deterioration we saw in the ship has also affected the planes; swimming past one, I pushed off it with two fingers and inadvertently punched holes in the skin of the wing.

Aft of the third plane, the compartment was blocked abruptly by a mound of debris where the flight deck above and wreckage from the stack had collapsed into the hangar, which was open to the sea. It was marked by the sloping sides of the square hole in the deck, above which the once sealed shaft of the No. 2 elevator stood. Beyond it the hangar loomed as a dark space. There to starboard we found the fourth plane, a TBM-3E "Avenger" torpedo-bomber. It too is an identified aircraft; its Bureau of Aeronautics serial number is 69190. Avengers were armed with a single aerial torpedo and .50- and .30-caliber machine guns. The TBM-3E was a General Motors Corporation, Eastern Aircraft Division-built identical version of the Grum-

Divers are dwarfed by *Sara*'s blunt bow. The overhanging flight deck casts shadows on the lagoon floor, while anchor chains broken free of their 10-ton mooring blocks by Baker's blast droop listlessly. (©Bill Curtsinger)

man TBF; in all, 4,664 were built. The TBM-3E was a late war, antisubmarine detection radar equipped aircraft that became "the principal operational version of the Avenger after 1945." A postwar version, the TBM-3R, carried nuclear weapon components to aircraft carriers in the postwar years. It was an ironic sight to see the same type of plane broken and sunk by Baker.

Aft of the Avenger, we followed the hangar for another hundred or so feet, the overhead sloping down as the dent in the flight deck above began and deepened the farther aft the hangar was penetrated. More ordnance littered the decks. On the starboard side near the torpedo elevator, Mark 13 torpedoes, a few lashed to bomb carts, lay tumbled and loose on the deck. These one-ton instruments of destruction were used to good effect in several battles, par-

An island in the sea. *Saratoga*'s flight deck was supported by a wide hull. The bow ended abruptly in the squared form of a blunt nose. (Naval Institute Photo Library)

ticularly the sinking of the Japanese super-battleship *Yamato* at the war's end. Now a score of them lie tumbled and broken on *Sara*'s hangar deck. Nearby, Lenihan and Murphy found other drowned weapons, including a rack of five-inch High Velocity Aerial Rockets and "Tiny Tim" rockets.

As we swam through the hangar, everyone noticed that the deck overhead was bowing down, weighted by the collapsed stack and the pressure of the depths. The heavy girders that sup-ported the flight deck were cracked, and when we returned in 1990, one major disappointment was finding that some of the girders had fallen into the hangar, partially crushing two of the planes. The flight deck is increasingly bowing under the weight of the fallen stack, and in the immediate future it will collapse into the hangar. *Sara* is slowly falling apart. Between 1989 and 1990 a section of sponson with a tub that mounted a Mark 51 gun director gave way and fell to the lagoon floor.

Nonetheless, the mass of steel that was the *Saratoga* will remain upright and intact on the bottom of Bikini Atoll lagoon for some time to come. In 1992, the waters of Bikini were opened to the diving public. All the ships, including the *Saratoga*, now receive submerged visitors, who come to inspect the vessels deposited on the bottom, more or less frozen in time. One of the U.S. Navy's most famous and historically significant vessels, the *Saratoga* was not spared by Joint Task Force One for use as a floating memorial, as was the USS *Texas* and, in later years, scores of other floating combat veterans of the Second World War. Ironically, the atomic bomb that sank the ship saved it from scrapping. The *Saratoga* now rests quietly in a watery grave, awaiting hordes of scuba-diving visitors who are drawn to her—the only carrier in the world for divers to explore.

8

The Ghost Fleet

Every day at Bikini began with a morning dive and a several-hour interval until the next, the last dive of the day taking place in the late afternoon. I spent those "off-hours" exploring the island on one of the four-wheeled "quad bikes" used as station runabouts. A dirt road ran from one end of the island to the other, and a few minutes' drive took one past the empty and overgrown shells of concrete homes, rusted and abandoned trucks, and the always smoldering dump where our trash was burned each day. Palm trees and low brush covered the island. Forays into the back areas led to modern testing stations for radioactivity, a large concrete bunker, and a small graveyard, all reminders of what lies in the soil. The bones of previous generations of Bikinians are there, marked by graves left behind when the people were moved to Rongelap in 1946. These ancestral bones are irradiated by fallout that has filtered down into the sandy loam of the island. The soil holds the radioactive legacy of many blasts. Cesium-137, cobalt-60, strontium-90, americium-240, plutonium-239, and plutonium-240 are trapped in the ground and in the water, accumulating in the co-conuts and plants. The cesium has reached its half-life of thirty years, but the plutonium-239, with a half-life of 24,065 years, is as potent now as it was in 1946.

It is a sad truth that the bomb, in displacing the Bikinians, destroyed much of their traditional culture. Even more harsh is the decision to remove the "poison" of cesium and plutonium by scraping off the soil, a patch of the island at a time. With the soil goes the record of a long past. The decision is a bittersweet one for the Bikinians, however, who see it as the only means of assuring that the poison is removed from their islands.

Bikini is a land of ghosts. A small monument near the field station records the tragic end of a five-man Japanese weather detachment that stayed on Bikini through the war. They killed themselves when American forces reached the island. But this small remnant of a time of war is not as haunting as the homes of the Bikinians. The empty shells of houses built by the U.S. government for the returning Bikinians are filled with debris, most of it sodden fiberboard. Geckoes walk up the whitewashed concrete walls, while rotting benches face the ocean from over-grown verandas. It is a beautiful land without people. David Bradley wrote about Crossroads, and Willard Bascom reminisced about the days after Bravo's deadly rain of fallout. Both present a chilling view of Bikini as a metaphor of a world in the aftermath of nuclear war. E. B. White, writing in the pages of the *New Yorker* in 1946, saw the islands and their displaced people as harbingers of a time after the final war when "the rest of us will leave our Bikinis for fair—some in the heat of stars, some in the remains of human flesh in a ruined earth." I knew what he meant during my stay in this land of brightly colored fish, waving palms, and radioactive death.

The Bikinians, promised that their atoll would be used for the betterment of mankind, left in 1946 after an emotional goodbye to their ancestors at the cemetery. From the deck of an LST, they sang songs of farewell. Most would never return. But in 1968 President Lyndon Johnson declared Bikini safe, and several Bikinians did come home. The U.S. government erected forty prefabricated concrete houses on Bikini and planted 50,000 coconut trees. But studies in 1975 showed dangerous levels of contamination in the island's interior and concentrated levels of cesium in breadfruit and pandanus. Further studies discovered that the people living on Bikini had ingested more radioactive material than any other people on the planet, and in August 1978 the island's 139 residents were again evacuated.

A sad legacy remains: empty houses, wells lined with concrete that penetrate to a plutonium-contaminated water supply, and regimented rows of radioactive coconut trees. In 1989 and 1990, on Enyu and the other islands, we found massive concrete bunkers with thick steel cables running from them into the sea. The rusted and loose corrugated metal of the Bravo assembly buildings rattle in Enyu's wind, while the dark bunkers are littered with wiring, broken equipment, and shattered glass. Every cable, every bunker, and every coconut tree is a material record of the nuclear legacy of the United States at Bikini Atoll. My forays to these sites, coupled with the dives, made it clear to me that Bikini is an unparalleled and unaltered museum of the atomic age. It is also, as E. B. White wrote in the *New Yorker* in 1946, "unspeakably precious, like a lovely child stricken with a fatal disease."

The Landing Craft

While walking on the beach on a blazing hot August afternoon in 1989 I saw a piece of wreckage sticking up out of the water about fifty feet offshore. Stripping to my trunks, I walked past the flat coral and sand edge of the island into deeper water, swimming up to the flat deck of a landing craft whose mooring cables stretched out below me on the bottom, then snaked toward the shore to disappear into the sand near where I had laid my clothes. I could see the bottom ten feet down and the greenish outline of the rectangular craft. It was an LCT (Landing Craft, Tank), one of a few dozen brought to Bikini and used for the tests. This was obviously one of six LCTs beached off Bikini during Baker. Swamped and pounded on the coral ledges by the tidal wave that swept out from the detonation, this LCT was an accessible and interesting

Torn free from the deck by ten- to fifteen-foot atomic tidal waves, this winch lies next to the wreck of a landing craft immediately off Bikini. Several landing craft were moored offshore to see how they would fare in the test, and two of them remain in place to this day. One lies directly atop a reef considered sacred by the Bikinians, much to their distress. (Larry Murphy, National Park Service)

diversion. I snorkeled it again and brought the rest of the team back in 1990 to photograph and draw it.

By comparing the position of the LCT with 1946 aerial photos of the beached landing craft, I was able to put a name to the wreck: it was LCT-1175. One of several hundred extremely rugged craft designed for direct "on-the-beach" loading and unloading of tanks, LCTs were the smallest U.S. landing craft to merit numbers in their own right. Carried on attack transports like the *Gilliam*, the LCTs were 134-ton, 117-foot-long vessels with bow ramps and triple 225-hp

Gray marine diesel engines. The engine-room hatches of LCT-1175 were open, and I dropped inside the cramped compartments to examine the diesels. A narrow passageway, too tight for me to fit through, connected the engine rooms, and looking down it I was able to watch Dan Lenihan flash his dive light down the corridor at the other end. Battered and sunk into the sand, the LCT's superstructure was missing, leaving a flat deck with stubs where a deckhouse and bulwarks had once stood.

LCT-1175 lies in ten feet of water off the sloping beach, its bow angled toward shore with the port side facing offshore. Atomic tidal waves stripped 50,000 tons of sand off the beach during Baker. Some of this sand has piled up against the wreck, so that only a foot or so of wreckage rises from the bottom on the portside, while the starboard side is scoured down to a cobbled coral bottom littered with wreckage, including a tumbled deck winch. The bow has nearly torn free, leaving a small hole that we pushed through. Shallow and an easy walk from the beach, the LCT was a fun dive that allowed us to play and relax while doing our work. We discovered we could stand up on the deck and our chests and faces would be out of the water, so we could talk to each other, and we excitedly compared notes for over an hour. The LCT wreck was interesting because it was placed at Bikini as an expendable piece of equipment, not a vessel. Whereas we daily explored ships littered with traces of scientific and military interest in the form of bent lead plates, blast gauge towers, or field guns, the LCT, like the two concrete craft on the lagoon floor and the submarines *Pilotfish* and *Apogon*, were test instruments.

The Concrete Ships

Navy divers rediscovered the wrecks of the concrete floating drydock ARDC-13 and the fuel barge YO-160 in 1988. We didn't dive them in 1989, but Kitty Courtney of Holmes and Narver made a brief reconnaissance of the ARDC, which she found flipped upside down, one of its wing-walls collapsed to make an inverted concrete triangle rising from the bottom. Penetrating it is

like diving into a long, dark cave. The 389-foot-long, 84-foot-wide drydock capsized after Baker, and the navy sank it with demolition charges on August 6, 1946. Its concrete hull, strained and cracked by Able, is now slowly breaking apart. We didn't think it important to dive, so ARDC-13 was left alone in 1989 and 1990.

In 1990, Dan Lenihan, with John Eliot of *National Geographic*, made a quick dive on YO-160. Battered by Able and instantly sunk by Baker, the concrete hulk sits on an even keel, its deck at 140 feet broken and separated in some areas. The remains of the deck house amidships, its overhead blown in, was damaged by Able. Bulkheads, some cracked, still retain their doors, one hanging cockeyed from a single hinge. Ventilators for the fuel tanks are missing—probably blown off—and only the stubs of the elevated catwalk run from the forecastle and poop decks. Pipes run fore and aft across the deck, littered with steel plates and broken equipment. A 12-inch-diameter fuel hose snakes across the deck. The hose and three pairs of large globe valves are reminders of this utilitarian vessel's function. In one brief dive, Lenihan and Eliot captured the mundane concrete ship on video. Though it has none of the glamour of the nearby carrier, battleships, or submarines sunk during Baker, this ugly fuel barge is nonetheless an impressive testimonial to Bikini's bombs.

The Submarines

The target group of submarines included two destined to become the bomb's victims, the

Apogon and the *Pilotfish*. We made a dive on the *Pilotfish,* and an ROV from the navy swam over the hulk of the *Apogon.* Diving the submarines again was difficult because the mooring buoys had been lost and needed to be relocated in 1990, but several divers visited the *Pilotfish* again that year. The other ships on the bottom lie in incongruous circumstance, but the submarines have the appearance of belonging on the seabed. Sleek and sinister as sleeping sharks, the two submarines looked at first glance as if they might rise for one last patrol. But they are forever shackled by anchor chain and cable, and a closer look showed impressive damage from Baker.

Diving the *Pilotfish*

Eerily rising out of the murk of the lagoon, the USS *Pilotfish* is a boat that shouldn't be at Bikini, according to most historical accounts. After all, some historians said that the submarine, after a month on the bottom, was raised, towed away, and sunk on October 16, 1948, as a target at Eniwetok. But in fact the boat never left. The *Pilotfish* lies in 175 feet of water, its deck at 150 feet and the shears atop the sail at 130 feet. Upright and listing heavily to starboard, it is intact but battered. Dick Laning, the sub's last skipper, was also one of the last men to see it in 1946, when he dropped into the lagoon in a hardhat diving rig to survey his sunken command. "She had been thrown to the bottom, twisted, bent and listing about 30 degrees," and partially buried by chunks of coral and silt. "Before I lost my yeoman," Laning later reminisced, "I signed a

An innocuous-looking tear proved deadly. This 1946 underwater photograph shows a small rupture in the hull of Pilotfish where a highly pressurized bubble of air shot through the sub as it was squeezed by Baker's blast. The bubble sank the submarine. (National Archives)

half-page report of the loss of my first command."

The most striking evidence of the bomb's damage to the *Pilotfish* is almost subtle. The hull was wrapped around its frames, or ribs, for nearly half its length, as the submarine was squeezed by the incredible pressure of Baker's burst. The high-tensile steel of this pressure-resistant vessel, built to withstand as much as 300 pounds per square inch at an emergency submergence of 600 feet, now looks like it was "shrink-wrapped" around the circular frames. The superstructure is intact but heavily dented. In front of

Marine worms have eaten the wood deck, and the metal superstructure of *Pilotfish* has collapsed, revealing the round, reinforced steel hull of the submarine. (Larry Murphy, National Park Service)

the sail or conning tower, the hull superstructure is broken. Deck beams have collapsed, and debris litters the lagoon bottom along the starboard side. This damage may not have come from the blast, because in 1946 it was more intact. That year divers noted that the superstructure had "shifted to starboard about six inches amidships and one inch at the stern. This shift makes salvage connections inaccessible unless part of the deck is cut away." Weakened and battered, this section of the submarine has slowly collapsed in the corrosive ocean.

The teak decking of the superstructure is missing, consumed by voracious marine organ-isms that left stubs of the deck around the metal fastenings holding the planks to the steel deck beams. Numerous fittings remain in place on the deck, including the portable capstands fore and aft, and a hydrophone sonar. Atop the sail, the shears, amid a tangle of white whip coral and schools of tiny fish that live there, are missing the periscopes, which were removed as part of the pre-Crossroads stripping. The shears mount radar antennae almost obscured by the marine growth. I dropped past the shears to the open navigation bridge where the submarine's officers once stood watch when cruising on the surface. I was disappointed to see that the hatch into the conning tower was sealed shut. The only hatch open is aft, leading into the torpedo room at the stern, and we would have had to take off our tanks and push them ahead of us as we wriggled down the narrow hatch. It was a risk no one cared to take.

The torpedo tube doors are shut, but the submarine's deck armament is in place. A single 40 mm gun is mounted on the fairwater, slightly elevated and canted to port. On the aft deck is a twin 20 mm gun with its barrels elevated and pointed toward the surface. The guns were a reminder that in the last months of the war the *Pilotfish* served a more noble purpose, saving the lives of young airmen who had ditched or bailed out of their shot-up planes after bombing Japan. On "lifeboat" duty, the *Pilotfish* was armed with fast and efficient anti-aircraft guns. The 20 mm's barrels remain elevated, forever frozen, as if recalling for eternity its last wartime assignment.

Although we didn't penetrate the *Pilotfish* in 1989 or 1990, navy reports in 1946 said that the passage of air through the submarine as it sank ruptured every bulkhead and hatch inside; the *Pilotfish* was squeezed by as much as 5,200 psi, seventeen times the maximum pressure the hull could take. The sub was built to operate at a maximum depth of 412 feet, with a "crush depth" of 600 feet, or 300 psi. It comes as no surprise to find that in 1947, when resurveyed, the boat was described as "destroyed," with "major failures in pressure and tank plating, scantlings, closures, piping, and miscellaneous fittings. Damage was so thorough throughout the boat that no one section or piece of damage can be considered the most serious." During the war, submarines were pounded for hours by depth charges that

wrought considerable damage and, in some cases, sank them. More severe damage was done to the *Pilotfish* in less than two seconds.

The *Apogon*

The *Gilliam* and the *Carlisle* were identical ships damaged in unique ways by the atomic bomb. What the two transports demonstrate in that way for Able, the submarines *Pilotfish* and *Apogon* demonstrate for Baker. All the target submarines were modified to submerge and surface without a crew aboard. "The method used was to fill part of the ballast tanks with water, then suspend heavy weights from the bow and stern by cables of carefully chosen length. These weights overcame the submarine's residual buoyancy and drew her down to the desired depth. She could be surfaced again by pumping air back into her ballast tanks." Moored at different depths for Baker throughout the array, these "useful instruments" were placed there to subject them to "the enormous pressures created by the atomic bombs, since their hulls are expressly designed to withstand high pressures." The *Apogon*, 850 yards from the bomb, was suspended at a depth of 100 feet, nearly twice the depth of the *Pilotfish*, and moored 363 yards from the zeropoint. Both submarines were thus within the thousand-yard "fatal zone" of the blast and were sunk by the shock wave's peak overpressure, but in a different manner.

Resting upright, slightly listed to port, the *Apogon* mounts two single 40 mm guns, one forward and the other aft of the sail on the cigarette decks. The periscopes, like *Pilotfish*'s, are missing, removed for the tests. The teak decks are now gone, eaten by voracious sea worms. The hatches are all closed, but the access plates for several salvage connections lie open. At one connection near the stern, a rubber hose is coupled. At first I thought it was a hose left in place to blow air back into the ballast tanks to surface *Apogon* as part of the ingenious unmanned mooring system, but research showed that it was left by divers attempting to salvage the wreck in 1946 or 1947, as it connects to the aft torpedo room, flooded and in need of being "blown out with air to surface the boat."

Nearby, the stern mooring fairleads have a wire cable wrapped around them that runs off both sides of the hull to the bottom. The cable is part of the mooring system and ran to a ten-ton navy anchor that moored the submarine at the stern. Another cable and anchor at the bow held the boat in position. Dive after dive we were confronted by anchor chains or cables that held the ships in position—direct evidence that the target fleet had been sunk "like fish in an atomic barrel."

The *Apogon* was found in 1946 by navy divers in 180 feet of water, leaking fuel oil and air bubbles. "All compartments were flooded or partially flooded with the exception of the conning tower." All the bulkheads except one were ruptured, and the pressure hull gave way in the forward torpedo room, blasting out into the sea. The hatch leading into the after torpedo room failed, slightly tearing the superstructure around it and rupturing its double lip "T" gasket. The navy was mystified over the hatch failure, as pre-Crossroads tests with 300-pound TNT charges at close range had not damaged similar hatches, even when the pressures generated by the TNT charges were greater than the 1,200 psi over-pressure recorded at the *Apogon* by gauges submerged in the water. Theories to explain the gasket failure included the greater duration of the nuclear-induced shock wave, localized peaks in the pressure distribution "caused by reflections from the bottom and other sources," or a force that elastically flattened the spherical hatch cover plate then followed by "vibrational deflections which caused the gasket to be rubbed back and forth rapidly." Simply stated, the submarine was shaken and bounced, beating the hatch against its gasket.

That damage admitted the full force of the blast wave, rupturing bulkheads as highly compressed air and water shot through the eight separate compartments before bursting out of the hull forward when it could go no farther. The worst damage to the *Apogon* is inside, and is not as noticeable as the *Pilotfish*'s wounds. However, both submarines were fascinating dives, and there was an unforgettable moment of awe as I saw the narrow, sleek hull of the *Pilotfish* rising up below me as I dropped as fast as I could to meet it, video camera in hand. She looked as deadly as a shark, sleeping on the sand, seemingly ready to rise in an instant.

The Enemy Ships

The two Japanese ships at Bikini were brought there to die, and both did. We never found the cruiser *Sakawa*, although divers who came after us in 1991 located a crumpled mass of battered

With pomp and ceremony, *Prinz Eugen* passes from German to American control at Bremerhaven on January 5, 1946. The U.S. crew, to the left, was joined for the voyage to the States by members of the German crew, now sailing as "employed enemy personnel." The huge swastikas on the decks were painted over, Hitler's portrait was removed from the wardroom, and, as one astonished German crew member recalled, coffee urns were installed everywhere aboard the ship. But then, "we knew that the Americans were a coffee drinking nation." (U.S. Naval Institute Photo Library)

metal that had been pounded into Baker's crater. I believe it was the *Sakawa*. Sunk by Able, the wreck was close to the suspended Baker bomb, ninety feet off the bottom. My guess is

that the bomb hammered the steel light cruiser into a flattened mass just now becoming visible as silt washes out of the crater.

An important aspect of Operation Crossroads,

Battered by aerial bombs and partially awash, the Japanese battleship *Nagato* is formally surrendered on Tokyo Bay on September 6, 1945. The original caption, when the photo was published by the U.S. Navy in 1945, stated that the "Stars and Stripes Replace Rising Sun on Jap Warship—symbolizing the complete domination of the U.S. Navy over the Jap Navy." In less than a year, *Nagato* was taken to Bikini and sunk by an atomic bomb in yet another act of domination. (U.S. Naval Institute Photo Library)

the atomic destruction of the remaining vessels of the defeated Imperial Japanese Navy, is evident when contrasted with the fate of the other enemy vessel, the German-made *Prinz Eugen*. The U.S. Navy took care during Able and Baker to keep the German cruiser out of the fatal zone, whereas the Japanese ships were placed well within the zone. It was a racist act made all the more incomprehensible by the fact that the *Prinz Eugen* was favored despite its association with

Nazism. Los Alamos engineer Bob Henderson, preparing for Crossroads at the Long Beach Naval Shipyard, worked next to the *Prinz Eugen.* Every morning the German crew mustered on deck and goosestepped on drill, as their commander stared at Henderson with a smile on his face. The Japanese were allowed no such freedom as their crippled battleship was towed into Bikini with shattered decks and waterlogged corpses on board. References to the *Nagato* reinforced the popular racist view of the Japanese in the Pacific War. David Bradley offered a first impression to his readers of an "ugly anthropoid creation. . . . This many-storied, buttressed pile of junk looks as though it had been thrown together without plan or purpose out of odds and ends of American scrap iron." Yet the *Prinz Eugen,* a seemingly potent symbol of the vanquished Nazi foe, was described as "graceful," "beautiful," and "as sleek and cavalier a ship as ever sailed the seas."

The German master of the *Prinz Eugen,* Captain H. J. Reinicke, was interviewed about his ship's impending doom in 1946 and said, "I'd rather see the ship atomized than go to the scrap heap. It's a sad thing being the last captain of such a fine ship, but better she is sunk than left to rot." Asked in 1992 if his vessel was taken to Bikini as a symbol of a defeated Germany, *Prinz Eugen* crew member Otto Schoetzow said, "Definitely no." In his opinion, the ship "was tested to see which one is the better ship and which one will survive an atom bomb attack. I was interested in the outcome to see how the ship would do in the test. One can be proud of being tested, of the durability of the material people built."

Unlike the *Prinz Eugen,* the *Nagato* was brought to Bikini and moored with few test instruments aboard as a symbolic representative of the vanquished enemy. Its location close to surface zero for each test, the ship's undocumented sinking, as well as the lack of attention paid to it in post-blast assessment dives, are indicative of its unique role at Bikini. The *Nagato* alone stands apart from the other ships as the only vessel whose pre-Crossroads history established its importance at Bikini. "Captured" at war's end in Tokyo Bay on August 30, 1945, to symbolize the "unconditional and complete surrender of the Imperial Japanese Navy," the *Nagato* was brought months later to Bikini, this time to represent the Imperial Japanese Navy under the fatal blow of the atomic bomb. It was a calculated insult to a people who had already experienced the power of two nuclear detonations and now, in a symbolic sense, were forced to feel another.

The *Nagato* had been the scene of many conferences and planning sessions for the attack on Pearl Harbor. The flagship of Admiral Yamamoto Isoruku, Commander-in-Chief of the Combined Fleet, the *Nagato* remained in harbor when the Pearl Harbor strike force sortied. With the fleet sailed 16-inch shells from the *Nagato* and its sister ship the *Mutsu* that had been specially modified as aircraft bombs. These missiles, dropped on Pearl Harbor, are credited with sinking the battleship USS *Arizona.* Yamamoto received news of the successful attack while aboard the *Nagato.* Larry Murphy, Dan Lenihan, and I were keen to dive the *Nagato* because of all the time we had spent diving the *Arizona.*

Five years of work at Pearl Harbor had made Lenihan and Murphy, Jerry Livingston, and Larry Nordby intimate with the sunken American

The main bridge level on *Nagato*, lying to one side of the ship in the silt. It was here that Admiral Yamamoto heard the radio broadcast "Tora, Tora, Tora," signaling a successful surprise attack on Pearl Harbor. (Larry Murphy, National Park Service)

battleship, and they had introduced me to the *Arizona*. Now we dropped down on the Japanese battleship whose shells had inflicted the terrible damage we had all thrilled to while groping through Pearl Harbor's murk. Swimming underneath the capsized *Nagato*, Lenihan and I stopped in front of the muzzles of the first 16-inch turret. It was the end of a quest, the closing of a book. We had traced the instrument of the *Arizona*'s destruction back to its place of origin. Our excitement peaked when we came upon the broken superstructure and the *Nagato*'s bridge. I yelled into my face-mask's microphone, "It's the bridge . . . this is where Yamamoto heard 'Tora, Tora, Tora!'"

Fifty years later, the battleship, scarcely visited and described in 1946, yielded many secrets, including how it had gone to the bottom in the darkness of the night of July 29. Lying inverted and listing 180 degrees to starboard, the

The bow of *Nagato* rises up from the lagoon bottom, the anchor cable that once moored it draped across the hull. It looked as if the ship were shackled to the bottom and reminded me that these targets were literally "fish in an atomic barrel." (Larry Murphy, National Park Service)

Nagato had capsized and sunk by the stern, moving backward slowly as it settled. The stern hit bottom and dug in, stopping the ship's momentum. It then slowly settled by the bow. The transom, caught in the sediment, was torn free of the hull as the wreck folded across the deck aft of the "D" turret and the screws. Past the rudders, the hull is torn and twisted, exposing floors and the aft collision bulkhead, which marks the breaking point. The transom sticks into the bottom at a sharp angle. Forward, the anchor chains stretch into the gloom, running straight out of the hawsepipes.

The most dramatic evidence of the slow sinking is the ship's foremast and superstructure, which includes the bridge. This massive tiered structure is bent just above the main deck level and folds out beyond the gunwale to starboard, intact to its uppermost levels, with signal, search-light, and gun-director platforms rising toward the surface out of its starboard side. The *Nagato* evidently capsized on its starboard side, rolling and moving slowly back to push the superstructure free of the hull, rather than crushing it directly beneath the ship. We found this structure during our last dives at Bikini. The *Nagato*'s

Torn open by bombs and twisted by fire, the bridge of *Nagato* was already devastated before the ship was atom-bombed at Bikini. Nearly fifty years later, we floated above the rounded windows near the top of the picture. (U.S. Naval Institute Photo Library)

Dan Lenihan floats over the bridge of *Nagato* with cameraman Nick Caloyianis. Once rising more than a hundred feet above the deck, the bridge, with the rest of the battleship's superstructure, now lies on the lagoon bottom. It bent to one side and came to rest there when *Nagato* capsized and sank. (Larry Murphy, National Park Service)

inverted hulk became the mecca for our last dive, as we passed once again underneath it in the gloom to gaze at the 16-inch guns, pause by the bridge, and peer inside. The deck above our heads mounted capstans and anchor chain that hung from its cable brakes. At the stern, close to where the deck suddenly tilts down and thrusts into the silt, a hatch lies open, with equipment that fell from it resting on the lagoon floor below. As one swims up out of the gloom and along the ship's side, damage from the blast becomes noticeable. Dents, some large enough for several divers to fit inside, line the bilges. The bow has a large hole, nearly ten-by-ten feet, where it has collapsed into itself. Just before the tear in the stern, the four massive screws remain in place, each with three blades and the two balanced rudders. The blades of the screws tow-

The guns of *Nagato*. The huge 16-inch guns of the Japanese battleship were photographed at Bikini with two Los Alamos scientists atop them. Dan Lenihan and I crawled under the overturned battleship to visit the same guns, hovering near the muzzles with only a few feet to spare between the deck and the bottom. (Los Alamos National Laboratory)

ered above us, dwarfing the divers who swam past them.

We left the *Nagato* reluctantly in May 1990. As we drifted up from the bottom, sharks darted around us as we passed the broken stern and hovered for a second by the propellers. Then, one by one, we gazed into the gloom toward the bridge and slowly ascended the buoy line. Gradually the *Nagato* receded, its large massive bulk becoming toylike as the water grew lighter, clear and warm. Hanging on the line at 30, then 20 and 10 feet as we "outgassed," I realized that we had just accomplished a difficult and wonderful feat.

Like other ships with famous pasts that served as settings for great and terrible events, the *Nagato* has an almost ghostly presence. World War II, with all its drastic consequences, began for

Japan on the *Nagato*. In certain measure, it also ended there. Japanese journalist Masanori Ito later wrote of the extreme irony of the *Nagato's* role in 1941 and its ultimate fate, which seemed to mirror that of his nation: "When World War II began, the Japanese Navy—the third most powerful in the world—included some of the mightiest ships in naval history and was a force worthy of the pride and trust of the Japanese people. Then, in less than four years, this great war machine fell from glory to oblivion. Of ten battleships riding in Hiroshima Bay in December 1941, nine were sunk. The lone survivor, *Nagato*, died at Bikini Island as a target in an atomic bomb test."

We packed our bags on Bikini and waited a day before riding the speedboats that had served as dive platforms to Enyu. Handing our gear up the side of a broken concrete wharf built for Operation Castle, we waited in the heat for the Air Marshall Islands plane to appear. Like our predecessors of 1946, we had come to Bikini to learn about ships and the bomb. Armed with this strange and terrible knowledge, we boarded the plane for the flight to Kwajalein and then, in a few days, home. Everyone was silent as we shot down the bumpy runway and climbed into the sky. Looking out the window, I saw the lagoon stretching below me, outlined by the atoll's narrow strips of sand and greenery. I caught the faint outline of the *Saratoga*, reminding me of David Bradley's view of the target ships as a "dead fleet," with "something of the mute sadness and mystery of the cemetery" hanging around them. Then it was gone, and in an hour we were on the concrete and asphalt strip of Kwa-

jalein, gazing at the missile base and its Star Wars facilities with a new and different perspective.

The *Prinz Eugen*

In 1989 we had prepared for our visit to Bikini while waiting in Kwajalein. During a two-day period we were able to visit the wreck of the *Prinz Eugen* and dive it. Standing on the shore of Enubuj Island, we gazed out into the lagoon of Kwajalein Atoll at the screws of the sunken hulk of the German cruiser. I insisted on making a dive on the famous "little brother" of the *Bismarck*, little realizing that our first Crossroads target ship dive was in fact a reflection of the end of the saga of the Bikini bombs. The *Prinz Eugen* lies upside down, stern in to shore at a 40-degree angle, in 26 to 120 feet of water, 200 yards off the north end of Enubuj Island in Kwajalein Atoll's vast lagoon. The vessel rests on its starboard gunwale and crushed superstructure. The stern rises to the surface, the rudder and one bronze screw protruding above the water. The shaft for the port screw rests high and dry, but the propeller once attached to it was cut free and presented to the West German government in 1974. Submerged, the starboard shaft and screw lie in a few feet of water.

When our boat approached the wreck, we decided to make the first dive a snorkel around the hull. The water was clear and we could see down thirty feet or more. I swam up past the hull and waded over to the bottom of the cruiser, taking off my fins so that I could walk on the wreck. The hull bottom had badly rusted. Holes pock-

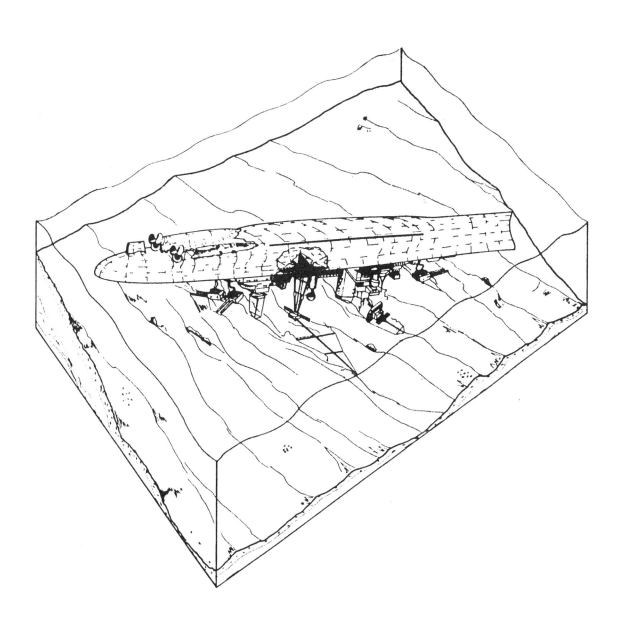

The capsized hulk of *Prinz Eugen* at Kwajalein, as drawn by navy divers in 1973. (U.S. Naval Historical Center)

marked the steel plates, some of them large enough to admit a person into the voids of the bottom and the shaft tunnels. Stepping cautiously out of fear that I might drop through the rotten steel into the ship, I investigated the stern before sliding off the *Prinz Eugen* and returning to the boat.

The second dive, this time with scuba gear, began when Lenihan and I dropped into the water behind the wreck. The cruiser stern of the *Prinz Eugen* stands proud on the bottom, garlanded by a cable that rings the hull below the waterline. I searched but could find no trace of the ship's name. As we dropped past the stern counter, we were inexorably drawn under the stern to the fantail, where a hatch stood open, leading into crew compartments.

The wreck of the *Prinz Eugen* has been heavily dived by the residents of Kwajalein, and two dive books offer detailed assessments of the ship. We knew what to expect in some cases, such as when we dropped to the bottom aft to see the two 8-inch gun turrets. The barrels lay in the sand, pointing aft. The last turret had partially dropped free of its barbette. It remained attached, however, by its entrails of cable and wiring and shell-feeding mechanisms, and by a ladder welded to the turret sideplates. Nearby was a small gun house for a pair of the Eugen's 4.1-inch anti-aircraft guns.

Dan Lenihan, on a later dive with *National Geographic* photographer Bill Curtsinger, found something no other diver had reported. While penetrating farther starboard close to the buried gunwale, Dan found a Crossroads "Christmas tree" blast-gauge tower wedged in tight between the deck and lagoon floor. Lying in the gloom, its upper portions buried and bolted to the deck, the tower was a solitary reminder of how this ship came to be here.

The sides of the hull were lined with portholes fixed with aluminum deadlights set into them. The hull's graceful cruiser lines swept forward and down into the gloom, unbroken until nearly amidships. Considerable damage to the freeboard amidships, including a large hole where rusted plating had given way and collapsed, marked where the *Prinz Eugen* had hit the reef as it capsized and grounded. This damage was seen by navy salvage divers in 1974, but at that time the shell plating was merely cracked and dented. Within sixteen years' time, the damaged hull has given way to the inexorable force of the ocean. Underneath the damage Lenihan found that the superstructure was partly crushed. The loading rails for the ship's 21-inch torpedo tubes hung from the deck; inside the port magazine for the torpedo tubes a rack held five torpedoes, some missing their bronze propellers, probably removed by souvenir-hunting divers, who at the time of our visit were busily engaged in scavenging artifacts from the wreck.

The presence of the torpedoes was a surprise, given the focus of effort on the target ships at Kwajalein to remove ordnance left aboard after the tests. The failure to remove the torpedoes is probably not due to the fact that the *Eugen* sank early in the two-year lay-up period for the ghost fleet of Kwajalein. Ammunition and ordnance removal was reportedly completed at the end of November, nearly a month before *Eugen*'s loss. Rather, the presence of the torpedoes is probably evidence of fear of radiation on a ship whose then unmeasurable alpha emitters had sounded the death knell for the Bikini decontamination effort.

The stack, the airplane hangar, and the fire-control director towers were crushed or broken off to port. One of the characteristic "mushroom" head-gun directors lay off the wreck's port side. The *Prinz Eugen*'s mainmast, bent out from beneath the wreck, lay on the bottom near the director head. Beneath the ship, forward, the "B" turret, trained forward, had dropped from its barbette. Forward of it, the "A" turret remained seated, welded to the barbette, as the heavy tubes of its two 8-inch guns would no longer gravity seat it. The guns had been removed for testing at the Philadelphia Navy Yard prior to the cruiser's sailing for Bikini. Past the turret, the bow rested some ten to fifteen feet off the bottom, the stem rising toward the surface. Lenihan and I did not want to spend much time on the bottom, so we "bounced" down to the bow very quickly before swimming up the ship's bottom and traced the hull where it flared out from the bow and rose up from the depths toward the surface.

During our few dives we did not go inside the *Prinz Eugen* except for a quick look into compartments open to the sea. The interior of the ship has occasionally been entered by divers from the nearby missile base at Kwajalein. Some of the *Prinz Eugen*'s compartments were described by diver-historian Dan Bailey. The crew's berthing and messing areas have lockers, cabinets, and bunks, as well as scattered pans, bowls, and platters lying on the overhead. A large table

in the officer's mess, bolted to the deck, hangs upside down, while red glass-covered lights that also survived the Able and Baker blasts line the overhead of the central passageway of the ship. In the ship's crew heads, the sinks, commodes, and urinals hang upside down, their unusual placement now normal for the overturned ship.

By 1990, however, the *Prinz Eugen* had become a dangerous wreck. The bulkheads and compartments, built of aluminum, have not fared well after more than four decades' immersion in salt water. The ship is slowly collapsing inside, and in time the hull, no longer supported by its internal members, will also collapse. As we surfaced near the stern, the broken hull confirmed that the final disintegration of the once proud German cruiser has begun.

The Continental Airlines jet, as it roared down Kwaj's runway, banked so that our row of seats caught a glimpse of the needlelike form of the *Prinz Eugen* as we circled and flew to the east and home. Starting and ending the last leg of our trips to Bikini at Kwajalein had unwittingly brought us into contact with the most instructive target ship. Lying off Enebuj, the long, dark outline of the cruiser dominates the island's shores. The *Prinz Eugen* is a visible tombstone for the scores of other ships that were scuttled in the deep ocean where, although the technology exists, we shall probably never visit them. The *Prinz Eugen* alone represents them, a forgotten fleet consigned to the deep despite the fact that they "survived" the bomb, only to find a watery grave because they were too hot to handle.

Three days later, after stops in Honolulu, San Francisco, and Chicago, I was back in Washington, D.C. I had confronted the nuclear beast of my childhood fears and come away unscathed. We had measured radioactivity while diving, and the silt and metal samples showed very little remaining contamination. The two years of work at Bikini had been intense. The deepest and most difficult diving I had ever done, the pro-ject had flown me a distance of nearly eighteen thousand miles and carried me almost fifty years back in time. Back home, in the darkness of my dimly lit room, I watched video and slides and slowly began to sort out the meaning of what I had been through.

9

Monuments to the Nuclear Age

Many sites, objects, and structures have been memorialized as monuments to the nuclear age. Casings and mock-ups of the "Fat Man" and "Little Boy" atomic bombs reside in museums throughout the United States. The B-29 bombers that delivered the deadly weapons to Hiroshima and Nagasaki have been preserved. The *Enola Gay* remained in storage until 1949, when it was donated to the Smithsonian Institution. Restoration of the plane began in 1984, and in 1995 a portion of the fuselage went on display at the National Air and Space Museum in Washington, D.C. amidst considerable controversy. *Bockscar* was also saved. Flown in September 1961 to the U.S. Air Force Museum outside Dayton, Ohio, at Wright-Patterson Air Force Base, *Bockscar* is one of several historic aircraft displayed there. The loading pits that each bomber rolled over to be fitted with its atomic bomb have also been preserved. Filled in, with trees growing from each, atomic bomb pits Nos. 1 and 2 on Tinian Island's North Field are unprepossessing monuments that attract many history-minded visitors to the Commonwealth of the Northern Marianas.

A more impressive monument to the dawn of the atomic age is the Trinity Site in New Mexico. As early as 1946, the effort to memorialize and celebrate the bomb began with a proposal made by New Mexico Senator Carl Hatch, a staunch supporter of the development of atomic weapons, to create an "Atomic Bomb National Monument" at Alamagordo in the southern part of the state. Hatch's proposal, offered seven months after Hiroshima and Nagasaki, was a recognition of the tremendous significance of the atomic bomb and the changes it had wrought and the impact it would continue to make on America and the world. Hatch sought to add the site of the Trinity test to the roster of national monuments, memorials, and historic sites administered by the National Park Service, as the epitome of the American experience. Clearly, others besides Hatch thought the site important, if not sacred. Relics like Trinitite, the fused and melted pale-gray-green sand at ground zero, were gathered and fashioned into costume jewelry in late 1945.

The Trinity site, located in the White Sands Missile Range, is fenced off, and in 1965 it was marked by the missile range command with a bronze and stone monument. Designated a National Historic Landmark by the secretary of the interior in 1975, the site is open to the public once a year, and thousands gather for a sunrise ceremony inside the crater before viewing exhibits on the bomb, the tests, or a glassed-in exposed deposit of "undisturbed" Trinitite.

Other monuments to the beginning of the atomic age do not commemorate historical significance or national pride in a technological achievement. The blasted remains of the Industrial Exhibition Hall in Hiroshima, whose twisted metal dome has become a symbol of the destructive power of the atomic bomb, now known as the "A-Bomb Dome," is one such site. Termed both a monument "left behind by the bomb" and a memorial to the city demolished by Little Boy, the dome is the only tangible remnant of August 6, 1945, apart from the scars of the survivors. The dome's preservation was controversial as Hiroshima was rebuilt. According to journalist Peter Wyden, many survivors and "peace groups wanted it preserved as a reminder of human vulnerability, especially for human visitors to see." Others found it a painful, constant reminder for many who wanted no reminder. The dome was left to disintegrate slowly without demolition until 1965, when the Hiroshima City Council voted to preserve the ruin. Money was raised throughout Japan over the next two years as a "national act for peace," and in 1967 work to stabilize the dome began. Today the ruins, part

of an atomic peace park, are the backdrop for a museum that offers souvenirs of another sort—the charred, twisted relics of life disrupted or ended by the bomb—watches, shoes, books, a human hand's bones fused to a melted pane of glass, and other personal items, interspersed with photographs of August 6, 1945, and the days, weeks, and years of ghastly effects that followed.

The sunken ships of Bikini Atoll are also a memorial and monument of the atomic age. Yet, unlike all the others, they are neither monuments to technology's impact nor memorials. They are now, in their isolation from the rest of the world in a depopulated land, simply evocative artifacts, the material record of Operation Crossroads as well as the fundamental human behaviors that brought the world to a crossroads. The Able and Baker blasts were more than the world's first nuclear-weapons tests. They were a statement made by the United States on many fronts, a demonstration of U.S. pride in our great and terrible achievement, and a striking material example of great wealth and power. More important, the Bikini tests were part of a swift and complete absorption of the atomic bomb into the new and vastly altered landscape of American politics and national defense. Operation Crossroads was one of the first chills of the Cold War. What followed it was a world where constant vigilance, even at home, suspicion, and the concept of the best defense being a strong offense was confirmed both by the atomic secret and by the power of the bomb to change America's foreign and domestic policy.

Operation Crossroads was also a source of pride

Admiral W. H. P. "Spike" Blandy, Mrs. Blandy, and Rear Admiral F. J. Lowry celebrate the end of Operation Crossroads and the dissolution of Joint Task Force One in Washington, D.C., in November 1946. The widely reproduced photograph, entitled "Atomic Age Angel Food," drew criticism from throughout the nation and from around the world. Mrs. Blandy's hat certainly complements the cake. (Pictorial Histories)

for Americans. Many considered the tests a tremendous national achievement of considerable significance reflective of the powerful, rich, and democratic society that had harnessed the atom to win the war. At the same time, the president, the Congress, the military, and the majority of the American people feared that the "atomic secret" would be stolen by spies; hence the classification of many aspects of Operation Crossroads and subsequent decontamination efforts. Bikini and the ships were declared off-limits for fear of an enemy analyzing the bomb residues to determine how the weapons were made or, worse yet, to garner enough plutonium particles for a bomb of their own. For the same reason, the decontamination efforts in San Francisco were off-limits for fear that fallout and other bomb resi-

dues washed off the contaminated ships might be analyzed by the enemy.

There was distress over the tests, not only from the Soviets, but also from within the United States itself, particularly from those who saw U.S. overtures at the United Nations to seek international control of the bomb and the peaceful use of nuclear power as being at odds with the military message of Operation Crossroads. Harsh words were spoken by the Reverend A. Powell Davies. Davies, a Washington, D.C., Unitarian pastor, thundered from his pulpit that a widely distributed photograph of Admirals Blandy and Lowry cutting a mushroom-cloud-shaped cake with Mrs. Blandy to celebrate the success of Crossroads on the occasion of its dissolution, was "utterly loathsome":

Stewards of relics representing a past that forever changed their destinies, members of the Bikinian dive team worked with us to map and document the sunken ships of Operation Crossroads. Here, they stretch a measuring tape to pinpoint the location of a rangefinder blasted loose by Baker and lying on *Saratoga*'s flight deck. (Larry Murphy, National Park Service)

Try to imagine yourself for a moment a continental European, wondering, brooding, asking yourself a hundred times a day, will America lead us? Then imagine yourself being shown this picture. If I had the authority of a priest of the Middle Ages, I would call down the wrath of God upon such an obscenity. I would damn to hell . . . these traitors to humanity who could participate in such a monstrous betrayal of everything for which the brokenhearted of the world are waiting.

Operation Crossroads had some impact in refocusing nuclear apprehension from the initial blast to the danger of the radioactive "toxins" left behind by the bomb. This lesson was driven home in the era of the hydrogen bomb, which introduced not only the capacity to vaporize fleets and devastate vast regions, but to destroy nations and dust the globe with highly radioactive fallout. In an age of megatonnage, the pre-1954 "simpler" age of kilotonnage has now faded from memory, with the exception of key dates such as the Trinity explosion or the wartime use of the bomb. As one historian notes, Operation Crossroads is now obscure, its role in the nuclear arms race for the most part forgotten, scarcely cited in standard histories of the bomb or the Cold War, and its role in accelerating the Cold War is still the topic of debate. Bikini Atoll is now better remembered for the Bravo test shot of 1954 that ushered in the new, more terrible era of the H-Bomb—and for the French-named bathing suit.

The Sunken Fleet as Artifacts

The test ships represent more than historic vessels whose physical survival on the ocean floor are reminders of Operation Crossroads. Our reason for diving the shipwrecks of Bikini Atoll was not merely to satisfy historical curiosity about these vessels and their fate. Rather, an emphasis was placed on using the wrecks as artifacts, then applying an archaeological perspective not only to assess the historical record but also to derive perspectives based solely on the material record, and to compare that with the basic patterns of human behavior.

The dished hulls, broken masts, and abandoned test instruments are all archaeological records that preserve the reality of Operation Crossroads in a way that can never be fully comprehended through written accounts, photographs, or even films of the tests. Even in light of a vast amount of information available from those most public and publicized of nuclear-weapons tests, myths and misunderstandings abound, such as that the *Arkansas* stood on end in the Baker blast column, or that the *Hughes* did a somersault and landed upright on the lagoon surface, not sinking. The legends that arose can be refuted only by the reality of the material statement.

The value of the ships as artifacts that evoke basic messages of human behavior is imperative when assessing events as recent as Operation Crossroads, whose implications and repercussions have a direct effect on the lives of every living being on the planet. With the development of nuclear weapons, for the first time in human history, technology provided humanity with the perceived means for the extinction of life. The bombs detonated at Bikini, tested at first in a context of ignorance, did not have the capacity to vaporize ships, or set off a self-sustaining chain reaction in the ocean, or kill everyone who witnessed the explosions. Yet those powerful weapons did have the power to sink ships within seconds or, in the case of the *Arkansas*, in less than a second, that otherwise would have taken hours or even days to go down, as the staunch refusal of the *Nevada* to sink in 1948 demonstrated.

More important, the testing set into motion in 1946 at Bikini escalated into tests of infinitely more powerful weapons, culminating in the 15-megaton Bravo blast of 1954, also at Bikini, the largest acknowledged nuclear detonation set off by the United States. The progeny of "Gilda" and "Helen of Bikini" were more effective killing machines, both in punch and radioactive aftermath. Now, thanks to the refinement of these tests, we are faced with the very real possibility of a lifeless planet or vast wastelands of slag lashed by the fierce storms of a nuclear winter. Such grim scenarios compel us to examine the physical evidence of what an atomic bomb can do at its most "nominal yield" and the behaviors that motivated the testing, refinement, and production of these weapons after their ostensible purpose of ending World War II had been accomplished. Confronting the archaeology of the atomic bomb is important in a world where nuclear weapons are being developed in such an atmosphere of denial that a deadly weapon is called a "device" and mutual nuclear devastation is termed "collateral damage."

Social anthropologist Hugh Gusterson of the School of American Research argues compellingly that the anthropology of nuclear weapons tests represents an ancient initiation rite of passage for the scientists who build the bombs. The tests are also an important means by which these same scientists simulate "human knowledge and control over events that otherwise seem mysterious and uncontrollable." So the ships of Operation Crossroads embody the first human attempts to control the bomb by confronting it and surviving, as represented by the "can-do" attitude of the crew of the battered, radioactive USS *Skate*, who boarded, pumped out, and fired up their half-sunken boat. At another level, the ships, particularly the *Prinz Eugen*, in their most compelling role represent the ultimate solution to the uncontrollable problem of contamination—part of "living with the bomb." When the problem was found to be insurmountable, the only option left was the "illusion of escape," as it was derisively termed by David Bradley, which left them at Bikini as wrecks or took them to Kwajalein to rust and eventually sink out of sight and out of mind.

The large number of test gauges and instruments we found on the *Saratoga* indicate the adaptation of technology to comprehend the incomprehensible. Through instruments as sophisticated as the inclinometer gauges that litter the *Saratoga*'s bridge, to the simple and somewhat crude "ruptured foil peak" pressure gauges on the "Christmas trees" and the lead sheets of the indentation pressure gauges that litter the flight deck, the "elemental forces" of a chain reaction gone wild were measured and quantified to provide the first detailed view of the forces and effects of the bomb. The gauges are compelling microartifacts of humanity's first attempts to grapple with the bomb, just as the ships themselves are the larger macroartifacts. The fact that the gauges were abandoned on the sea bottom reflects the fear of radiation that panicked the scientists and military in 1946. It was not so much fear of contamination that brought about the decision to abandon the project and sink the contaminated ships left afloat; it was fear of being unable to control what had happened.

The Future of the Shipwrecks of Bikini Atoll

In visiting the wrecks of Operation Crossroads and trying to conjure a possible future for them, another basic human behavior comes to mind. There is an attraction to horror and horrible things, a part of the human need to confront the fear they evoke. Bikini offers us the opportunity to face the ultimate horror of our society—nuclear destruction—with artifacts of a time when the power of the unleashed atom was merely sufficiently powerful to rend steel, vaporize water, and sink capital ships, not to leave a deep crater as the only remembrance of human life. The ships provide a human scale of reference, a checkpoint where we can begin to comprehend what Able and Baker's progeny could now reap. The power of these "nominal yield" bombs to sink and maim a ship beyond recognition is demonstrated in the remains of the *Gilliam,* in the twisted, half-smashed hulk of the *Arkansas,* or to a lesser extent in the split bottom, toppled stack, and dented flight deck of the *Saratoga.* The greater power of the bomb is even more dramatically demonstrated in the intact, irradiated, and capsized hull of the *Prinz Eugen* at Kwajalein.

The implications and reality of the bombs at Bikini are too much for some people. While a few confront their fears, others deny them. Some focus on the non-nuclear history of the ships, a phenomenon that actually began before the tests and continued in their immediate aftermath as the war records and symbolism of the great and famous ships were touted. The *Saratoga* most demonstrates this focus as the most eulogized of Crossroads' victims. The *Saratoga* at Bikini was to a great extent not the same *Saratoga* commissioned in 1927, nor was it the same ship that had fought pitched sea battles during the war. To remain those, the carrier would have to have been sunk during those times, in those places, and in those roles. Changed and modified for Operation Crossroads, the *Saratoga* fulfilled a new reality and role. Yet the fascination with this great ship remains firmly focused on its wartime role.

Oceanographer Willard Bascom, diving at Bikini during the various nuclear tests of the early 1950s, wrote in his memoirs how he and his colleagues eagerly sought the *Saratoga,* "famous for its exploits in World War II." The need to dive the ship was not to see what the bomb had done but simply to see and touch it. In this, Bascom and his friends were no different from anyone else who has ever dived at Bikini, including the National Park Service team, as well as those who have focused submerged archaeological efforts on famous ships like the *Monitor, Titanic,* or *Bismarck.* There is a compelling aura that surrounds a famous ship. The need to see and touch the ship was powerful for Bascom and his colleagues. "Most important, we walked, or at least touched down, on the flight deck, stirring up wisps of dust." The images evoked in their minds were not of Crossroads, or the bomb:

> Back aboard our LCM the four divers were unusually pensive, our minds still communicating with the spirits of the Saratoga's long-gone pilots and crew. Having visited their old haunts, our minds reconstructed the ship as it had been in its glory days. We could see the uniformed figures on the rail of the bridge and the A-5s on the deck, as the ghost ship streamed through the fourth dimension, running into the wind like the Flying Dutchman to launch phantom aircraft.

The need to deny the bomb's impact on the ships, and perhaps by extension its impact on our lives, is also reflected in the reaction of some of the USS *Arkansas'* crew. The 26,100-ton battleship, popularly but incorrectly thought to have been lifted up, end over end, in the Baker blast column, was nonetheless smashed half flat and capsized. Viewing color slides and video of the wreck at the annual reunion of the ship's company in 1990, some of the *Arkansas'* crew questioned the ship's identity. One man insisted that he had seen previous footage of the battleship on an even keel, guns pointing forward in their turrets. Another wrote that he was "amazed and spellbound," because "somehow, I had always imagined that our Grand Old Lady . . . was sitting upright on the bottom of the ocean floor still looking as gallant as she did the day I last went ashore in 1946."

The future of the ships might be more secure if advertised and promoted as a collection of great and famous World War II vessels or a museum of wartime ship types. Yet tourism of the site may in the long run hinge more on its unique role as monument and museum of the dawning of the atomic age. The human need to confront the past, even its most unpleasant aspects, is ingrained in our psyche, as the tourism of battlefields and other sites sanctified by great loss of life in war or other disasters demonstrates. The tourism of Pearl Harbor, the Alamo, Dachau, and Hiroshima allows us to confront our human limitations and perhaps reaffirm our joy in personal survival. Bikini, without loss of human life, faces a difficult challenge in making the same association. As I floated nearly 180 feet below the surface of Bikini Lagoon, the massive hulk of overturned battleships nearby in the dim twilight, I was struck by the power of the ghost fleet to convey what had happened to them in 1946.

As a member of the world's first generation born under the nuclear sword of Damocles that was swung at Trinity, Hiroshima, Nagasaki, and Bikini, I am a person who, despite my scientific training, nonetheless remains a product of those times and their fears. The ships of Operation Crossroads, more so than any other site or battlefield, even the blasted hulk of the USS *Arizona*,

gave me the first true opportunity to assess my fragile mortality, as well as the world's. They also reminded me that we need to preserve them, and the bunkers at Bikini, to commemorate a past that reflects not only humanity's triumphs, but its tragedies.

The Legacy of Crossroads

Two days before the Able test, Vice Chief of Naval Operations Admiral DeWitt C. Ramsey spoke to the Jacksonville, Florida, chamber of commerce. The subject was, of course, Operation Crossroads. After outlining the basic and by then well-known aspects of the test's planning and imminent execution, Ramsey stressed that Bikini would convey no aggressive or militaristic message, and that the "information yielded by 'Operation Crossroads' will never be used by this country to intimidate or dominate any other country." And yet Crossroads was just that—part of a shift in the strategic policy of the United States that was to capitalize on public apprehension of the new weapon to deter future wars. The bomb was not an instrument of war so much as it was an instrument of statecraft, of nuclear political blackmail. Admiral Ramsey's remarks, intended for a domestic audience, were soothing while subtly threatening, invoking the concept of "the plummeting missile and the mushrooming explosion spreading out once again to encompass the future of mankind. The only certainty is that on this lonely Pacific Atoll, amid a curious welter of hope and fear, another signpost is being erected along the building highway of the nuclear age."

Thus Operation Crossroads signaled the new U.S. policy of political strategic use of the bomb. The message was clear to some, particularly the Soviet Union, which responded by taking every step to reach nuclear parity with the United States. The flames of the Cold War were fanned by the blasts at Bikini. In a way, the detonations were the first shots fired in the Cold War. The process was aided in large part by focusing public attention on an aspect of the bomb that had previously received little to no attention—radiation. Crossroads' results, presented at the same time that John Hersey published *Hiroshima*, with its graphic depiction of the injuries wrought by the bomb on the victims, made the bomb an even more powerful psychological weapon. Operation Crossroads had minimized the fear of the explosion, but its aftermath, like those of Hiroshima and Nagasaki, was one of radioactive "sacrilegious violation." Thus, radioactive fears meant that the "abhorrent results of modern warfare had been nearly symbolized by one particular effect."

Operation Crossroads inspired fear even though the atoll and ships were not vaporized; "relief was not the only reaction . . . for Bikini became a sort of ideological battleground, as its symbolism was appropriated for different polemical purposes." The issue that ultimately induced fear, even among some members of the military, and in time reached the public, was not the destructive power of atomic blasts but the radiation that followed. As Admiral Blandy noted, "the atomic bomb is definitely not 'just another weapon'; its destructive power dwarfs all previous weapons. Observers at Bikini saw the bomb sink great steel warships and, with its penetrat-

ing nuclear radiations, reach into ships' interiors to kill test animals."

The day after Baker, the *New York Times'* editors wrote that the test had introduced a new factor into nuclear war: "the huge mass of radioactive water which may fall on a ship." The final accounting of ships lost to contamination, first alluded to in Crossroads releases in September 1946, fed a growing fear of radioactivity that was spurred by vivid color photographs of atom-blasted internal organs and blood-swollen brains of irradiated test animals published in *Life* magazine in August 1947. The selection of goats and pigs for test exposure because of their similarities to humans reinforced the grim if not devastating impact of the photos—these could be the radiation-destroyed remains of *people*.

To underscore the message, *Life* reported that human casualties at Bikini would have been 35,000 people. The same issue carried a report from Dr. Stafford Warren, head of the radiological safety team at Bikini. His report on the dangers of the radioactive contamination of the ships and the atoll itself were grim reminders of a possible future. "It was Bikini, rather than Hiroshima or Nagasaki, that first brought the issue of radioactivity compellingly to the nation's consciousness." Public awareness and wariness over Crossroads, which declined after the seeming "failure" of the tests to devastate the world or sink the entire fleet, surfaced again in 1948. In that year David Bradley, M.D., a radiological safety monitor at Bikini, published his journal of the tests as *No Place to Hide*, which was syndicated as a prepublication release by the *Atlantic Monthly*, condensed by *The Reader's Digest*, made into a Book-of-the-Month-Club release, and stayed on the *New York Times* best-seller list for ten weeks. *No Place to Hide* was a forceful book that conveyed the "real" message of Bikini. Operation Crossroads, "hastily planned and hastily carried out . . . may have only sketched in gross outlines . . . the real problem; nevertheless, these outlines show pretty clearly the shadow of the colossus which looms behind tomorrow." Bradley's metaphor was the target ships rusting at Kwajalein, including "the beautiful *Prinz Eugen*, intact and unbroken by the tests but nevertheless dying of a malignant disease for which there is no help."

The "cure," enacted by the navy as Bradley's book was being printed, was the sinking of the contaminated ships. That message, only alluded to in 1946, was first directly reported in a February 1949 column by Drew Pearson in the *Washington Post* that termed the tests a "major naval disaster." Pearson reported that "of the 73 ships involved in the Bikini tests, more than 61 were sunk or destroyed. This is an enormous loss from only two bombs." Thus Pearson reinforced David Bradley's conviction of the radioactive menace that Crossroads had revealed. Pearson, like Bradley, pointed to what he viewed as a military effort to keep the true lesson of Crossroads—the virtual destruction of the target fleet by radioactivity—from being fully comprehended by the public. Yet the story had ultimately leaked. The navy and Joint Task Force One could not keep the fate of so many capital ships and lesser craft out of the public eye after so publicized a test, even by keeping most of the contaminated ships at far-off Kwajalein. Leaving the ships there, said Bradley, provided only the "illusion of escape."

One official response was an attempt to shift the public's fears about radioactivity to bombs delivered on or in the water, a possibility far less likely than air attack. P. M. S. Blackett, a prominent British physicist and government advisor writing in 1948 in an attempt to alleviate the "nuclear neurosis," drove home the misleading point stressed by the U.S. government that, "at Hiroshima and Nagasaki, where the bombs were exploded well up in the air, it has been stated that very little radioactivity remained. . . . On the other hand, after the underwater test explosion at Bikini, intense radioactivity remained for several months in the water and on the ships which had been deluged with active water, and would have killed all living things remaining there for any length of time." This message, which downplayed the damage in Japan, also muted the fact that the deadly radioactivity remained at Bikini for more than several months and led to the sinking of nearly every target ship within four years of the tests, in part because the costs of decontamination did not outweigh the scrap value of the ships, and in part because the U.S. government was determined to avoid contaminating the world steel supply with metal exposed to the bomb. One way or another, fear of radioactivity sank the surviving target ships.

The danger of the initial burst of radiation during a nuclear detonation was not fully understood by the public. Radiation fears inspired by Operation Crossroads, particularly the Baker test, pictured a base surge rolling across a fleet or a harbor city after a nuclear detonation. The 1950 civil defense handbook, written by Crossroads veteran Richard Gerstell, discussed at length the effects of an atomic attack on a harbor and the deadly "radioactive mist" that would follow. Well into the 1950s and the advent of a deliverable H-bomb, the worst-case scenario envisioned by defense planners was a bomb delivered in shallow water in a crowded port.

The message of long-term contamination was at first downplayed, however. The decontamination efforts on the support ships at San Francisco were kept classified, and one wonders if it was time and cost which ultimately backed up David Bradley's assertion that "no such rigamarole as rubber boots and gloves and oxygen rebreathing masks could conceivably be used if San Francisco were atomized, its population struggling to escape from the blazing debris, the smoke and the terror of the man-made emanations."

Some veterans of Crossroads have suffered and died of cancer and numerous other ailments brought on by exposure to the fallout and contaminated ships. The Defense Nuclear Agency, in congressional testimony, pointed out that approximately 9,000 people (21 percent of the total Crossroads contingent) boarded the target ships after they had been irradiated by Able and Baker, and that 4,900 boarded ships between July 25 and July 31, a time when the vessels were at the peak of radioactivity. Yet the government denies that the exposures were harmful, stressing that these "personnel were scientists . . . damage inspection teams, and accompanying radiation safety monitors . . . most . . . knowledgeable concerning radiation safety." There was, therefore, "no reason to assume that the . . . people . . . who actually boarded received any additional exposure as a result of inadequate decontamination." But photographs show large numbers of inexperienced sailors with their

sleeves rolled up, or barefooted, scrubbing contaminated ships. Subsequent inquiry has shown that fallout was accurately plotted, that an inadequate number of badges were provided to the men, and that a Crossroads-accepted "safe" exposure rate of one-tenth of a roentgen per twenty-four hours is now considered excessive. David Bradley testified in a congressional hearing that as a monitor he flew through a 30-to-50 roentgen area with a badge that failed to register his exposure to the radiation.

A November 1985 report by the General Accounting Office pointed in hindsight to inaccuracies in the film badges issued to some but not all of the ships' crews. The GAO also criticized the lack of comprehensive decontamination procedures until weeks after Baker. No estimates were made for ingestion through cuts and other open wounds, or inhalation, for which there was a probable error factor of five or ten. Thus, there are cases like the late John Smitherman, a fireman on the USS *Allen M. Sumner* (DD-692), who went aboard the *Independence* after Able to put out fires. Smitherman was on deck after the Baker test nineteen miles from surface zero, when "mist from the mushroom fell on our deck [with] little pieces of metal and rocks." Smitherman developed lymphedema that swelled his feet and hands and later required the amputation of his limbs. He died of cancer of the liver, spleen, and lungs.

As for the Bikinians, not only were they taken from their homeland and relocated on Rongelap, but they were also exposed to high levels of radiation. After being neglected and nearly starved from lack of food in their new home in 1947, they were subjected to the deadly fallout of the

Prefabricated houses for a returning population. After the U.S. Government declared Bikini "safe," the islands were bulldozed, new trees planted, and rows of concrete and fiberboard houses were erected. When it was belatedly discovered that the islands were still "hot," the Bikinians were again hastily relocated. The now empty houses are slowly crumbling, home only to the occasional bird and gecko lizard. (James P. Delgado, National Park Service)

1954 Bravo shot at Bikini, which also killed a member of the Japanese fishing vessel *Fukuryu Maru*'s crew and put the rest of the crew in the hospital for a year. The Bikinians on Rongelap were heavily contaminated by the fallout: 90 percent were so severely burned that their blisters and scars took a year to fade. Evacuated three days after the test, they were later returned to contaminated Rongelap. The Bikinians now live on isolated Kili Island. The Rongelapese, who remained on their contaminated islands, were evacuated to Mejato Island, part of Kwajalein Atoll, in 1985 by the Greenpeace vessel *Rainbow Warrior*.

Compensated by the U.S. government with $90 million and the dubious gift of the sunken ships, bunkers, and the detonation and measurement cables from the atomic tests, the Bikinians feel they have been used as human guinea pigs. Nineteen of the twenty-one people on Rongelap who were under the age of twelve when Bravo detonated developed thyroid le-

The scientific field station on Bikini Island is a constant reminder that while decades have passed since the last nuclear detonations at Bikini, many more years of inquiry remain, as scientists grapple with the unresolved issue of how to neutralize the radioactive contamination of the islands. (James P. Delgado, National Park Service)

sions and other radiation-induced diseases. Isolated on Kili, hundreds of miles from Bikini, the Bikinians have now lost their culture as well as their home. Efforts by some, notably scientist Dr. William L. Robison of the University of California, are seeking to reduce or stop the intake of cesium into the food chain through using high-potassium fertilizer to block the fallout. In the end, though, the Bikinians decided to remove the irradiated topsoil. It is a tremendously complex and expensive task to return the Bikinians to their homes. The Bikinians care little

about *how* the "poison" is removed from their islands. They only want to know when. Kilon Bauno, the "king" of Bikini in 1990, said upon his visit to the island that year that, as soon as "we know that this place is safe for us to come back, we'll all swim out to the ships from Kili. We'll swim to the ships and get on."

After his 1946 visit to the displaced Bikinians on Rongelap Island, David Bradley wrote that they "are not the first, nor will they be the last, to be left homeless and impoverished by the inexorable Bomb. They have no choice in the matter, and little understanding of it. But in this perhaps they are not so different from us all." In 1978, Tomaki Juda, leader of the Bikini Council, told the U.S. Congress that his people had been relocated on the premise that they were to be like "the Children of Israel, whom the Lord led into the Promised Land." Juda observed, "we were naive then. . . . We are, sadly, more akin to the Children of Israel when they left Egypt and wandered through the desert for forty years." The home they left behind is now a monument to their long exile, to the broken promise of re-settlement in the 1960s, and to the continuing power of the bombs at Bikini to deny a home-coming.

Notes

Chapter 1: "It Is an Awful Responsibility Which Has Come to Us"

There is a considerable bibliography on the development of the atomic bomb and its combat use against Japan. In preparing this chapter, I relied on a number of sources, but found excellent overviews in Jones, *Manhattan: The Army and the Atomic Bomb;* Rhodes, *The Making of the Atomic Bomb;* Kurzman, *The Day of the Bomb;* Lansing, *Day of Trinity;* and Marx, *Seven Hours to Zero.* Also very helpful in providing various perspectives were accounts from participants in the Manhattan Project, such as Sanger and Mull, *Hanford and the Bomb;* Nichols, *The Road to Trinity;* Russ, *Project Alberta;* and Laurence, *Dawn Over Zero.* For the atomic bombings, I relied on Tibbets, *The Tibbets Story;* and Thomas and Witts, *Ruin from the Air.*

The perspective of the Japanese is outlined in Hersey, *Hiroshima;* The Pacific War Research Society, *The Day Man Lost;* Shohno, *The Legacy of Hiroshima;* and Wyden, *Day One: Before Hiroshima and After.* Estimates of casualties and damage come from Committee for the Compilation of Materials on Damage Caused by the Atomic Bombs, *Hiroshima and Nagasaki;* and Glasstone, *The Effects of Nuclear Weapons.* For the background of the bombing campaign against Japan, and for American attitudes, I relied on Schaffer, *Wings of Judgement;* Holmes, *Acts of War;* Edoin, *The Night Tokyo Burned;* Geddes, *The Atomic Age Opens;* Fussell, *Thank God for the Atomic Bomb;* Tibbets, *The Tibbets Story;* and LeMay, *Superfortress.*

7   "great ball of fire": Laurence, *Dawn Over Zero,* pp. 10–11. Whether or not Oppenheimer thought of the *Bhagavad Gita* during Trinity has been the subject of some debate. The best modern biography of the complex character of Oppenheimer is Goodchild's *J. Robert Oppenheimer: Shatterer of Worlds.* The *Bhagavad Gita,* a book of Hindu scriptures, was written sometime around the fifth century B.C. in the form of a poetic dialogue between Prince Arjuna and Krishna.

9   The character and career of "Deak" Parsons was gleaned from his biographical file at the U.S. Naval Historical Center at the Washington Navy Yard, several of his memoranda in the Los Alamos National Laboratory Archives, and a December 20, 1990, interview with Robert "Bob" Henderson of Albuquerque, a Los Alamos and Operation Crossroads veteran, who offered the comment of Parsons that "if a weapon didn't have a lanyard on it, it wasn't a weapon."

14   "A column of smoke rising fast": Thomas and Witts, *Ruin from the Air,* p. 326.

14   "Clear-cut, successful in all respects": Ibid., p. 328.

14   "It is an awful responsibility which has come to us": Truman as quoted in the Pacific War Research Society, *The Day Man Lost: Hiroshima, 6 August 1945*, pp. 299–300, and Geddes, *The Atomic Age Opens*, p. 42.

16   "After looking at the damage done": LeMay and Yenne, *Superfortress*, p. 161.

Chapter 2: Operation Crossroads

17   "No nation will be invulnerable": Sarnoff, as quoted in Geddes, *The Atomic Age Opens*, pp. 162–163.

17   "not only the most important single announcement" and "the victory or defeat of armies": in Geddes, *The Atomic Age Opens*, p. 43.

17   "Seldom, if ever, has a war ended": Murrow, *In Search of Light*, p. 102.

17   "It should make an end of marching": *New York Times*, August 12, 1945.

17   "In order to test the destructive powers": McMahon, as quoted in Shurcliff, *Bombs at Bikini*, p.10

18   "a number of Japanese vessels be made available": Arnold, as quoted in Shurcliff, *Bombs at Bikini*, pp. 10–11.

19   On *Ostfriesland*: Graybar, "Bikini Revisited," p. 118.

19   "that ships were not excessively vulnerable" and "Navy carrier aircraft could be just as useful": Davis, *Postwar Defense Policy and the U.S. Navy, 1943–1946*, p. 243.

20   "a comprehensive program for testing high explosives": Shurcliff et al., "Historical Report, Atomic Bomb Tests Able and Baker," 1:viii.

20   "to undertake broad-scale experiments" and "full-scale testing . . . both underwater and above water": Ibid., pp. ix–x.

20   "control of the sea by whatever weapons": Forrestal, as quoted in the *New York Times*, August 24, 1945.

20   "to test the effects of the new atomic bomb against warships": *New York Times*, August 25, 1945.

20   "a few of our own modern naval vessels": Shurcliff, *Bombs at Bikini*, p. 11.

20   "have been working aggressively": *New York Times*, December 11, 1945.

21   "battleship mentality": *New York Times*, July 30, 1946.

21   "imaginative but thorough planner": Lloyd Graybar, "William Henry Purnell Blandy," in Garraty, ed., *Dictionary of American Biography*, pp. 65–67.

21   "I named the project": Blandy, "Remarks . . . Before the 47th National Encampment, Veterans of Foreign Wars, at Boston, Massachusetts, September 5, 1946."

21   Blandy's orders: Shurcliff, "Technical Report," pp. 1.6–1.7.

22   "it is indeed routine to test each new weapon": Shurcliff, *Bombs at Bikini*, p. 9.

22   "help us to be what the world expects": Blandy, "Address . . . On New York Herald-Tribune Youth Forum, Over Columbia Broadcasting System, Waldorf-Astoria Hotel, New York City, April 13, 1946: Why Test the Atom Bomb?"

22   "the first of the atomic era war games": As quoted in Boyer, *By The Bomb's Early Light*, p. 83.

22   requires such major expenditures": Bush, *Modern Arms and Free Men*, p. 92.

23   "Some people fear that these tests": Blandy, "Statement . . . On Purposes of Atomic Bomb Tests."

23   "there was some danger": Shurcliff, *Bombs at Bikini*, p. 52.

23 "to help those correspondents who were starting off 'cold'" and press statistics: Shurcliff, *Bombs at Bikini*, pp. 36–38 passim.

24 "suspicion and disapproval of the planned experimental use": *New York Times*, May 9, 1946.

25 "We want ships that are tough": Blandy, as quoted in Shurcliff, *Bombs at Bikini*, p. ix.

25 "The tests stand out clearly as a defensive measure": Blandy, "Background Material, Operation Crossroads," Distributed to U.S. Naval Forces in Europe by the Public Information Section, Joint Task Force One and cited in Daly, "Crossroads at Bikini," *Proceedings*, July 1986, p. 68.

25 "other nations with even a moderate degree": Blandy, "Why Test the Atom Bomb?"

26 "The ultimate results of the tests": Shurcliff, "Historical Report, Atomic Bomb Tests Able and Baker," 1:xiii.

26 "a large number of scientists": Kincaid, "Bikini," p. 41.

26 "At Hiroshima and Nagasaki": Shurcliff, *Bombs at Bikini*, p. 7.

26 "grandiose display of atomic destruction": Sen. Lucas' remarks appear in the *Congressional Record*, 79th Cong., 2d sess., 1946, 92, pt. 3: S 2790 (daily ed., March 29, 1946).

27 "I would like to have a real PT boat": Letter, Max Ladewasser and Gang to the President, April 14, 1946, filed in Protest Letters, Joint Task Force One, National Archives Record Group 374, Records of the Defense Atomic Support Agency, Washington, D.C. All letters in this group are hereafter cited as Protest Letters. The answering correspondences are also filed here, and are hereafter cited as Protest Answers.

27 "do not need to kill elephants": Letter, John P. Howe to the President, April 16, 1946, Protest Letters.

27 Costs of tests: *New York Times*, March 20, 1946. The navy's Bureau of Ships, when totaling the costs of the target ships, was ordered *not* to include the cost of armament. Also untallied were the costs through the years for each ship's modification, modernization, and repairs.

27 "one large new ship": *New York Times*, April 17, 1946.

27 "in excess of the number required" and "those badly damaged": Letter, Brig. Gen. T. J. Betts, USA, to Alexander Wilde, April 2, 1946, Protest Answers.

27 "New York may lose forever" and "I don't see why": *New York Times*, January 26, 1946.

28 "While it is regretted": Letter, Brig. Gen. T. J. Betts, USA, to Peter Brambir, March 21, 1946, Protest Answers.

28 "many other ships": Letter, Brig. Gen. T. J. Betts, USA, to Lt. Herbert B. Leopold, USN, February 11, 1946, Protest Answers.

29 "No provisions are indicated": "The Effect of the Atomic Bomb on Naval Power," *Bulletin of the Atomic Scientists of Chicago*, February 15, 1946, p. 1.

29 Test animal statistics: Shurcliff, *Bombs at Bikini*, p. 84.

29 "chosen from special strains" and "their psychoneurotic tendencies": Ibid., p. 85.

30 "Germans and Japanese who have been condemned": Letter, R. Lee Page to George Lyons, Commissioner of Atomic Research, Navy Department, March 15, 1946, Protest Letters.

30 "In lieu of the 4,000 innocent animals": Letter, Jeanne Robinson to Adm. W. H. P. Blandy, May 1, 1946, Protest Letters.

30 "We are more interested in preserving the lives of men": Blandy, "Scientific Data to be Gained through Use of Animals in Crossroads Project."

30 "If we are making plans to outlaw": Sen. Lucas' remarks are in the *Congressional Record*, 79th

Cong., 2d sess., 1947, 92, pt. 1: S 624 (daily ed., January 31, 1946).

Chapter 3: Bikini: The Place to Test the Atomic Bomb

33 Statistics on Crossroads personnel: Shurcliff, "Technical Report," pp. 3.1–3.16.

34 "people who wanted to be in on what promised to be," "There were a lot of chiefs," and "The normal wartime complement": Waters, "As I Recall Crossroads," p. 72.

34 "very tired, unshaven and dirty": Peterkin, "Personal Log," March 20, 1946.

34 "was especially clear after it had been decided": Shurcliff, "Technical Report," p. 6.7.

35 "considerable public feeling developed": Ibid.

35 "over-age or of obsolete design": Ibid., p. 6.4.

35 "those scheduled for the reserve fleets": Ibid.

35 "catchers to collect samples": Shurcliff, "Historical Report," 1:21.

35 "the damage of reinforced concrete structures": Ibid., pp. 72–73.

35 "the day the Admiral was coming over": David S. Bill was interviewed by John Poehl, a shipmate, at the first USS   reunion at St. Louis, Missouri, in June 1980. Bill's remarks were transcribed by another shipmate, Alan S. Evans, and a typescript "History" of the ship was prepared by the USS *Hughes* Reunion Association, Inc., for the June 1985 reunion. A copy was presented to the Naval Historical Center, Washington, D.C. Hereafter cited as Bill, "Interview."

36 "great, dirtless farm": Shurcliff, *Bombs at Bikini*, p. 50.

36 "Venice-like transportation system": Ibid., p. 58.

36 Statistics on facilities at Bikini: Shurcliff, *Bombs at Bikini*, pp. 94–96.

37 "certain items of historic interest": Shurcliff, "Historical Report," 1:67.

37 "as closely as possible to the battle": Ibid., p. 68.

37 "hamper the collecting of samples": Ibid.

38 "This type of instrument was roughly representative": Shurcliff, "Technical Report," p. 7.9.

38 Statistics on gauges: Glasstone, ed., *Radiological Defense*, 2:5.

44 "to run her for a couple of months": Interview with Capt. A. H. Graubart, Palm Beach, Florida, May 23, 1992.

46 Bikinian names "were difficult to spell": Shurcliff, *Bombs at Bikini*, p. 89.

47 "The outside world they knew little about": Markwith, "Farewell to Bikini," p. 97.

48 "Civilization and the Atomic Age had come to Bikini": Ibid., p. 116.

48– "We also had Japanese coming alongside in
49 boats," "almost a hulk," and "that was filled with dead Japanese": Letter, George Culley to the author, October 10, 1991. Also, interview with Mr. Culley, Kent, Washington, February 24, 1991.

51 Sabotage aboard the *Sakawa: New York Times*, May 8, 1946, and August 26, 1946.

Chapter 4: Able and Baker

53 "the queen of the atoll": Interview with Robert Henderson, Albuquerque, New Mexico, December 20, 1990.

53 "Well, she was the sexiest thing around": Interview with Leon D. Smith, Albuquerque, New Mexico, December 21, 1990.

53 "Helen of Bikini," *Time*, August 5, 1946, p. 27.

53 *Gilda* (Columbia Pictures, 1946), starred Rita Hayworth, Glenn Ford, and George McReady.

53 Sex and the bomb: Boyer, *By the Bomb's Early Light*, pp. 11–12.

55 "to provide the best instrumentation": Shurcliff, "Technical Report," pp. 6.7–6.8.

55 "All hands face aft": Unsigned article in "Crossroads Crosstalk," mimeographed newsletter "By

and for the Staff, Electronics Coordinating Officer," vol. 2, no. 1 (July 2, 1946), p. 3. Copy in the Peterkin papers.

55–56 "Bomb away, bomb away!": Shurcliff, *Bombs at Bikini*, pp. 104–105. Also, interview with Woodrow Swancutt, San Antonio, Texas, December 20, 1990.

56 Characteristics and position of Able detonation: Shurcliff, "Technical Report," pp. 10.5, 10.9–10.10.

56–57 "Then, suddenly, a whole hemisphere of air catches fire": Unsigned article in "Crossroads Crosstalk," mimeographed newsletter "By and for the Staff, Electronics Coordinating Officer," vol. 2, no. 1 (July 2, 1946), p. 3.

57 "Look at that, captain": Letter, Capt. Richard B. Laning to Lloyd Graybar, January 27, 1983, and interview with Dick Laning, Orlando, Florida, December 12, 1990.

57 "having been addicted to science fiction": Ibid.

58 Col. Sutherland's black eye: Leon D. Smith interview, Albuquerque, New Mexico, December 20, 1990.

58 Characteristics of Able release of heat and pressure: Shurcliff, "Technical Report," pp. 12.3–12.4, 13.20, 16.5, 17.3, 18.3, 28.9., and Glasstone, *The Effects of Nuclear Weapons*, pp. 29, 36.

58 "for a few minutes, it looked like a giant ice cream cone": Press pool report on Able, dispatch from USS *Appalachian*, July 1, 1946, National Archives.

59 "Once the mushroom cloud": Waters, "As I Recall Crossroads," p. 73.

59 "We still couldn't make out" and "bent masts": Peterkin, "Personal Log," July 1, 1946.

61 Damage to the *Gilliam* and the *Carlisle:* Shurcliff, "Technical Report," p. 13.6.

61–62 Damage to the *Anderson* and "several seams": Director of Ship Material, Joint Task Force One, "Bureau of Ships Group, Technical Inspection Report, USS ANDERSON (DD411), Test Able, Operation Crossroads," pp. 5, 9.

62–63 Damage to the *Lamson* and "twisted and torn almost beyond recognition": Director of Ship Material, "Technical Inspection Report, USS LAMSON (DD367), Test Able," pp. 6, 8, 9.

63–64 Damage to the *Sakawa* and "the stern was most badly damaged": Director of Ship Material, "Technical Inspection Report, SAKAWA (Ex-Jap CL), West Able," pp. 5, 6, 8.

64 "I don't like it": Bradley, *No Place to Hide*, p. 101.

64 "Then, as that disappeared": Peterkin, "Personal Log," July 2, 1946.

64 Pig 311's story was told, with a photograph of the lucky porker, then a "350-pound sow," in "What Science Learned at Bikini: Latest Report on the Results," *Life*, vol. 23, no. 6, August 11, 1947, pp. 78–79.

65 "blown in and there was buckling": Bradley, *No Place to Hide*, p. 64, Shurcliff, "Technical Report," p. 13.5, and Shurcliff, *Bombs at Bikini*, pp. 132–133.

66 "Soot and burnt gear" and "This blast was so hot": Peterkin, "Personal Log," July 2, 1946.

66 Damage to the *Skate:* Shurcliff, "Technical Report," p. 13.6, and *Bombs at Bikini*, pp. 133–134, and interview with Captain Enders Huey, Orlando, Florida, May 23, 1992.

67 Damage to the *Arkansas*, and "but the shock wave did the worst damage": Shurcliff, *Bombs at Bikini*, p. 134.

67 YO-160 damage: Director of Ship Material, "Technical Inspection Report, USS YO-160, Test Able," pp. 3, 5.

67 the bomb "only" sank two ships: *New York Times*, July 1, 1946.

67 Observer reactions: Ibid. and Boyer, *By the Bomb's Early Light*, p. 83.

67 Combat readiness assessments: Shurcliff: "Technical Report," pp. 13.2–13.3.

67 "blown to hell": Dick Laning interview, Orlando, Florida, December 12, 1990.

69 "a solid slimy seagoing bucket" and "Those who had seen the hulk": Bradley, *No Place to Hide*, p. 74.

70 "with great difficulty through the almost formless wreckage": Director of Ship Material, "Technical Inspection Report, USS GILLIAM, Test Able," p. 5.

70 "heavily built and heavily armored ships are difficult to sink": Forrestal, as quoted in *New York Times*, July 2, 1946.

70 "dying like flies": *New York Times*, July 15, 1946. Also see Director of Ship Material, "The Gross Autopsy Findings and a Statistical Study of the Mortality in the Animals Exposed at Bikini."

70 "As usual, the day before the blast" and "We are now veterans of atomic bombing": Peterkin, "Personal Log," July 15–26, 1946.

71 Caisson details and preparation: Henderson interview, Albuquerque, New Mexico, December 20, 1990.

71 LSM-60 arrangements for detonation: Shurcliff, "Technical Report," p. 5.12.

71 "a flash of a small boat exploding": Letter, Lieut. Commander Robert W. Underwood to "Babe Darling," July 25, 1946. Photocopy provided by USS *Saratoga* Reunion Association.

71 Characteristics of Baker detonation: Glasstone, *The Effects of Nuclear Weapons*, pp. 45–46, 52; Shurcliff, "Technical Report," pp. 28.3, 28.7.

73 Damage to the *Pilotfish*, Shurcliff, "Technical Report," p. 26.3, and Director of Ship Material, "Technical Inspection Report, USS PILOT-FISH (SS386), Test Baker," p. 6.

73 Blast-generated wave data: Shurcliff, "Technical Report," pp. 28.5–28.6.

73 "like the spray at the base of Niagara Falls": Glasstone, *The Effects of Nuclear Weapons*, p. 46.

73 Radiation levels: Shurcliff, "Technical Report," pp. 27.3–27.7, 28.4.

73– Director of Ship Material, "Technical Inspection Report, USS ARKANSAS (BB33), Test Baker," includes an extremely slow-motion photo sequence and radar images taken from an overflying PBY that shows the capsizing and overwashing sequence of the *Arkansas*' sinking.

74 "flopped end over end" and "not a single soul": Bill interview.

77– *Saratoga*'s sinking and "There were many who had served in her": *New York Times*, July 25, 1946.

78– "radiological hazards prevented salvage": Shurcliff, "Historical Report," 1:54.

79 "I, for one, am not sorry": Bradley, *No Place to Hide*, p. 102.

79 "before Bikini the world stood in awe": "Bikini 'Dud' Decried for Lifting Fears," *New York Times*, August 4, 1946.

Chapter 5: The Radioactive Aftermath

80 "that taking them in tow": Director of Ship Material, "Technical Inspection Report, Radiological Decontamination of Target and Non-Target Vessels," 1:4.

80– "the nature and extent of the contamination" and "water might take up": Ibid.

81 the *Hughes*' radiation readings: Ibid., p. 5.

82 "available means" for decontamination: Ibid., pp. 9, 11.

83 "The main deck forward had not been touched": Bradley, *No Place to Hide*, pp. 109–110.

83 "apply detailed scrubbing" and "painting over the surface": Director of Ship Material, "Radiological Decontamination of Target and Non-Target Vessels," p. 8.

84 "No successful suits could be brought": Hacker, *The Dragon's Tail*, pp. 119–120; see also Draeger and Warren, "Medicine at the Crossroads," pp. 219–225.

85 "I noticed the coxswain": Dick Laning interview, Orlando, Florida, December 12, 1990.

85 On the overwhelmed "Rad Safe" effort, see Hacker, *The Dragon's Tail*, pp. 123–124. On inadequate personnel, equipment, and difficult conditions, see Catherine Caufield, *Multiple Exposures: Chronicles of the Radiation Age* (Chicago: University of Chicago Press, 1989), p. 97, and Weisgall, *Operation Crossroads*, pp. 230–242. The Rad Safe limit that was exceeded was aboard the destroyer *Allen M. Sumner* (DD-692). Although the ship was told that its "present situation [was] not dangerous," it was ordered to sea to flush with fresh sea water (Hacker, *The Dragon's Tail*, p. 141).

85 "which were not detectable": Director of Ship Material, "Radiological Decontamination of Target and Non-Target Vessels," p. 13.

86 "although all waters and land areas": Blandy, as cited in Hacker, *The Dragon's Tail*, pp. 146–147.

86 "recovery of instruments": Shurcliff, "Historical Report," 1:55.

87 "the classification of this memo": Memorandum, Col. A. W. Betts, USACOE, to Brig. Gen. K. D. Nichols, MED, USACOE, August 10, 1946. F-3-5, Test Baker Results, Box 26, National Archives Record Group 377, Records of the Manhattan Engineer District, Washington, D.C.

87 "although successful to a certain extent": Director of Ship Material, "Radiological Decontamination of Target and Non-Target Vessels," p. 17.

87 "to establish facilities there for continued examination": Shurcliff, "Historical Report," p. 57.

87 "to restrict entry": Shurcliff, "Technical Report," p. 31.6.

88 "It is a very peculiar sensation" and "We walk around these deserted ships": Peterkin, "Personal Log," July 26–August 9, 1946.

88 Authorization to sink the ships: Director of Ship Material, Technical Inspection Report, Radio-

logical Decontamination of Target and Non-Target Vessels," 3:14.

89 Only "9 of 92 ships escaped": *New York Times*, September 5, 1946.

90 "crippled, gaunt, silent": Bradley, *No Place to Hide*, p. 142.

90 Sinking of the *Prinz Eugen:* Dickey, "The End of the Prinz," *United States Naval Institute Proceedings* (August 1969).

90 "for further study of damage": Memorandum, CNO to CINCPAC, "Removal of Equipment and Supplies from Contaminated CROSSROADS Target Ships," February 18, 1947, Serial 034P36, Operational Archives, U.S. Naval Historical Center.

91 "Since the New York was towed here" and "stern low and covered with rust": *New York Times*, May 11, 1947.

92 Decontamination laboratory established: see C. Sharp Cook, "The Legacy of Crossroads," *Naval History* 2, no. 4 (Fall 1988).

92 The *Independence*'s gradual voyage by towing to the West Coast and its subsequent sinking dates are provided by the Bureau of Ships file card for the vessel, now on file in the Ships' Histories Branch of the U.S. Naval Historical Center. The ship was reported sunk at 37 degrees, 20 minutes N—123 degrees, 04 minutes W, in 500 fathoms of water. A 1990 seafloor mapping by the U.S. Geological Survey of the Gulf of the Farallones National Marine Sanctuary, twenty-six miles west of San Francisco, disclosed 47,000 barrels of radioactive waste, some of it from the Crossroads decontamination efforts at Hunter's Point and Mare Island, and the hulk of the *Independence*, in 470 fathoms, at 37 degrees, 28 minutes N—123 degrees, 07 minutes W, which is not a major discrepancy in position for a ship drifting while being fired at before sinking. See Jane Kay, "N-Waste Litters Farallones," *San Francisco Examiner*, November 18, 1990, pp. A-1, A-26.

92 "radiologically contaminated material" and "real and ever-present hazard": Memorandum, CNO to Chiefs of the Bureau of Ships, Bureau of Ordnance, Bureau of Aeronautics, Bureau of Medicine and Surgery, Bureau of Docks and Yards, Bureau of Supplies and Accounts, "Handling and Control of Radiologically Contaminated Material from Crossroads," June 10, 1947, Serial 0138P36, Operational Archives, U.S. Naval Historical Center.

93 Statistics on ship sinkings: Cook, "The Legacy of Crossroads," p. 29.

93 The *Nevada*'s sinking was front-page news in a number of cities. For example, see the *San Francisco Call-Bulletin*, "A Gallant Ship Is Sunk," August 2, 1948.

93 The *Salt Lake City*'s sinking and career were summarized in the *Christian Science Monitor* on May 28, 1948. The author of the eulogy was Captain Frederick L. Oliver, USN (Ret.), the commissioning commander of the vessel.

93 "When I saw that single stack": Joseph Zuccaro was interviewed by John Poehl, a shipmate, at the first USS *Hughes* reunion in St. Louis, Missouri, in June 1980. Zuccaro's remarks were transcribed by another shipmate, Alan S. Evans, and a typescript "History" of the ship was prepared by the USS *Hughes* Reunion Association, Inc., for the June 1985 reunion. A copy was presented to the Naval Historical Center, Washington, D.C.

94 "a sponge for radioactive particles" and special orders for ships from Bikini: Waters, "As I Recall Crossroads," p. 73.

94 "even in damage repair": Ibid., p. 73.

94 Decontamination of the *Laffey*: Hacker, *The Dragon's Tail*, p. 144.

95 Ship decontamination statistics: Waters, "As I Recall Crossroads," p. 72. See also Cook, "Legacy of Crossroads," pp. 31–32, and Hacker, *The Dragon's Tail*, p. 146.

95–
96 "From a military viewpoint" and "If used in numbers": "The Evaluation of the Atomic Bomb

as a Military Weapon: The Final Report of the Joint Chiefs of Staff Evaluation Board for Operation Crossroads," June 30, 1947. CCS 471.6, 10-15-46, Section 9, Part 1, p. 60, 73. National Archives Record Group 218.

96–
97 "the Navy's determined, frustrating, and ultimately futile efforts": Boyer, *By the Bomb's Early Light*, p. 92.

97 "what it had argued all along" and "properly dispersed": Davis, *Postwar Defense Policy and the U.S. Navy, 1943–1946*, p. 246.

97 "the results at Bikini": Hanson W. Baldwin, dispatch of 22:02 to the *New York Times*, July 25, 1946, from on board the USS *Appalachian*. See also Baldwin, "Atom Bomb Is Proved Most Terrible Weapon: Surveys in Japan and Bikini Test Are Enough to Change Concepts of War," *New York Times*, July 7, 1946.

97 "perhaps she might have been saved": Baldwin, "Lessons Learned in Bikini Tests," *New York Times*, August 1, 1946.

97 "crews doomed to slow death": Ibid.

98 "The results may be": Cochrane as quoted in "Guided Missile Warships on Way for Redesigned Atomic-Age Navy," *New York Times*, September 8, 1946.

98 "it will not be a serious hazard": Glasstone, *Radiological Defense*, p. 165.

98 "atomic-driven and equipped with atomic warhead missiles": Hanson W. Baldwin, "Atomic Age Augurs New-Style Navy," *New York Times*, July 1, 1946.

99 "It is too soon to attempt": Joint Chiefs of Staff Evaluation Board, "Preliminary Statement by the Evaluation Board on Test B; Section III, Observations and Conclusions, Both Tests" (August 2, 1946), reproduced in Shurcliff, *Bombs at Bikini*, pp. 198–199.

99 "in order to determine": Memorandum to Op-36 from Op-33 and Op-38 (Parsons), April 9, 1947, as well as undated attached draft memorandum from the Joint Crossroads Committee to

the Joint Chiefs of Staff, the Secretary of the Navy, and the Secretary of War. Serial 106P36, Operational Archives, U.S. Naval Historical Center.

99 "the story of cooperation": "Bikini Resurvey Plan, 1–47, Annex L, Public Information Plan," National Archives Record Group 374, Entry 4B, Box 156, Folder A4. Hereafter cited as "Operations Plan."

99 "to determine the amount and nature of radioactivity": Ibid., Annex D, "Sunken Ship Inspection Plan."

100 "blasted loose from ships": Armed Forces Special Weapons Project, *Technical Report, Bikini Scientific Resurvey,* vol. 2, "Report of the Technical Director," pp. 47–54.

100 "few visible effects of the blast": "Bikini Backtalk," vol. 1, no. 16, September 10, 1947; copy on file in National Archives Record Group 374, Box 28, Folder 212.

100 "divers today walked up and down. . . ." from "Divers Examine Sunken Aircraft Carrier in Bikini Lagoon," Joint Army–Navy Release No. 11, July 17, 1947. Department of Energy Archives, Las Vegas, Nevada, Document number 100940.

100 Radiation levels on dives, "Report of the Director of Ship Material," in *Technical Report, Bikini Scientific Resurvey,* Vol. III, pp. 1–2. Also see the press release, "Divers Examine Sunken Aircraft Carrier. . . ."

100– "sun-tanned sailors and scientists": Joint Army–
101 Navy Release No. 16, July 24, 1947, as quoted in Hines, *Proving Ground,* p. 61. See also "Report of the Technical Director," 2:59.

101 Damage to the *Saratoga:* "Report of the Director of Ship Material," 3:1–2.

101 On thickness of radioactive mud: Van Arx, *Circulation Systems of Bikini and Rongelap Lagoons (Bikini and Nearby Lagoons, Part II: Oceanography (Physical),* p. 271.

101 "possible radiological or blast effects": "Opera-

tions," in *Technical Report, Bikini Scientific Resurvey,* 1:10–12, 67.

101 "a comprehensive survey" and "revealed no changes in population": "Report of the Technical Director," Annex IV, p. 102.

101 "after a few more years": Ibid.

101 "a set of problems": Hines, *Proving Ground,* p. 75.

Chapter 6: Diving at Ground Zero

108– Many of the observations made about the condi-
109 tion and appearance of the wrecks are mine. They do reflect, however, hours of comparison and discussion with my colleagues at Bikini. I am particularly indebted to Larry Murphy and Dan Lenihan. A number of the observations were first reported in Delgado, Lenihan, and Murphy, *The Archaeology of the Atomic Bomb.*

109 "as though the blast [had] acted like the hammer": Director of Ship Material, "Technical Inspection Report, USS GILLIAM (APA57), Test Able," p. 5.

112 "throughout the ship": Director of Ship Material, "Technical Inspection Report, USS CARLISLE (APA69), Test Able," p. 9.

113 "in sinking, she carried": Shurcliff, *Bombs at Bikini,* p. 164.

113 "lying buried in the silt": Director of Ship Material, "Technical Inspection Report, USS ARKANSAS (BB33), Test Baker," pp. 5, 7.

Chapter 7: Exploring the Wreck of the *Saratoga*

122 "The new *Saratoga*": *Philadelphia Evening Star,* March 21, 1925.

122 "*Sara* is a queen": Halsey and Bryan, *Admiral Halsey's Story,* p. 62.

123 "perhaps her most brilliant strike": Mooney, *Dictionary of American Naval Fighting Ships,* pp. 340–341.

125 "very similar in arrangement": Shurcliff, "Technical Report," p. 6.5.

126, Many of the observations made about the condition and appearance of the *Saratoga* are mine.
128 But they do reflect hours of comparison and discussion with my colleagues at Bikini. I am particularly indebted to Larry Murphy, Dan Lenihan, Larry Nordby, Jerry Livingston, Eric Hiner, Lee McEachern, George Lang, and Kitty Courtney. A number of the observations were first reported in Delgado, Lenihan, and Murphy, *The Archaeology of the Atomic Bomb,* and in Delgado, "What's Become of *Sara?*", *United States Naval Institute Proceedings* (October) 1990.

128 "the indentation is gradual" and "the wood decking has been splintered": Director of Ship Material, "Technical Inspection Report, USS SARATOGA (CV3), Test Baker," p. 8.

129 "twisted about 20 degrees": Ibid., pp. 6–7.

131– We compared observations of what we saw in
132 1989 and 1990 with Colonel J. D. Frederick's "Final Report of Army Ground Group (Task Group 1.4), Operation Crossroads Atomic Bomb Tests" (1946).

132 Joe Louis fight: Interview with Alvin Brommer, by Lee McEachern, at the USS *Saratoga* annual reunion, Las Vegas, Nevada, September 1989.

132 "Christmas trees" and other gauges: Shurcliff, *Bombs at Bikini,* p. 69, and "Technical Report," p. 9.5.

138 The ordnance was carefully labeled in Bureau of Ordnance photographs, Record Group 74, Records of the Bureau of Ordnance, U.S. Navy, photographs labeled 74-BO-B4, USS SARATOGA (CV-3), Still Pictures Branch, National Archives, Washington, D.C. Originally labeled BACR-63-1563, these photographs are contact prints of 4 x 5 negatives; picture boards in each view indicate that they were taken on either June 17 or June 19, 1946. The legend BACR stands for "Before Able, Crossroads." The bombs

remained in the photographed positions for Test Baker.

138, The identification of the aircraft was done in
140 consultation with the report by the Director of Ship Material, "Final Report of Tests Able and Baker, Bureau of Aeronautics," October 11, 1946, National Archives Record Group 374. The characteristics of the aircraft are from Swanborough and Bowers, *United States Navy Aircraft since 1911,* pp. 166–168, 232–233, and Andrade, *U.S. Military Aircraft Designations and Serials since 1909,* p. 222.

Chapter 8: The Ghost Fleet

145 The identification of fallout particles at Bikini is from Robison, as cited in Delgado, Lenihan, and Murphy, *The Archaeology of the Atomic Bomb,* p. 179.

145 The plight of the Bikinians is recounted in Weisgall, "The Nuclear Nomads of Bikini," *Foreign Policy* (1980), Ellis, "A Way of Life Lost: Bikini," *National Geographic* (1986), and Weisgall, *Operation Crossroads.* A number of documentary films have been made, including the well-known *Radio Bikini* and, most recently, the award-winning film by William Livingston, *Bikini: Forbidden Paradise.*

146– Some of the observations made about the condition and appearance of the wrecks are mine.
147 Others were shared by my colleagues at Bikini. I am particularly indebted to Larry Murphy, Dan Lenihan, Larry Nordby, Jerry Livingston, Eric Hiner, Lee McEachern, George Lang, Bill Curtsinger, John Eliot, and Kitty Courtney. A number of the observations were first reported in Delgado, Lenihan, and Murphy, *The Archaeology of the Atomic Bomb.*

149 "She had been thrown": Dick Laning letter to Lloyd Graybar, January 27, 1983.

149 Damage to the *Pilotfish*: Ibid., pp. 5–6, and Director of Ship Material, "Bikini Scientific Re-

survey: Report of the Director of Ship Material," 3:1.

150 "shifted to starboard": Director of Ship Material, "Technical Inspection Report, USS PILOT-FISH, Test Baker," p. 6.

151 "The method used was to fill": Shurcliff, *Bombs at Bikini*, p. 147; see also plate 17, caption, between pp. 118–119.

151 "the enormous pressures": Shurcliff, *Operation Crossroads: The Official Pictorial Record*, p. 106.

152 Damage to the *Apogon* and "caused by reflections": Director of Ship Material, "Technical Inspection Report, USS APOGON (SS308), Test Baker," pp. 5–6, and Director of Ship Material, "Bikini Scientific Resurvey: Report of the Director of Ship Material," 3:1–2.

155 Goosestepping German crew: Henderson interview, Albuquerque, New Mexico, December 20, 1990.

155 "ugly anthropoid creation": Bradley, *No Place to Hide*, p. 12.

155 "graceful," "beautiful," and "as sleek and cavalier": Ibid., pp. 39, 147.

155 "I'd rather see the ship atomized": As quoted in Raumann, "Life as Employed Enemy Personnel," *Naval History* (1989), p. 32.

155 "was tested to see which one is the better ship": Interview with Otto Schoetzow, Seattle, Washington, May 23, 1992.

155 "unconditional and complete surrender" comes from a certificate awarded to one of the men who participated, now in the ship's history files at the Naval Historical Center.

160 "When World War II began": Ito and Pineau, *The End of the Imperial Japanese Navy*, p. 1.

160 "something of the mute sadness": Bradley, *No Place to Hide*, p. 13.

160 Observations made on the *Prinz Eugen* come from our dives, as noted in Delgado, Lenihan,

and Murphy, *The Archaeology of the Atomic Bomb*, and also from Bailey, *WWII Wrecks of the Kwajalein and Truk Lagoons*. I am particularly indebted to Dan Bailey, Bill Remick, and Mark Miller for sharing observations and photographs of dives on and into the *Prinz Eugen*.

Chapter 9: Monuments to the Nuclear Age

165 On efforts to commemorate Trinity, see "Atomic Bomb National Monument, Proposed," S.2054, 79th Cong., 2d sess., March 5, 1946. See also "First A-Bomb Blast Site to Be National Monument," *Washington Daily News*, April 3, 1952. The National Park Service's chief of its Museum Division urged the collecting of Trinity Site artifacts and "material evidence of the bomb explosion" on March 15, 1946. On October 7, 1947, the service's chief historian urged the same after a tour of the site, including saving the rapidly dispersing "atomsite" in the blast crater. The director of the National Park Service wrote to the Atomic Energy Commission on January 7, 1952, requesting a hundred pounds of Trinitite. This correspondence is in the Trinity Site National Historic Landmark File, Division of History, National Park Service, Washington, D.C.

165 Trinitite jewelry: Boyer, *By the Bomb's Early Light*, p. 4.

166 Hiroshima memorials and commemoration and "peace groups wanted it": Wyden, *Day One*, pp. 342–343.

168 "Try to imagine yourself": quoted in "Atomic Age Angel Food," *Time*, November 18, 1946, p. 31.

169 For the anthropology of weapons testing, see Gusterson, "Coming of Age in a Weapons Lab," *The Sciences* (1992).

171 "famous for its exploits," "Most important, we walked," and "Back aboard our LCM": Bascom, *The Crest of the Wave*, p. 169.

172 "somehow, I had always imagined": Letter from Roy Alton, President, USS *Arkansas* (BB-33) Association, to the author, June 4, 1990.

172 "information yielded by 'Operation Crossroads,'" and "the plummeting missile": quoted in "Address by Admiral deWitt C. Ramsey, USN, Vice Chief of Naval Operations, before the Chamber of Commerce, Jacksonville, Florida, 12:30 P.M. (EST) June 28, 1946," Navy Department Press Release, June 28, 1946. Copy on file in the Ships Histories Branch, U.S. Naval Historical Center.

173 "abhorrent results of modern warfare": Weart, *Nuclear Fear*, p. 111.

173 "relief was not the only reaction": Boyer, *By the Bomb's Early Light*, p. 84.

173 "The atomic bomb is definitely not 'just another weapon'": Blandy, as quoted in Shurcliff, *Bombs at Bikini*, p. ix.

173 "the huge mass of radioactive water": *New York Times*, July 26, 1946.

173 "It was Bikini, rather than Hiroshima": Boyer, *By the Bomb's Early Light*, p. 84.

174 "hastily planned and hastily carried out": Bradley, *No Place to Hide*, pp. 165–166.

174 "the beautiful *Prinz Eugen*, intact and unbroken by the tests": Ibid., p. 147.

174 "of the 73 ships involved": *Washington Post*, February 18, 1949.

174 "illusion of escape": Bradley, *No Place to Hide*, p. 166.

174 "at Hiroshima and Nagasaki": Blackett, *Fear, War, and the Bomb*, p. 71.

175 "no such rigamarole": Bradley, *No Place to Hide*, p. 145.

175 Crossroads radiation exposures: U.S. General Accounting Office, *Operation Crossroads: Personnel Radiation Exposure Estimates Should Be Improved*, and Del Tredici, *At Work in the Fields of the Bomb*, p. 177.

175 "personnel were scientists" and "no reason to assume": from the testimony of Lieutenant General John L. Pickitt, director of the Defense Nuclear Agency, before the Senate Committee on Veterans Affairs, Washington, D.C., November 14 and December 11, 1985, as quoted in Del Tredici, *At Work in the Fields of the Bomb*, p. 177.

175 David Bradley's estimate of his exposure is from his congressional testimony, December 11, 1985, as quoted in Del Tredici, *At Work in the Fields of the Bomb*, p. 179.

175 "mist from the mushroom fell": Smitherman was interviewed at his home in Mulberry, Tennessee, on July 31, 1983; quoted in Del Tredici, *At Work in the Fields of the Bomb*, p. 176.

175 Bikinians exposed to Bravo fallout: see Glasstone, *The Effects of Nuclear Weapons*, pp. 423–427, 483–488; Weisgall, "The Nuclear Nomads of Bikini," pp. 89–90; and Ellis, "A Way of Life Lost: Bikini," p. 83. See also Weisgall, "Micronesia and the Nuclear Pacific since Hiroshima," *SAIS Review* (Summer–Fall 1985).

177 "we know that this place": Interview with Kilon Bauno by William Livingston (trans. Jack Niedenthal), Bikini, February 3, 1992.

177 "are not the first, nor will they be the last": Bradley, *No Place to Hide*, p. 163.

178 "the Children of Israel": Tomaki Juda, as quoted by Weisgall, "The Nuclear Nomads of Bikini," p. 98.

Bibliography

Books, Articles, and Manuscripts

"Address by Vice Admiral W. H. P. Blandy, U.S.N., Commander Joint Task Force One. On New York Herald-Tribune Youth Forum, Over Columbia Broadcasting System, Waldorf-Astoria Hotel, New York City, April 13, 1946: Why Test the Atom Bomb?" Joint Army–Navy Task Force One, Crossroads Release No. 36. Department of Energy Archives, Las Vegas, Nevada, Document No. 101008.

"Address by Admiral deWitt C. Ramsey, U.S.N., Vice Chief of Naval Operations, Before the Chamber of Commerce, Jacksonville, Florida, 12:30 P.M. (EST) June 28, 1946." Navy Department Press Release, June 28, 1946. Copy on file in the Ships Histories Branch, U.S. Naval Historical Center.

Alden, John D. *The Fleet Submarine in the U.S. Navy: A Design and Construction History.* Annapolis, Md.: Naval Institute Press, 1979.

Alperovitz, Gar. *Atomic Diplomacy: Hiroshima and Potsdam.* New York: Penguin Books, 1985.

Andrade, John M. *U.S. Military Aircraft Designations and Serials since 1909.* Leicester, Pa. Midland Counties Publications, 1979.

Armed Forces Special Weapons Project. *Technical Report, Bikini Scientific Resurvey,* vol. 2. Washington, D.C.: Armed Forces Special Weapons Project, 1947.

"Atomic Age Angel Food." *Time,* November 18, 1946.

Bailey, Dan E. *WWII Wrecks of the Kwajalein and Truk Lagoons.* Redding, Calif.: North Valley Diver Publications, 1989.

Bascom, Willard. *The Crest of the Wave: Adventures in Oceanography.* New York: Harper & Row, 1988.

Berkhouse, L., S. E. Davis, F. R. Gladeck, J. H. Hallowell, C. B. Jones, E. J. Martin, F. W. MacMullan, and M. J. Osborne. *Operation Crossroads* (DNA 6032F). Washington, D.C.: Defense Agency, 1984.

Birdsall, Steve. *Saga of the Superfortress: The Dramatic Story of the B-29 and the Twentieth Air Force.* New York: Doubleday & Company, 1980.

Blackett, P. M. S. *Fear, War, and the Bomb: Military and Political Consequences of Atomic Energy.* New York: McGraw-Hill Book Co., 1949.

———. *Atomic Weapons and East-West Relations.* Cambridge: Cambridge University Press, 1956.

Boyer, Paul. *By the Bomb's Early Light: American Thought and Culture at the Dawn of the Atomic Age.* New York: Pantheon Books, 1985.

Bradley, David J. *No Place to Hide.* Boston: Little, Brown & Co., 1948.

Bruce-Briggs, B. *The Shield of Faith: Strategic Defense from Zeppelins to Star Wars.* New York: Simon & Schuster, 1988.

Bush, Vannevar. *Modern Arms and Free Men: A Discussion of the Role of Science in Preserving Democracy.* New York: Simon & Schuster, 1949.

Caufield, Catherine. *Multiple Exposures: Chronicles of*

the Radiation Age. Chicago: University of Chicago Press, 1989.

Chesnau, Roger, ed. *Conway's All the World's Fighting Ships, 1922–1946.* New York: Mayflower Books, 1980.

Clark, Ronald W. *The Greatest Power on Earth: The International Race for Nuclear Supremacy.* New York: Harper & Row, 1980.

Clevenger, Edward W. "Things That Happened While I Was in the Navy!" Diary, January 2, 1946–March 31, 1949. Edward W. Clevenger, Dover, Delaware.

Cochrane, Vice Admiral E. L., USN. "Crossroads and Ship Design." *Shipmate,* September 1946.

Commander, Joint Task Force One. "Report on Atomic Bomb Tests Able and Baker (Operation Crossroads) Conducted at Bikini Atoll, Marshall Islands, 1 July 1946 and 25 July 1946." Vol. 1. Operational Archives, U.S. Naval Historical Center.

Committee for the Compilation of Materials on Damage Caused by the Atomic Bombs in Hiroshima and Nagasaki. *Hiroshima and Nagasaki: The Physical, Medical and Social Effects of the Atomic Bombings.* London, Melbourne, Sydney, Auckland, Johannesburg: Hutchinson and Company, 1981.

Compton, Arthur Holly. *Atomic Quest: A Personal Narrative.* New York: Oxford University Press, 1956.

Cook, C. Sharp. "The Legacy of Crossroads." *Naval History* 2, no. 4 (Fall 1988).

Cousins, Norman. "The Standardization of Catastrophe." *Saturday Review of Literature,* August 10, 1946.

Cranwell, John Philips. "Sea Power and the Atomic Bomb." *United States Naval Institute Proceedings* 72, no. 2 (October 1946).

Daly, Thomas N. "Crossroads at Bikini." *United States Naval Institute Proceedings* 112, no. 7 (July 1986).

Davis, Vincent. *Postwar Defense Policy and the U.S. Navy, 1943–1946.* Chapel Hill: University of North Carolina Press, 1962.

Delgado, James P. "What's Become of *Sara?*" *United States Naval Institute Proceedings* 116, no. 10 (October 1990).

Delgado, James P., Daniel J. Lenihan, and Larry E. Murphy. *The Archaeology of the Atomic Bomb: A Submerged Cultural Resources Assessment of the Sunken Fleet of Operation Crossroads at Bikini and Kwajalein Atoll Lagoons.* Santa Fe, N. Mex.: National Park Service, 1991.

Del Tredici, Robert. *At Work in the Fields of the Bomb.* New York: Harper & Row, Perennial Library, 1987

Dibblin, Jane. *The Day of Two Suns: U.S. Nuclear Testing and the Pacific Islanders.* New York: New Amsterdam, 1990.

Dickey, Capt. George L. Jr., USN. "The End of the Prinz." *United States Naval Institute Proceedings* (August 1969).

Director of Ship Material, Joint Task Force One. "Bureau of Ships Group, Technical Inspection Report, USS *Anderson* (DD411), Test Able, Operation Crossroads." National Archives Record Group 374, Records of the Defense Atomic Support Agency. National Archives.

———, Joint Task Force One. "Final Report of Tests Able and Baker, Bureau of Aeronautics," October 11, 1946. National Archives.

Director of Ship Material. "Technical Inspection Report. . . ." Reports on the following ships can be found in the National Archives: USS *Apogon* (SS308), Test Baker; USS *Arkansas* (BB33), Test Baker; USS *Carlisle* (APA69), Test Able; USS *Gilliam* (APA57), Test Able; USS *Lamson* (DD367), Test Able; *Nagato* (Ex-Jap BB), Test Baker; USS *Pilotfish* (SS386), Test Baker; *Prinz Eugen* (USS IX-300), Test Able; *Sakawa* (Ex-Jap CL), Test Able; USS *Saratoga* (CV3), Test Able; USS *Saratoga* (CV3), Test Baker; USS YO-160, Test Able."

———, Naval Medical Research Subsection. "The Gross Autopsy Findings and a Statistical Study of the Mortality of the Animals Exposed at Bikini" (March 1, 1947). Available on microfilm from the National Technical Information Service.

———. "Technical Inspection Report, Radiological Decontamination of Target and Non-Target Vessels." Vol. 1, vol. 3, National Archives.

Director of Ship Material. *Technical Report: Bikini Scientific Resurvey: Report of the Director of Ship Material.* Washington, D.C.: Armed Forces Special Weapons Project, 1947.

Dower, John. *War without Mercy: Race and Power in the Pacific War.* New York: Pantheon Books, 1986.

Draeger, R. H., and Shields Warren. "Medicine at the Crossroads." *US Naval Medical Bulletin* 47 (1947).

Dull, Paul S. *A Battle History of the Imperial Japanese Navy (1941–1945).* Annapolis, Md.: Naval Institute Press, 1978.

Edoin, Hoito. *The Night Tokyo Burned: The Incendiary Campaign against Japan, March–August 1945.* New York: St. Martin's Press, 1987.

"The Effect of the Atomic Bomb on Naval Power." *Bulletin of the Atomic Scientists of Chicago,* vol. 1, no. 5 (February 15, 1946).

Eliot, John. "Nuclear Graveyard." *National Geographic* 181, no. 6 (June 1992).

Ellis, William S. "A Way of Life Lost: Bikini." *National Geographic* 169, no. 6 (June 1986).

"The Evaluation of the Atomic Bomb as a Military Weapon: The Final Report of the Joint Chiefs of Staff Evaluation Board Operation Crossroads," June 30, 1947. CCS 471.6, 10-15-46, Section 9, Part 1. National Archives Record Group 218, Records of the United States Joint Chiefs of Staff. National Archives.

Fox, Charles H. *Radioactive Wastes.* Oak Ridge, Tenn.: U.S. Atomic Energy Commission, 1965.

Frederick, Col. J. D. "Final Report of Army Ground Group (Task Group 1.4), Operation Crossroads Atomic Bomb Tests" (1946). National Archives.

Friedman, Norman. *U.S. Destroyers: An Illustrated Design History.* Annapolis, Md.: Naval Institute Press, 1982.

———. *U.S. Aircraft Carriers: An Illustrated Design History.* Annapolis, Md.: Naval Institute Press, 1983.

Fussell, Paul. *Thank God for the Atomic Bomb and Other Essays.* New York: Ballantyne Books, 1988.

———. *Wartime: Understanding and Behavior in the Second World War.* Oxford: Oxford University Press, 1989.

Garraty, John A., ed. *Dictionary of American Biography: Supplement Five, 1951–1955.* New York: Charles Scribner's Sons, 1977.

Geddes, Donald. *The Atomic Age Opens.* New York: Pocket Books, 1945.

Glasstone, Samuel, ed. *Radiological Defense: The Principles of Military Defense against Atomic Weapons.* Vol. 2. Washington, D.C.: Armed Forces Special Weapons Project, 1951.

———. *The Effects of Nuclear Weapons.* Washington, D.C.: Government Printing Office, 1957.

Goodchild, Peter. *J. Robert Oppenheimer: Shatterer of Worlds.* New York: Fromm International, 1985.

Gould, Richard A. "The Archaeology of War: Wrecks of the Spanish Armada of 1588 and the Battle of Britain, 1940." In *Shipwreck Anthropology,* ed. Richard A. Gould. Albuquerque: School of American Research/University of New Mexico Press, 1983.

Graybar, Lloyd. "Bikini Revisited." *Military Affairs,* October 1980.

Gusterson, Hugh. "Coming of Age in a Weapons Lab: Culture, Tradition, and Change in the House of the Bomb." *The Sciences,* May/June 1992.

Hacker, Barton C. *The Dragon's Tail: Radiation Safety in the Manhattan Project, 1942–1946.* Berkeley and Los Angeles: University of California Press, 1987.

Halsey, William F., and Joseph Bryan III. *Admiral Halsey's Story.* New York: McGraw-Hill Book Co., 1947.

Hansen, Chuck. *U.S. Nuclear Weapons: The Secret History.* Arlington, Tex.: AeroFax, 1988.

"Helen of Bikini," *Time,* August 5, 1946.

Herken, Gregg. *The Winning Weapon: The Atomic Bomb in the Cold War, 1945–1950.* Princeton, N.J.: Princeton University Press, 1981.

Hersey, John. *Hiroshima.* New York: Alfred A. Knopf, 1946.

Hewlett, Richard G., and Francis Duncan. *Nuclear Navy, 1946–1962.* Chicago: University of Chicago Press, 1974.

Hines, Neal O. *Proving Ground: An Account of the Radiobiological Studies in the Pacific, 1946–1961.* Seattle: University of Washington Press, 1962.

Holmes, Richard. *Acts of War: The Behavior of Men in Battle*. New York: Macmillan, 1985.

Howarth, Stephen. *The Fighting Ships of the Rising Sun: The Drama of the Imperial Japanese Navy, 1895–1945*. New York: Atheneum, 1983.

Humble, Richard. *U.S. Fleet Carriers of World War II*. Poole, Eng.: Blandford Press, 1984.

Irving, David. *The German Atomic Bomb: The History of Nuclear Research in Nazi Germany*. New York: Simon & Schuster, 1967.

Ito, Masanori, and Roger Pineau. *The End of the Imperial Japanese Navy*. New York: Jove Books, 1986.

Jentschura, Hansgeorg, Dieter Jung, and Peter Mickel. *Warships of the Imperial Japanese Navy, 1869–1945*. Annapolis, Md.: Naval Institute Press, 1986.

Joint Army–Navy Task Force No. 1. Press Release File. Department of Energy Archives, Las Vegas, Nevada.

Joint Chiefs of Staff Evaluation Board. "Preliminary Statement by the Evaluation Board on Test B; Section III, Observations and Conclusions, Both Tests" (August 2, 1946). National Archives.

Joint Task Force One. Telegrams to Los Alamos on Recovery of Test Instrumentation. Los Alamos National Laboratory Archives, A-86-019, Los Alamos, New Mexico.

Jolie, E. W. *A Brief History of U.S. Navy Torpedo Development*. Newport, R.I.: Naval Underwater Systems Center, 1978.

Jones, Vincent C. *Manhattan: The Army and the Atomic Bomb, The United States Army in World War II, Special Studies*. Washington, D.C.: Center for Military History, 1985.

Jungk, Robert. *Brighter Than a Thousand Suns: A Personal History of the Atomic Scientists*. New York: Harcourt, Brace & Co., 1956.

Kincaid, Eugene. "Bikini: The Forthcoming Atomic Bomb Test in the Marshalls Will Determine the Future of Man, Animals, Birds, Fish, Plants, and Microorganisms." *Life*, vol. 20, no. 1, July 1, 1946.

Kurzman, Dan. *The Day of the Bomb: Countdown to Hiroshima*. New York: McGraw-Hill Book Company, 1985.

———. *Fatal Voyage: The Sinking of the* Indianapolis. New York: Atheneum, 1990.

LaFarge, Phyllis. *The Strangelove Legacy: Children, Parents, and Teachers in the Nuclear Age*. New York: Harper & Row, 1987.

Lamont, Lansing. *Day of Trinity*. New York: Atheneum, 1985.

Laurence, William L. *Dawn Over Zero: The Story of the Atomic Bomb*. New York: Alfred A. Knopf, 1946.

LeMay, General Curtis E., and Bill Yenne. *Superfortress: The Story of the B-29 and American Air Power*. New York: McGraw-Hill Book Company, 1988.

Lenihan, Daniel J., ed. *Submerged Cultural Resources Study: USS Arizona Memorial and Pearl Harbor National Historic Landmark*. Southwest Cultural Resources Center Professional Papers, No. 23, Santa Fe, N. Mex.: National Park Service, 1989.

Lerager, Jim, Karl Z. Morgan, and Susan D. Lambert. *In The Shadow of the Cloud: Photographs and Histories of America's Atomic Veterans*. Golden, Colo.: Fulcrum, 1988.

Lifton, Robert Jay. *Death in Life: The Survivors of Hiroshima*. London: Weidenfeld and Nicolson, 1967.

Markwith, Carl. "Farewell to Bikini." *National Geographic* 90, no. 1 (July 1946).

Martin, Laurence. *The Changing Face of Nuclear Warfare*. New York: Harper & Row, 1987.

Marx, Joseph L. *Seven Hours to Zero*. New York: G. P. Putnam's Sons, 1967.

May, Elaine Tyler. *Homeward Bound: American Families in the Cold War Era*. New York: Basic Books, 1988.

May, John. *The Greenpeace Book of the Nuclear Age: The Hidden History, the Human Cost*. New York: Pantheon Books, 1989.

McBundy, George. *Danger and Survival: Choices about the Bomb in the First Fifty Years*. New York: Vintage Books, 1990.

Miksche, F. O. *Atomic Weapons and Armies*. London: Faber & Faber, 1955.

Millis, Walter, ed. *The Forrestal Diaries*. New York: Viking Press, 1951.

Mojtabai, A. G. *Blessed Assurance: At Home with the Bomb in Amarillo, Texas*. Boston: Houghton Mifflin Company, 1986.

Mooney, James L., ed. *Dictionary of American Naval Fighting Ships*. Washington, D.C.: Government Printing Office, 1967–1976.

Murrow, Edward R. *In Search of Light: The Broadcasts of Edward R. Murrow, 1938–1961*. New York: Alfred A. Knopf, 1967.

Nichols, Major General K. D., USA (Ret.). *The Road to Trinity*. New York: William Morrow and Co., 1987.

Noel, Capt. John V. Jr. USN (Ret.). "Homeward Bound." *Shipmate*, May 1984.

Office of the Historian, Joint Task Force One. *Operation Crossroads: The Official Pictorial Record*. New York: William A. Wise & Company, 1946.

Oliver, Douglas L. *The Pacific Islands, Revised Edition*. Honolulu: University of Hawai'i Press, 1975.

Pacific War Research Society. *The Day Man Lost: Hiroshima, 6 August 1945*. Tokyo and Palo Alto, Calif.: Kodansha International, 1972.

Parsons, Rear Admiral W. S., USN. "Atomic Energy—Whither Bound?" *United States Naval Institute Proceedings* 73, no. 8 (August 1947).

Patch, Irwin Jr. "Saratoga at Iwo Jima." *Shipmate* 52, no. 5 (June 1989).

Peterkin, Ernest W. "Daybook" [1946]. Ernest W. Peterkin Collection, Camp Springs, Maryland.

———. "Personal Log, Operation Crossroads, Joint Task Force One, Bikini Atoll, March–December 1946." Ernest W. Peterkin Collection, Camp Springs, Maryland.

———. Personal Papers [travel orders, notes, sketches, drawings, and paintings of Operation Crossroads]. Ernest W. Peterkin Collection, Camp Springs, Maryland.

Protest Letters and Protest Answers. Joint Task Force One, National Archives Record Group 374, Records of the Defense Atomic Support Agency. National Archives.

Raumann, Helmut. "Life as Employed Enemy Personnel." *Naval History* 3, no. 2 (Summer 1989).

"Remarks by Vice Admiral W. H. P. Blandy, U.S.N., Commander, Joint Task Force One, Before the 47th National Encampment, Veterans of Foreign Wars, At Boston, Massachusetts, September 5, 1946." Joint Army–Navy Task Force One, Crossroads Release No. 67. Department of Energy Archives, Las Vegas, Nevada, Document No. 100967.

Rhodes, Richard. *The Making of the Atomic Bomb*. New York: Simon & Schuster, 1986.

Rigg, E. H. "The Launch of the Airplane Carrier U.S.S. *Saratoga*." *Transactions of the Society of Naval Architects and Marine Engineers*, vol. 33. New York: Society of Naval Architects and Marine Engineers, 1925.

Rock, Rear Admiral George R., USN. "Some Observations on the Design of Airplane Carriers and Notes on the *Saratoga* and *Lexington*." *Transactions of the Society of Naval Architects and Marine Engineers*, vol. 38. New York: Society of Naval Architects and Marine Engineers, 1928.

Roscoe, Theodore. *United States Submarine Operations in World War II*. Annapolis, Md.: Naval Institute Press, 1949.

Russ, Harlow W. *Project Alberta: The Preparation of Atomic Bombs for Use in World War II*. Los Alamos, N. Mex.: Exceptional Books, 1990.

Sanger, S. L., and Robert W. Mull. *Hanford and the Bomb: An Oral History of World War II*. Seattle: Living History Press, 1989.

Schaffer, Ronald. *Wings of Judgement: American Bombing in World War II*. New York and London: Oxford University Press, 1985.

"Scientific Data to Be Gained through Use of Animals in Crossroads Project." Joint Army–Navy Task

Force Number One, Crossroads Release No. 7. Copy on file at Operational Archives, U.S. Naval Historical Center.

Semler, Eric, James Benjamin, and Adam Gross. *The Language of Nuclear War.* New York: Harper & Row, 1987.

Sherwin, Martin J. *A World Destroyed: Hiroshima and the Origins of the Arms Race.* New York: Vintage Books, 1987.

Ships Section, Office of Public Information, Navy Department. "History of USS *Saratoga* (CV-3)," August 29, 1946. Ships' Histories Branch, U.S. Naval Historical Center.

Shohno, Naomi. *The Legacy of Hiroshima: Its Past, Our Future.* Tokyo: Kosei Publishing Company, 1986.

Shurcliff, W. A. *Bombs at Bikini: The Official Report of Operation Crossroads.* New York: Wm. H. Wise, 1947.

———. *Operation Crossroads: The Official Pictorial Record.* New York: Wm. H. Wise, 1946.

———. "Technical Report on Operation Crossroads" (1946). National Technical Information Service.

Shurcliff, W. A., et al., "Historical Report, Atomic Bomb Tests Able and Baker" (1946). National Archives Records Group 374, Records of the Defense Nuclear Agency. Vol. 1.

Smith, Myron J., Jr. *Keystone Battlewagon: U.S.S. Pennsylvania (BB-38).* Charleston, W. Va.: Pictorial Histories, 1983.

Smyth, Henry D. *Atomic Energy for Military Purposes: The Official Report of the Development of the Atomic Bomb under the Auspices of the United States Government, 1940–1945.* Princeton, N.J.: Princeton University Press, 1948.

Spangler, Lieut. Cmdr. Wayne E., USN. "*Prinz Eugen,* Little Brother of the *Bismarck.*" *United States Naval Institute Proceedings* 72, no. 10 (October 1946).

Sprout, Harold, and Margaret Sprout. *Toward a New Order of Sea Power: American Naval Policy and the World Scene, 1918–1922.* Princeton, N.J.: Princeton University Press, 1940.

"Statement by Rear Admiral Thorvald A. Solberg, U.S.N., on Ship and Salvage Preparations for Bikini Tests." Joint Army–Navy Task Force Number One, Crossroads Release No. 35, April 10, 1946. Copy on file in the Ships' Histories Branch, U.S. Naval Historical Center.

"Statement of Vice Admiral W. H. P. Blandy, U.S.N., Commander Joint Task Force One, on Purposes of Atomic Bomb Tests." Joint Army–Navy Task Force Number One, Crossroads Release No. 37. Department of Energy Archives, Document No. 101007.

Swanborough, Gordon, and Peter M. Bowers. *United States Navy Aircraft since 1911.* Annapolis, Md.: Naval Institute Press, 1990.

Thomas, Gordon, and Max Morgan Witts. *Ruin from the Air: The* Enola Gay's *Atomic Mission to Hiroshima.* Chelsea, Mich.: Scarborough House, 1990.

Thursfield, Rear Admiral H. G., ed. *Brassey's Naval Annual, 1947.* New York: The MacMillan Company, 1947.

Tibbetts, Paul. *The Tibbetts Story.* New York: Stein and Day, 1978.

Titus, A. Constandina. *Bombs in the Backyard: Atomic Testing and American Politics.* Reno: University of Nevada Press, 1986.

Uhl, Michael, and Tod Ensign. *G.I. Guinea Pigs.* New York: Wideview Books, 1980.

United States General Accounting Office. *Operation Crossroads: Personnel Radiation Exposure Estimates Should Be Improved* (GAO/RCED-86-15). Washington, D.C.: Government Accounting Office, 1985.

Van Arx, William S. *Circulation Systems of Bikini and Rongelap Lagoons (Bikini and Nearby Lagoons), Part II: Oceanography (Physical).* Geological Survey Professional Paper 260-B. Washington, D.C: Government Printing Office, 1954.

Waters, Rear Admiral Odale D., Jr., USN. "As I Recall Crossroads: A Tin Can Perspective." *United States Naval Institute Proceedings* 112, no. 7 (July 1986).

Weart, Spencer. *Nuclear Fear: A History of Images.* Cambridge, Mass.: Harvard University Press, 1988.

Weisgall, Jonathan M. "The Nuclear Nomads of Bikini." *Foreign Policy* 34 (Summer 1980).

———. "Micronesia and the Nuclear Pacific since Hiroshima." *SAIS Review* 5, no. 2 (Summer–Fall 1985).

———. *Operation Crossroads: The Atomic Tests at Bikini Atoll*. Annapolis, Md.: Naval Institute Press, 1994.

"What Science Learned at Bikini: Latest Report on the Results." *Life*, vol. 23, no. 6, August 11, 1947.

Whitley, M. J. *German Cruisers of World War II*. London, New York, and Sydney: Arms and Armour Press, 1985.

Wyden, Peter. *Day One: Before Hiroshima and After*. New York: Simon & Schuster, 1984.

Yergin, Daniel. *Shattered Peace: The Origins of the Cold War*. New York: Penguin Books, 1990.

Crossroads Participants: Interviews and Correspondence

Roy L. Alton, Maryland (USS *Arkansas*)

Kilon Bauno, Bikini (interview conducted by William Livingston)

Alvin Brommer, Turlock, California (USS *Saratoga*)

Edward W. Clevenger, Dover, Delaware (USS *Saratoga*)

George B. Culley, Kent, Washington (*Nagato*)

Harold H. Demarest, New Jersey (USS *Hughes*)

W. R. Dill, Duncan, Oklahoma (USS *Carteret*)

Joe Fetherston, Thousand Oaks, California (USS *Saratoga*)

Captain A. H. Graubart, USN (Ret.), Palm Beach, Florida (commanding officer, *Prinz Eugen* as USS IX-300)

Robert W. Henderson, Albuquerque, New Mexico (Los Alamos Group)

Captain Enders Huey, USN (Ret.), Orlando, Florida (commanding officer, USS *Skate*)

Captain Richard B. Laning, USN (Ret.), Orlando, Florida (commanding officer, USS *Pilotfish*)

Jack Lehman, North Charleston, South Carolina (USS *Saratoga*)

Roger Meade, historian/archivist, Los Alamos National Laboratory

Captain Ernest W. Peterkin, USN (Ret.), Camp Springs, Maryland (BuShips Physical Measurements Group)

Otto Schoetzow, Seattle, Washington (KMS *Prinz Eugen*)

Leon D. Smith, Albuquerque, New Mexico (weaponeer, *Dave's Dream*)

General Woodrow Swancutt, San Antonio, Texas (pilot, *Dave's Dream*)

Lewis Talley, Ringgold, Georgia (USS *Carlisle*)

Index

About the Author

James P. Delgado is executive director of the Vancouver Maritime Museum in Vancouver, British Columbia. Formerly he headed the U.S. maritime preservation program as maritime historian of the National Park Service in Washington, D.C. A trained maritime archaeologist, Delgado has dived all over the world on wrecks as diverse as Revolutionary War ships and the USS *Arizona* at Pearl Harbor. He is the author of numerous books and articles and has lectured widely on maritime archaeology.